The STRANGE Woman

The STRANGE Woman

Power and Sex in the Bible

Gail Corrington Streete

Westminster John Knox Press
Louisville, Kentucky

© 1997 Gail Corrington Streete

All translations of scripture and other ancient literature
are the author's unless otherwise indicated.

Scripture quotations from the New Revised Standard Version of the Bible are copyright
©1989 by the Division of Christian Education of the National Council of the Churches of
Christ in the U.S.A. and are used by permission.

Book design by Jennifer K. Cox
Cover design by Alec Bartsch
Cover illustration: Philistines Visit Delilah,
by James Tissot. Jewish Museum
New York. Courtesy SuperStock

First edition
Published by Westminster John Knox Press
Louisville, Kentucky

This book is printed on acid-free paper that meets the
American National Standards Institute Z39.48 standard. ♾

PRINTED IN THE UNITED STATES OF AMERICA
97 98 99 00 01 02 03 04 05 06 — 10 9 8 7 6 5 4 3 2 1

Library of Congress Cataloging-in-Publication Data

Streete, Gail P., date.
    The strange woman : power and sex in the Bible / Gail P.
Streete. — 1st ed.
        p.   cm.
    Includes bibliographical references and indexes.
    ISBN 0-664-25622-8 (alk. paper)
    1. Sex role—Biblical teaching.   2. Women—Biblical teaching.
    3. Power (Social sciences)—Biblical teaching.   4. Feminist
theology.   I. Title
BS680.S5S77   1997
220.8′330542—dc21   97-23140

For Jack
and in memory of Jim

Contents

Acknowledgments

I have a confession to make, and to quash anyone's expectation that it might have to do with adultery, it doesn't. I confess that I love reading other people's acknowledgment pages, primarily because I can never decide how to write my own. Fearful that I might omit thanking someone whose help has been instrumental in some way to the production of a book, I tend to err on the side of acknowledging my debts to everyone and anyone who has been instrumental in developing my thoughts over a lifetime of scholarship. In these pages, therefore, the two-legged, the four-legged, libraries, and even cities will receive thanks. (I do, however, draw the line at acknowledging a particular brand of coffee!)

First, I want to thank the Faculty Development Endowment Committee of Rhodes College for the generous grant in 1994–1995 that enabled me to embark upon the preliminary investigation at the heart of this book, which was completed during my sabbatical leave in the fall of 1996. As ever, I am indebted to my colleagues in the Department of Religious Studies for their support and companionship, but I especially wish to thank Carey E. Walsh, for her insights into and assistance with the Song of Songs, and for her perspectives on wine and viticulture that do not appear in this book but that have nevertheless enriched my life. My thanks also to Ellen T. Armour for taking over directorship of Rhodes Women's Studies program while I was on sabbatical, and for assuming the office of High Priestess of the Society of Beatrice de Silva, whose members also have my gratitude. Additional thanks to Greg Carey for provoking me in many directions: I will not read the Gospel of Luke ever again in the same way. Karen Winterton has also proven a witty and insightful critic of my ideas. Thanks go to my students at Rhodes for their encouragement, enthusiasm, and even pride in my work.

I will never be able to think about writing this book without keeping two cities in mind: Memphis, Tennessee, whose Interstate 40 provided me with the inspiration for the introduction and whose Mississippi River continues to nourish my life, my prose, and occasionally my poetry; and Boulder, Colorado, where much of this book was written during summers of 1995, 1996, and 1997, and whose atmosphere—physical and intellectual—has proven a rare stimulus. My thanks also to the library of the Harding Graduate School of Religion in Memphis and Norlin Library of the University of Colorado, Boulder, for their collections and the helpfulness of their respective staffs.

Special thanks to my two families, the Patersons and the Streetes, particularly to my sister Wendy, whose support and encouragement continue to amaze me, and to my husband, Jack, in whose love I enfold myself. Thanks also to my friend and Shakespearean sparring partner of thirty years, Linda E. Laufer, whose conversations helped me articulate concepts behind this book. My thanks also to William R. Walker, Ph.D., who has served as my spiritual guide. Without him, the person who wrote these pages could not have emerged.

The four-legged members of my family, Yukon Jack and Keetah, merit my thanks for their wholehearted and tail-wagging acceptance of me in all moods, and their canine wisdom in keeping me down to earth.

Introduction

Adultery—Hell. Rev. 21:8
—Anonymous highway sign

SIGNS OF THE TIMES?

Driving from my home to work in Memphis, Tennessee, I sometimes encounter a series of homemade signs at the ramp entrance to Interstate 40, signs which are the religious equivalent to the Burma Shave signs that once clustered so abundantly along rural highways. Neatly lettered in red, green, and black against a stark white background, these placards proclaim equally forthright judgments. On one occasion, at the fork of ramps that leads west to Little Rock, Arkansas, and east to Nashville, Tennessee, I saw this grim proclamation: **Adultery—Hell. Rev. 21:8.** A few feet farther to the east, in case the traveler might miss the point, was an equally bald sign: **Hell Hurts. Rev. 21:8.**

I was intrigued by this local variant of the ubiquitous "Jesus Saves" signs and eventually looked up that particular Bible reference. In Revelation's vision of the new heaven and new earth, which will only be created after a series of terrible battles between the righteous and the wicked, the "One seated on the throne" who is the all-powerful Lord God pronounces a "second death" in the "lake burning with fire and sulfur" for "cowards, unbelievers, the polluted, murderers, the unchaste (in Greek, *pornoi*, translated by NRSV as "fornicators"), sorcerers, idolators, and all liars."[1]

I had several reflections on this verse and its importance to some anonymous modern prophet, who was so exercised by the need to proclaim this selection from the Apocalypse of John that the risk of being hit by traffic on a busy interstate highway or of possible arrest was of little consequence. First, I was struck by the fact that, out of all the possible transgressions that could land a person in the infamous "lake of fire," adultery was singled out for special mention by the sign maker. Even accounting for the fact that sorcery and idolatry are not sins that occupy the modern religious imagination, lying certainly remains contemporary, at least in election-year rhetoric. But telling lies seemed not to be the "great sin" that adultery was. Second, I found equally striking the idea that for this latter-day apocalyptic

1

prophet, the English translation "fornicators" clearly meant adulterers, persons who commit the sin that guarantees top-price admission to hell. I had a vision of streams of cars, filled with potential adulterers, who would read the prophet's homemade "signs," recognize themselves, and repent, provided they were not so startled that they crashed into a guardrail and ended up in an actual position to test these proclamations. The signs also seemed to me unusual in a time when most of the road signs and bumper stickers that focus on sexual transgressions are preoccupied not with sexual unchastity but with abortion, which, though it may be a consequence of unchastity, is certainly placed in a different category of sin: murder.

Adultery, I thought, the Scarlet **A**, the transgression meriting death in biblical law, has seen its day as the monster it once was, useful only for plots on daytime television, in which it figures as a stock form of intrigue. Nevertheless, according to a recent opinion survey, while Americans no longer find homosexuality and premarital sex as abhorrent as they did in 1974, 78 percent still find adultery, defined somewhat broadly as intercourse of a married person with someone other than husband or wife, wrong.[2] An article in the September 30, 1996, issue of *Newsweek* titled, "Adultery: New Furor over an Old Sin," declared, "In the 90's [marital] infidelity sparks more outrage than it did a few decades ago. And more of the cheaters are women."[3] The recent furor generated by the case of Lt. Kelly Flinn, an Air Force bomber pilot charged with adultery, has reminded many Americans that the military still considers adultery a criminal sexual offense. In countries like Iran and Afghanistan, where Islamic revivalist movements have reinstituted capital punishment for adultery, women and their partners are still publicly stoned for violation of religious law.[4]

While not considered a capital crime in the United States, adultery nevertheless still exists in American legal codes as the prime reason for the termination of a marriage. For many years it was the only legal reason for divorce, and many continue to consider it a moral crime. In some recent debates over ending "no-fault" divorce, adultery is again being considered as one of the few serious reasons for ending a marriage. "Adultery" has usually been understood in Western religio-legal codes as a married woman having sexual intercourse with a man who is not her husband, or a man (married or unmarried) having sexual intercourse with another man's wife. Historically, a married man having sexual relations with an unmarried woman has sometimes been defined as adultery, but more often has not.

The purpose of making adultery a legal crime in addition to a moral one has been to protect heterosexual marriage and the rights of the husband to the exclusive enjoyment of his wife's sexuality. Such a marriage, in short, becomes a "sacred" sexual script.[5] As in the case of prostitution, where a legal category is also a moral one, a "double standard" prevails. An ideology of male heterosexual needs and their satisfaction supports this standard, in which "frequenting prostitutes, perhaps more than other forms of promiscuity, is forgiveable in the male, while being a prostitute, again perhaps more than other forms of promiscuity, is totally reprehensible in the female."[6] Thus, the category of "adultery" is charged with perceived differences between male and female sexual desire, and with different limits to satisfying that desire. These limits have been set by heterosexual and socially dominant males, in a discourse in which the moral becomes the legal and vice versa.[7] Anything that does not fit this script, like same-sex marriages, is perceived as both morally, and thence legally, unacceptable.

Merely two ephemeral signs along a Tennessee interstate—but as signs, whether divine or human, often do, they conjured up a whole train of thoughts and images of the link between sexuality, immorality, and evil in the religious imagination. As a twice-married heterosexual woman who was raised within a Protestant biblical tradition, as a feminist who is both a biblical scholar and teacher, and as a citizen of a region where, despite the nominal separation between church and state, public policy is often informed and critiqued by competing biblical traditions, I have more than a superficial concern with such matters. In a sense, they serve to define and therefore to limit both my perceptions of the world and others' perceptions of me.

It seems to me, however, that there is something about sexuality and the need to control and direct it that preoccupies us. It is as if that part of our nature is an unruly inner evil, the *yetser ha-rah*, the "perverse spirit" or "evil inclination," as the rabbis called it, or the "perversity of will," as the Christian Augustine described it. And it is as if that unruly part needs to be named, objectified, and personified in order to be dealt with sufficiently.[8] Thus we often link "sin" with individual violation of communally defined sexual morality, a "transgression" in the most literal sense of "stepping over" boundaries drawn for sexual behavior. Sexual boundaries are of great importance in social formation, since the primary tool necessary to ensure human continuity—sex—is at the same time the most essential and the most problematic. With Paul Ricoeur,

> one is struck by the importance and the gravity attached to the violation of interdictions of a sexual character in the economy of defilement. The prohibitions against incest, sodomy, abortion, relations at forbidden times—and sometimes places—are so fundamental that the inflation of the sexual is characteristic of the whole system of defilement; so that an indissoluble complicity between sexuality and defilement seems to have been formed from time immemorial.[9]

There is a further link. The passage from Revelation previously quoted (21:8) belongs to a series of spectacular destructions of evil opponents of the righteous and the salvation of the latter. Among these destructions, that which causes the greatest "wonder" (*thauma*, Rev. 17:6) is the fall of "Babylon," a cipher for all evil dominion, which is characterized as a woman, the "Great Whore" (*porne te megale*), with whom the "kings of the earth" commit *porneia* ("unchastity," usually translated "fornication," and often understood as "adultery"; Rev. 17:1–2). While the kings of the earth may be presumed to come to bad ends, perhaps in the "lake of fire" reserved for fornicators (*pornoi*) among other iniquitous persons, the Whore of Babylon herself comes to a graphic and horrific end, "left desolate," stripped naked and eaten by her vassals, and then burned with fire (Rev. 17:16), like the poor wretches in the burning lake.[10] As a figure of power, the Whore of Babylon represents female sexual power "out of control," as perceived from the framework of male heterosexual desire. The "mother of whores and of the abominations of the earth" (17:5), she is not only the originator of all (illegitimate) female seductiveness but the source of its power to lure men into delusion and to destruction.

Since the Whore is equated in these passages with Babylon, the pagan city that itself symbolizes the captivity and martyrdoms of the righteous, she is also symbolic of a foreign, "outsider" power that disrupts and shatters the peace of the people of God, as Babylon did of Judah in the sixth century B.C.E. and as Rome, in the view of the writer and audience of Revelation, was doing to the Christians of Asia Minor in the first century C.E. There is no corresponding male figure in Revelation—not even Satan—whose evil is characterized primarily in sexual terms. The monstrous symbol of the evil empire, the foreign power that seeks to destroy the people of faith, is female—and what a useful and enduring symbol of feminized evil the Great Whore has proven! As feminist art historian Elena Ciletti has put it, "Whenever women exert power over men, it is by definition sexual and lethal."[11]

Of course, like every enduring literary symbol, especially those of biblical literature which have also entered the iconography of the sacred, the Great Whore has a long heritage. According to Gale A. Yee, "The powerful but insidious symbol of a woman seducing a man sexually to sin, resulting in any number of dire consequences, is one that has been ingrained in the literature of Western Civilization ever since Eve gave the fateful fruit to Adam in the garden," despite, one might add, the silence of Genesis 2—3 on any kind of explicit sexual seduction.[12] The strength of apocalyptic writing like that represented by the book of Revelation, moreover, is that it presents itself as timeless. Using symbolic language from the past, apocalyptic text can cite past triumphs over evil forces while foreshadowing future victory, the continuity of symbols furnishing a sense of the eternal realm of the divine, in which past, present, and future are the same. To develop the image of the Great Whore, the Christian seer John draws upon images from his own scriptural past, primarily the adulterous Israel portrayed by the prophets as desolate, stripped naked, and sexually shamed, and the seductively lethal adulteress or "strange woman" (*'iššah zarah*) of Proverbs 1—9. As the one who is "mother of abominations," moreover, the Whore, like Hosea's "wife of Whoredom" (Hos. 1:2), is also the symbol of heterodoxy and apostasy in an equation of "wrong" religious behavior with "wrong" sexual behavior. In the apocalyptic work of Zechariah, written just after the end of the exile (ca. 520–518 B.C.E.), the prophet sees a woman in a basket and is told she is the "Wickedness" that comes out of Judah to be deposited and worshiped in Babylon (Zech. 5:5–11). Here again a male writer personifies evil as a female character, while defining religious apostasy as sexual infidelity and "iniquity."[13]

From what needs do that equation and its strength derive? Mark Taylor has noted that the maintenance of "intellectual and moral" hegemony derives from the ability to create a "dialectic between monster-making and monster-slaying." This means that the construction of an identity of power often entails the creation of a monstrous "other" and its exaggeration into such a threat that it must be "slain."[14] Further, according to Michael L. Satlow's examination of ascetic behavior in late antique Judaism, "sanctioned sexual deportment" is determined by the societal values and institutions enshrined and privileged in the discourse of communities. This discourse becomes codified in literature,[15] and in turn sanctions and dictates the appropriate behavior of those societies for which this literary code is a divine code. In other words, if both adultery and apostasy are defined as transgressions in the religious code known as the Ten Commandments, those communities of faith for which this and other passages in scripture are normative and prescriptive will continue to regard them as sins. Adultery, a sexual "sin" and a violation of the social code, is thus seen as equal in severity to a religious "sin," apostasy. Both are serious offenses against God. The unknown apocalyptic prophet of Interstate 40 and the intended audience for his or her messages need no "hermeneutical circle" to relativize their conviction that adultery is a sin tantamount to idolatry though much more immediate, and that both are equally punishable by hellfire.

ADULTERY: FROM LEGAL
TO MORAL CATEGORY TO SYMBOL OF EVIL

Why has adultery, as defined in the "great code" of biblical literature, so often been synonymous with all unsanctioned sexual behavior and even with unsanctioned nonsexual behavior, like apostasy? Why do we also so frequently think of women in connection with this "deviance"? I suggest, with Nancy Jay, that in early Middle Eastern societies, where tribal and ethnic identity and survival continued to depend on endogamy (marriage within the kinship group), patrilocality (residence with the husband's family), and patriliny (descent reckoned through the father's line), the ability both to circumscribe female fertility and to establish biological paternity was important.[16] Under these circumstances, adultery becomes a legal category, whereas, for a group in less precarious circumstances, it might be regarded simply as an exchange of sexual partners. Narrowly defined first as sexual intercourse with another man's lawfully possessed wife and conversely (later and more important) as a married or betrothed woman's sexual intercourse with any man not her husband, adultery is thence translated into the language of a moral transgression that has serious consequences. Carol Meyers suggests that the "survival and . . . the prosperity of any group is dependent upon three major activities: (1) procreation (reproduction), (2) production (subsistence), and (3) protection (defense)," and that in the transitional period from the Bronze to the Iron Age, Israelite gender roles had already become disproportionate, with females exclusively responsible for the first activity, males for the second and third activities.[17] It was important for the dominant males, therefore, to circumscribe female sexual activity in order to control reproductive integrity or "purity."[18]

As the seventh of the ten apodictic commandments indicates (Ex. 20:1–17), the commission of adultery is plainly an offense that violates the covenant between God and Israel. It is later defined in Deuteronomy (Deut. 5:1–21) and the Holiness Code of Leviticus (chapters 17—26), composed around the seventh or six century B.C.E., as a capital crime. According to Henry McKeating, adultery was originally a matter of family law, but during the exilic (597–538 B.C.E.) and postexilic (post-538 B.C.E.) periods, it came to be regarded as a "pollution," like homicide, a violation of the integrity of the entire community. Hence the community had a responsibility and even an obligation to punish it.[19] Marriage and marital fidelity were no longer familial, private concerns, but elements of a communal ideal, for which infidelity came to be viewed as worthy of capital punishment, "a sexual crime." [20]

Although both the Seventh Commandment and the other provisions in the Covenant, Deuteronomistic, and Holiness Codes are addressed to men, they are about women who belong to men. Adulterous women in particular threatened community stability from within because of the wife's responsibility for securing the production of legitimate (Israelite male) heirs, and from without, because the adulterous women were married women of another tribe or nation, and male Israelites might produce offspring that were not only illegitimate but non-Israelite. Group identity would thus be eroded and eventually lost. The woman's task was to secure the stability of the family and the community through reproduction. This task became the arena of most concern to the biblical writers, especially during and following the exile, when proof of legitimate Israelite descent provided a claim to property abandoned by those who had been taken to Babylon and now wished to return.

The adulterous or sexually promiscuous woman had thus already become the symbol of religious and social chaos for biblical writers by the sixth century B.C.E. In the revisionist history of the people of Israel from Joshua to 2 Kings known as the Deuteronomistic History, exilic and post-exilic scribes sought a theological explanation for the fall, first of Israel (the northern ten tribes) and later that of Judah (the southern two tribes and the capital at Jerusalem), and the latter's captivity in Babylon. They found it in the non-Israelite women ("foreign women" or *nokriyyoth*), whom they blamed for causing Israelite and Judahite kings to follow "other" deities, causing an angry YHWH, the God of the Israelites, to take away the land that was their promised inheritance (Gen. 12:1–9). On the return of some of the courtly Judahites from Babylon to Judah in the sixth century B.C.E., the "purging" of foreign wives and their children from the body of Israel became a prime concern to males of the scribal elite like Ezra and Nehemiah who had gained or retained religious power among the exiles. Although the "problem" was essentially one of inheritance of the land by non-Israelite issue (see the genealogical lists in Ezra 8 and Nehemiah 7), in the rhetoric of these postexilic books, the cause of the loss of the land is defined as the result of ignoring YHWH's prohibition of intermarriage with Gentiles. Deuteronomy 7:3–4, a text composed or at least edited during the exile, expresses the fear that daughters given in marriage to non-Israelites, and non-Israelite daughters married to Israelite sons will "turn away" the hearts of their husbands from YHWH to follow other deities. The language of this prohibition echoes that of the covenant renewal in Exodus 34:15–16, where YHWH explicitly says that marrying the daughters of the inhabitants of the land will cause the sons of Israel to "prostitute" themselves before other deities. In either case, the women—through sexual intercourse—are assumed to be responsible for the turning. It is no accident that the infamous figure of the adulteress, the seducer of foolish young men, also called the "strange" or "outsider" woman (*'iššah zarah*) is also developed in this postexilic period as a seductive, lethal monster against whom the young men of Proverbs (chapters 1–9) must be warned.[21]

The portrayal of Israel as the adulterous whore-wife of YHWH by Hosea as a warning against religious apostasy in the mid–eighth century B.C.E. was eagerly adopted by the Judahite prophets of the exile—Ezekiel, Jeremiah, and to a lesser extent, Second Isaiah—as a symbol of the faithless nation that had to be hideously punished for "her" flagrant amours with lovers other than her legitimate husband, YHWH. Israel, as the collective of the people of YHWH, is thus the scriptural prototype for the Whore of

Babylon and is punished in much the same way. Not being a foreign or strange woman, however, Israel is not consigned to total destruction, but she needs to be punished and once more brought under the control of her legitimate authority, her husband YHWH.[22]

Female adultery, from the perspective of the exilic and postexilic writers and editors of the Tanakh, thus represents a dangerous subversion of the hegemony of familial, ethnic, and religious male authorities and of the male God of Israel. Even when Israelite males are themselves charged with committing adultery, it is because they are seduced by powerfully alluring "strange" or "outsider" women. When they commit apostasy, the religious crime often spoken of as adultery, the same "foreign" or "strange women" are again responsible. Temptation to do evil, to stray from the path indicated by the scribes and other interpreters of the legal and moral covenant between YHWH and Israel, proceeded, in the form of sexual temptation, from women not legitimately possessed by the men of Israel. In fact, these women seemed not to be possessed by any man, husband or deity. These are outsiders who are most wholly "other": female rather than male, non-Israelite rather than Israelite, worshipers of "other" gods and goddesses than YHWH.

Female adultery, rather than male, continued to be portrayed as threatening the social and moral order of the Jews right through the Hellenistic period, from the fourth to first centuries B.C.E. Indeed, as Léonie Archer observes, the entire period of postexilic Judaism, from the return to the "Second Commonwealth" (Second Temple), is marked by "an all-embracing morbidity where sexual relations were concerned."[23] The first-century B.C.E. moral exhortations known as the Wisdom of Solomon praise Wisdom (Sophia) as the God-given female possession of the righteous man (8:21), while treating idolatry and apostasy as adultery (Wisd. Sol. 3:13; 14:12, 24–26). The misogynistic wisdom text from the second century B.C.E. known as the Wisdom of Ben Sira (Ecclesiasticus) lauds Wisdom in a way similar to that of Proverbs 1—9, equating Wisdom with the commandments of God (24:23), but precedes this praise with dire warnings against the adulteress (23:22–27). The positive portrayal of divine female Wisdom is moreover offset by Ben Sira's condemnation of women as beings who excel in iniquity (25:19), who generally make uncontrollable and therefore wicked wives, and are the source of sin and death (25:24).

More positive portraits of women are contained in the apocryphal tales of Judith, Susanna, and, to a lesser extent, Tobit. Virtuous Jewish wives (Susanna) and widows (Judith, Sarah [Tobit]) support and defend the honor of their nation and of their husbands by the strength of their chastity. Judith, a chaste Jewish widow, plays the seductress in order to defeat the Assyrian enemy Holofernes, whose unchecked desire to possess both Judith and her town, Bethuliah, results in his death. Susanna, whose fidelity to her husband is threatened by the lechery of Jewish elders, is ultimately vindicated by another Jew, the young Daniel, on the very point of her stoning as a condemned adulteress. Sarah, the hapless bride in the book of Tobit, attracts the lecherous demon Asmodaeus, but never succumbs to his sexual advances despite the death of seven husbands, and in the end marries a groom who follows the advice of his wise father and survives. In the hagiographic 2 Maccabees and its philosophical partner 4 Maccabees, another virtuous widow watches with "a man's courage" (2 Macc. 7:21; 4 Macc. 15:29–30) the death by torture of her seven sons and, still faithful to God, is martyred also. In the apocryphal (Greek) additions to the canonical book of Esther, the Jewish virgin becomes the favorite of the Gentile Artaxerxes, after the deposition of the disobedient wife, Queen Vashti. Esther is able to achieve the difficult feat of remaining faithful to God despite being in a Gentile court, saving the lives both of her foolish royal husband (Gk. Esth. 2:22–23) and of her people. The virtue thus prescribed for Hellenistic Jewish women is a single one, fidelity: fidelity to one husband, dead or alive, foolish though he may be (although having a wise wife helps), and fidelity to the God of Israel. Adultery and apostasy are, even in the more syncretistic context of diaspora Judaism, still regarded synonymously as the chief violators of this virtue.

These chaste, at times ascetic, and always faithful heroines of the Apocrypha have much in common with the women of the New Testament. It has often been argued that Judaism, in contrast to Christianity, is much more body- and sex-affirming. Christianity has been portrayed as fatally infused with Greco-Roman philosophical ideas of the separation of soul and body, with a corresponding disdain for all bodily appetites, especially sexual impulses. While one might argue endlessly against this rather simplistic and thus inaccurate distinction, one thing is clear: for the male authors of the New Testament and early Christianity, just as for those of the Tanakh, the Apocrypha, and formative Judaism, sexual behavior, male as well as female, remains problematic.[24] Judith Plaskow observes that, "Though Jewish attitudes toward sexuality are often contrasted favorably with Christian asceticism, one might argue that the energy the church fathers devoted to worrying about sexuality, the rabbis devoted to worrying about illicit sexuality—with similar implications."[25]

The eschatological perspective of the followers of Jesus and early Christianity, in which men and women "neither marry nor are given in marriage, but are like the angels in heaven" in the life of the "age to come" (Mark 12:25; Matt. 22:30; Luke 20:34–35), calls earthly marital and familial arrangements, including sexual behavior and reproduction, into question (Matt. 10:26–27; Luke 14:26). In the Gospel of Matthew, Jesus characterizes the present age, in prophetic vein,[26] as "a wicked and adulterous (*moichalis*) generation" (Matt. 12:39; cf. Luke 11:30). The Christian apostle

Paul's advice to the Corinthians on such matters as marriage, intermarriage, adultery, abstinence, and intercourse in 1 Corinthians 7 has at its root the firm conviction that "the present form of this world is passing away" (1 Cor. 7:31, NRSV). In the same passage (1 Cor. 7:10–11), Paul nevertheless mentions a "commandment of the Lord" against marital separation and divorce, and elsewhere assumes that the biblical laws against adultery are still in place (Rom. 2:22; 7:2–3). In his catalog of those who will not be saved because they are "of the flesh," he includes both those who commit *porneia* (unchastity; Gal. 5:19–21) and *moicheia* (adultery; 1 Cor. 6:9–10) specifically. Paul commands the Corinthian man living with his stepmother in violation of biblical law to be handed over to Satan (1 Cor. 5:1–5), and he condemns those Corinthian men who consort with prostitutes because they are prostituting the body of Christ, in effect committing adultery against him (1 Cor. 6:15–17). Here again, adultery and apostasy are equated in gender-bending metaphorical language that presents the community as male (the church at Corinth) betraying the bride (Christ).

Jesus' teachings, as related in Matthew's Gospel particularly, do not abrogate the laws about adultery and divorce that are found in the Torah, but rather expand them (Matt. 5:27–30, 31–32) and apply them again primarily to men as the responsible parties. A man who divorces his wife for reasons other than "unchastity" (*porneia*, a looser, possibly more inclusive category than adultery, perhaps applying to the case where a man finds his bride is not a virgin; cf. Ex. 22:13–21)[27] forces *her* to commit adultery (*moicheuthenai*). Likewise a man who marries a divorced woman himself commits adultery, perhaps because she is still regarded as another man's wife (Matt. 5:31–32; cf. Matt. 19:7–9). The parallels in Mark (10:11–12) and Luke (16:18) do not mention divorce as allowable even on the grounds of *porneia*. At various times in the Synoptic Gospels, Jesus is criticized for having table fellowship with prostitutes, included in the more general category of "sinners" (cf. Matt. 11:18–19; Luke 7:33–34), but prostitutes are not usually regarded as being in the same class as adulterous women.

In the Gospel of John, however, female adultery becomes a point at issue in two ways, one indirect and one direct. In John 4:7–41, Jesus encounters a woman in Samaria who has had five husbands (or male companions) and is now living with a man not her husband. While according to the standards of the Synoptics, this would surely constitute adulterous or at the very least unacceptably promiscuous behavior, the author does not dwell on this fact, using it as other evidence of Jesus' prophetic powers. Considering the rejection of Jesus by "his own" in John, it is all the more remarkable that a woman, a Samaritan, and one whose marital status is irregular becomes the first to preach Jesus as the messiah in an area traditionally off-limits to faithful Judeans. In the second episode (John 7:53–8:11), the status of which as part of the Gospel of John has long been in dispute, the so-called Pericope on the Adulteress, the "scribes and Pharisees," Jesus' opponents, bring before him a woman whom they claim they caught "in the very act" of adultery. Much can be and has been made of the fact that her partner was not also caught, but the point of the story seems to be whether Jesus will agree with those who bring the woman to him that the death penalty—here, by stoning—enjoined by the law of Moses should be exacted. Jesus' famous reply, that "The one among you without sin should be the first to cast a stone at her" (8:7), has seemed to some commentators to condone or at least excuse the woman's action, but, in fact, the sentence is only commuted. Jesus commands her, "Go, and do not sin any more" (8:11). The dispute is not over whether adultery is a sin or whether the woman is guilty: it is, and she is. Once again the focus, as in all of John's Gospel, is upon Jesus' authority, not the woman's sexual history.

As has been shown, neither the Gospels nor the letters of Paul seem to be overly occupied with female sexuality, nor do they demonize female sexual promiscuity. Where female adultery is an issue, it is not the focus of the narrative. Male sexual misbehavior comes in for a greater share of attention and condemnation, probably because male heterosexual hegemony is assumed. But it may also be because the necessity for the continued existence of the familial unit is not an issue in the family of disciples (Mark 3:34–35 and parallels), and biological parenthood (motherhood or fatherhood) is therefore not a great concern.

Where female sexual misbehavior again becomes a preoccupation is in the later-written portions of the New Testament. Texts written at the end of the first and beginning of the second century C.E., like 1 and 2 Timothy, Titus, and Revelation, insist on female chastity and male hegemony and resist the authority of even ascetic women in the church. The most demonic of all women, actual or imaginary, are those of Revelation. These include a female prophet in Thyatira called "Jezebel," in terms reminiscent of the foreign queen of Israel (2:19), and the "Great Whore," both of whom are characterized as practicing and luring their "servants" to practice *porneia*, which represents apostasy. In terms of this work, however, where the one hundred forty-four thousand redeemed companions of the Lamb (Christ) "have not defiled themselves with women" (Rev. 14:4), *porneia* includes any form of sexual intercourse, including "sanctioned" marital intercourse, a view that makes adultery doubly damning.

ADULTERY:
DEVIANCE AS SUBVERSION

We will return to the various biblical texts in which adultery and its connection with the control of female sexuality are either central or important

albeit peripheral themes, but I hope to have indicated, however briefly, that
the canonical texts of the Bible, including the Tanakh, Apocrypha, and New
Testament, despite differences in time, beliefs, and social context, exhibit a
surprising diachronic consistency in their treatment of the subject. Such a
consistency is not all that startling, however, when we consider that this "paradigmatic meta-narrative"[28] is, as womanist theologian Delores Williams has
it, "a male story populated by human males, divine males, divine male emis-
saries and human women mostly servicing male goals."[29] This series of male
stories is moreover concerned with the "discourse of the body, and especially
sexuality."[30] Female sexuality, including female desire and sexual activity, is
thus seen through a male lens, as it affects and encounters male heterosexual
concepts of normative sexual desire and behavior.

All of this makes it difficult for feminist readers and interpreters of the
Bible who want to discover some form of liberating word for women or to
salvage a past for those for whom this metanarrative, if no longer normative, is nevertheless still a significant part of their heritage. As Williams observes, "Both feminist and womanist Christian women agree that the Bible
cannot be 'scrapped' because it has been and continues to be fundamental
in the life, faith, and hope of many women."[31] Alicia Ostriker puts it more
grimly: "I strive for healing. And so I must confront what is toxic."[32] Recent readings and rereadings of scripture such as *The Women's Bible Commentary* (1992) and *Searching the Scriptures* (1994) represent the combined
effort of feminist and womanist biblical scholars to examine and challenge
ideas of canonicity and the androcentric portrait of women presented in the
canonical Jewish and Christian scriptures. This activity indicates the hope
that even from what is toxic, as from a waste dump, with proper handling,
something retrievable and potentially salvageable may be found.

Confronting toxicity, however, often appears to be merely a process of
naming it and then dismissing it, putting it back in the "patriarchal" or
"kyriarchal"[33] waste, to be quickly disposed of. A case in point is the feminist treatment of the episode of the "woman taken in adultery" (John
7:53–8:11), the text that first led me to examine the image of the adulterous woman in biblical texts. My attention was caught when I advised a student who was presenting a paper on this passage in the Rhodes senior
seminar in religious studies. Although his paper focused on the textual dif-
ficulties of this passage and its patchy manuscript attestation, the student
asked me if I knew of any feminist commentary on this passage. I assumed
that I would find some but discovered that virtually no feminist scholarship
has given this passage or the woman as a character in it more than cursory
treatment.[34] Gail R. O'Day, the sole feminist commentator on this passage
to date, points out that centuries of androcentric scholarship have "misread" the text in order to establish "the unlawful sexuality of the woman"
as its heart.[35] Perhaps this is not a misreading of the text so much as it is a

correct reading of the assumptions about female sexuality and its "unlawfulness" embedded in the text, which constitute a threat to the solidarity of the male community that includes Jesus. At any rate, as O'Day concludes, "In fact the narrative evokes men's fear of what Jesus' teaching might suggest to their wives, of what might happen if women's sexuality passed out of men's control."[36]

The topic of adultery itself does not attract the attention of feminist scholars of biblical Judaism and Christianity, except as a means to expose yet another vestige of patriarchy. Laws and rules about adultery, like those about other realms of sexual behavior and its regulation (marriage, rape, incest, prostitution) are undeniably part and parcel of heterosexual male hegemony. The biblical laws are, according to Andrea Dworkin, "the basis of the social order as we know it" and "have not to this day been repudiated."[37] Like Dworkin, Mary Daly regards heterosexual marriage as rape and urges the (pure, female) self to reject "adulteration" by cleansing it of "the base ingredients that were assimilated through coerced adultery," an "adultery of the brain" that attempts to master and possess her mind.[38] But simply to assign these laws and rules, even while decrying or rejecting them, to a system accurately but dismissively categorized as patriarchal fails to give credit to fears and apprehensions that make these laws appear absolutely necessary to preserve the social order in the interests of the dominant group—necessary enough to legislate, if not always to execute, death for the violators. Moreover, to remove adultery from its association with the sexual body, as Daly does, while attempting to give women mental hegemony, also risks trivializing the very realm in which accusations of adultery have had their terrible power to define and therefore to control women. In the words of legal theorist Catharine MacKinnon, "A feminist theory of sexuality which seeks to understand women's situation in order to change it must first identify and criticize the construct 'sexuality' as a construct that has circumscribed and defined experience as well as theory."[39]

Radical feminist theorists, in their dismissal of marriage and adultery as parts of the heterosexual "rapist" system of patriarchy or kyriarchy, however justifiable such claims may be, do not give adequate attention to the fact that the perceived threat of women's violation of that system of male heterosexual hegemony is so great because the violation is itself a "strategy of resistance" to this ordering of society. In her analysis of female sexual repression, Patricia Murphy Robinson observes that women have "primarily submitted and even turned against themselves in the interests of those who have used and oppressed them. But they have also rebelled and these have been brief, historic moments . . . closely tied to sexual release."[40] Male-authored scripts, such as the majority of the biblical texts, reflect the views of those who dominate symbol systems, if not always the political and religious systems, of the various societies represented in them. Those who get

"out of place" threaten to subvert the entire social hierarchy of groups, especially groups like those represented in biblical literature that already perceive themselves as marginal and under threat from the outside. In such a
society, the deviance of no subgroup appears as dangerous as that of
women. "Woman" as a category transcends the boundaries both of nation
and class and is tied most closely to the anxiety-producing realm of reproduction. Upon "woman" then the ultimate integrity of the group is perceived to depend. In her study of heroines in male-authored literature,
Joanna Russ claims that rebellion for the female protagonist often takes the
form of adultery, this representing deviance from the depicted "social roles
women are supposed to play."[41]

Undeniably there are also times in the biblical texts, for example, the stories of Tamar (Genesis 38), Jael (Judges 4; 5), Ruth (book of Ruth), or Judith (book of Judith) when what is apparently adulterous or unchaste
behavior is either excusable or actually warranted by the situation, which is
to produce a male heir to continue an Israelite "line" or to protect the Israelites themselves. There are also stories, like those in which the patriarch
presents his wife to a foreign monarch as his own sister (Genesis 12; 20; 26),
in which the husband incites his wife to commit adultery (or at least to be
willing to do so) in order to protect his own skin. These stories, too, re-
bound negatively not on the patriarch or matriarch, but on the foreign king,
who is compelled to restore the jeopardized wife while sparing and enrich-
ing the life of her husband. In the story of the adultery of David with
Bathsheba, he is the one the narrative regards as the sole guilty party. The
death of their child and the subsequent sexual and political chaos of his
household are his punishment (2 Samuel 11—12), while Bathsheba bears
David's ultimate heir, Solomon, and helps engineer his ascent to the throne
(1 Kings 1—2).[42]

Even prostitutes, who because of their officially tolerated outsider status
do not bear the same awful stigma as adulterous wives or nonvirgin brides,
can sometimes be seen in a positive light. For example, Rahab "the harlot"
of Jericho rescues the Israelite spies and in turn is saved, with her family,
from the destruction of the city (Joshua 2; 6).[43] In the Gospels of the New
Testament, prostitutes make up part of the group of outsiders drawn to
Jesus so frequently that later interpreters assumed that female followers of
Jesus like Mary of Magdala and the "woman of the city" who anointed Jesus'
feet and dried them with her hair (Mark 14:3–9; Matt. 26:6–13; Luke
7:36–50), identified by Luke alone as "a sinner," were repentant prostitutes.

It must nevertheless be observed that two facts remain constant. First,
adultery (rather than prostitution, which never comes in for direct condemnation as an institution even in the New Testament) is portrayed as a
crime because it represents chaos in the foremost social institution, heterosexual marriage. It represents this chaos, moreover, because the wife's

sexuality is involved. Second, in the instances cited above in which women are used as sexual pawns (Sarah, Rebekah, Bathsheba), they are absolved of guilt because they do not initiate sexual contact out of a need to satisfy their own desires and because their actions often help to preserve the life of their husbands or continuity of their family line. In the case of Judith, Jael, and Ruth (the latter of whom, being literal foreigners and non-Israelites, already occupy a liminal status), their seductive behavior is practiced to preserve Israel (Judith, Jael) or to reconstitute an Israelite family line through marriage to an Israelite (Ruth). In none of these cases does female sexual behavior threaten to destabilize the community ruled by male interests, but in fact it is subordinated to those interests.

Seeing the biblical texts in this light does not end with examining and finally condemning definitions of adultery as tools of patriarchy or heterosexist kyriarchy. However legitimate such an enterprise may be, it ignores the strategies of women represented as demonic by the texts, women who, in a different reading, can be seen to have refused to be limited or controlled by these tools. They step over (transgress) boundaries, and therefore are labeled transgressors. They make their own choices of partners, not for marriage or the preservation of male life, the male line, or the continued interests of the male-dominated household or community, but for what can only be the satisfaction of their own desires, the fulfillment of their own pleasures on their own terms. Such women, in the eyes of the males who wrote and were the primary audience for these texts, are demonic precisely because they upset the desired power balance. The women are portrayed as seductive, where seduction equals destruction, because they have power over men who wish themselves to be in control, both of their own and of women's desires. As David Halperin has observed of the "sexualized rage" that surfaces par excellence in Ezekiel (and we might add, in Revelation as well), women when perceived as sexually powerful are also "cruel, sexually rampant, seductive and treacherous."[44] In many of the biblical texts, female adultery subverts—turns over from the underside—the hegemonic male heterosexual definition of and control over the proper direction of female desire, toward males. It is therefore a risky business for both sides.

READING SUBVERSIVELY

To regard female adultery as a strategy of resistance requires a different strategy of reading, one that feminist scholars have described as "counter-reading" (Mieke Bal, Ilana Pardes), or "reading like a trickster" (Claudia Camp).[45] This way of reading, according to Camp, "involves, first, claiming identity with those at the margins and second, willingness to read against the text, to read subversively."[46] If we read as tricksters, then, the

Adulteress becomes a kind of Adventuress in the nonpejorative sense of that
term, breaking out of the controls and norms of her social system to make
her own sexual choices, albeit at great risk, or breaking into an established
system that can only defend itself against her by condemning her as a monstrous "Other." Of course, as Judith Plaskow has pointed out, women need
to acknowledge that the "Otherness" of women is a projection of males:
"To ourselves, women are not Other."[47] The Adulteress or the Strange
Woman is a rare, exotic being who does not respect boundaries or limits
placed on her sexual freedom by others, but she is also "strange" because
she cannot be understood within the normative confines established by
male authority. In Israelite terms, she is not one possessed by a *ba'al*, a hus-
band/master. As portrayed by the prophets, even Israel as virgin/wife has a
series of sexual adventures in foreign realms with partners other than
YHWH. Israel as son/husband Israel has also given in to the seductions of
"strange women" and their gods, leaving YHWH, who at times is portrayed
as scolding father, at other times as abandoned wife.[48] In such texts, however, such dalliances are also cruelly punished just short of the prescribed
penalty for adultery: death. In prophetic terms, YHWH is portrayed as a
merciful God precisely because he does *not* punish the wayward wife to the
point of death, but instead restores her to him.

The Adulteress/Adventuress largely disappears in the Apocrypha except
for her role as a complement to the "good woman" Wisdom, perhaps in
continuation of her role in the canonical Proverbs. For the most part, however, the noble widow (the mother of 2 and 4 Maccabees; Judith in Judith;
Sarah, widowed seven times in Tobit) and the chaste (Susanna) and obedient (Esther) wife take her place. Even so, the seductive potential of women
is highlighted. Judith briefly takes on the role of an Adventuress to capture
and destroy the enemy general Holofernes; Esther dons the crown she
claims to "abhor as a filthy rag," putting on her most splendid robes to entice the favor of her husband to win life for the Jews and death for their enemies; and the temptingly beautiful Susanna attracts the lustful gaze of the
elders who falsely accuse her of adultery.

In the New Testament, where, as previously observed, even sanctioned
sexual behavior in marriage becomes problematic in the eschatological
viewpoint that calls prevailing social norms into question, the Strange
Woman is often eclipsed. In John 4 she emerges in the double outsider
Samaritan woman, who does not appear as threatening, perhaps because
she symbolizes the Johannine community's own double outsider status with
respect to both formative Judaism and other Christian groups. She appears
as the repentant sinner who anoints Jesus' feet with precious ointment and
her own tears, wiping them with her hair, in Luke 7:36–50. She also appears
in the much more shadowy and subdued guise of the potential victim of
male religious zealotry in the Pericope on the Adulteress in John 7:53–8:11,

only to reappear with a vengeance (as its recipient) as the Great Whore in Revelation. It seems ironically fitting that this nightmarish creation of androcentric literature and male hegemony should suffer the penalty of her *sexual freedom* —death. Notes Daly, "The harlot 'deserves' to be hated and destroyed, of course, for she symbolizes the uncontrollable."[49]

In sum, the biblical Adulteress is meant to be frighteningly, even deathly "Strange." She is Mark Taylor's monstrous "other" who must be slain to ensure hegemonic survival.[50] She serves as a warning, to those who would be defined as virtuous women and men who perceive themselves as vulnerable, that the risks of sexual freedom in the first case and sexual (or religious) experimentation in the second lead to death—death of the adulterous woman and death of her "victims." This happens because the power of female sexual desire in biblical texts has both "appropriate" and "inappropriate" uses. Female sexual desire is "appropriate" only when it is directed toward the building up of the patriarchal household and ultimately the community, which is likewise dominated by males. In that case, males may be the proper objects of female desire. Behavior that aims at the seduction of unsuspecting but appropriate males is the subject of praise rather than condemnation, like Tamar's seduction of Judah, Ruth's of Boaz, the solicitation of male guests by the street-walking Wisdom in Proverbs, and the bold initiative taken by the bride to satisfy her desire for the bridegroom in Song of Songs (cf. Song 3:1–4). Similarly, the stories in which women's sexuality is subordinated to the need for protection of the males of the household or of the community, like the wife/sister stories of Genesis, or those in which women use seduction against a perceived enemy, like the stories of Jael and Judith, serve because of their borderline status to reinforce the boundaries of what is appropriate. They condone deviance only in extraordinary and carefully limited situations, and do not act as exemplary endorsements of women's sexual freedom.

Female sexual desire is portrayed as disturbing and destructive to the community when it is perceived to aim at no benefit to husband or household, and the community must rid itself of such a threatening force to retain its proper identity and to confirm its boundaries. As Tina Pippin has noted of Revelation, and as is also true of other biblical texts, female desire for power is portrayed in wholly sexual terms, and "the affirmation of the female body and sexual desires and autonomy and erotic power" are utterly defeated and brought under the dominion of the appropriate male authorities.[51]

The problem for the male authors of the biblical texts (the origins of the book of Ruth in women's oral narratives are still a matter of dispute), whether they belong to the Tanakh, the Apocrypha, or the New Testament, is not female sexuality per se. That women do have sexual desires and experience sexual pleasure is not denied and at times is shown to be appropriate, if directed to an appropriate male, a husband for the virgin daughter

or wife, a master for the slave girl, a client for the prostitute. When regulated, directed, and controlled by male authorities (husbands, fathers, elders), female sexuality, like women themselves, is a male possession that
enhances male power, and thus is not a threat to male heterosexual hegemony in the way that "deviant" female sexuality is.

Indeed, as Howard Eilberg-Schwartz has suggested, the control of
women's sexuality, both in biblical Judaism and biblical Christianity, has
been pressed into service in finding "appropriate" definitions of masculinity and male sexual desire in monotheistic communities where YHWH and
Christ were envisioned as males, and in which the male-centered communities (Israel, the "church") were metaphorically gendered as female.[52]
Thus males create de-finitions (drawing of boundaries) of male sexual desire that cannot be disturbed by "others" without fundamental chaos. Notes
MacKinnon, "Law from the male point of view combines coercion with authority, policing society where its edges are exposed: at points of social resistance, conflict, and breakdown."[53]

What follows in this book is my approach as reader to the literary, biblical depiction of attempts to transgress these boundaries by adulterous/sex-
ually adventurous women and equal attempts by a largely androcentric
heterosexual body of literature to "confine" (confirm the boundaries for)
these women or to shut the borders against them by driving them out,
threatening to kill them, and warning members of the bounded community
against them. My interest, like my approach, is in showing how these texts
still have the power to define the categories of our dominant religious and
even political discourse about what is sanctioned and unsanctioned sexual
behavior, what is labeled masculine and feminine, what is considered normal and what is deviant.

I realize that in this attempt, I am dealing with gender categories in ancient literature and that there are two risks involved. One is to assume that
ancient concepts of gender are our own.[54] The second risk is that in speaking of gendered language and images of gender, ancient and modern, we
may inadvertently "re-valorize" the very categories we are attempting to
critique or deconstruct.[55] It is true that we have an irresistible tendency to
seek confirmation of our own particular worldviews, and the denial of those
views we oppose, in the literature that is meaningful for us. But it is also
true that in many ways these worldviews have been shaped by centuries of
"interested" readings of metanarratives like the Bible, which serve as a kind
of unconscious subtext for our own readings.

I intend neither to endorse nor to condemn adultery in women nor to
depict it specifically as yet another tool of patriarchy or kyriarchy, but to
show how the category "adultery" attempts both to define and confine
women in the societies represented by the biblical texts, and how it represents women's resistance to and transgression of such boundaries. I demon-

strate how adultery is defined in biblical, and to a certain extent, related extrabiblical law, how it is related to other laws about sexual crimes, including rape and incest, and particularly how adultery is linked to prostitution, "harlotry," or "whoring" (Heb., *znh*; Gk., *porneia*). This link will be specifically explored in the prophetic and apocalyptic literature, in which infidelity to the one God by "his" people through apostasy or syncretism is portrayed as marital infidelity and harlotry. Further, I will contend that such descriptions of female behavior as "harlotry" or "adultery" are applied in the biblical texts, not only to actual sexual behavior but to *any* independent female behavior that denies or rejects male control or that seeks its own power or autonomy.

Finally, I will suggest that there is a link between wisdom and transgression in the case of female biblical characters, since their wisdom is often presented as "feminine wiles" (i.e., seduction) and trickery. Their wisdom is treated positively when it deceives "outsiders" and helps to defend, protect, or build up the community and its males (Tamar, Rahab, Ruth, Jael, personified Wisdom, Judith, Esther). It is treated negatively, usually as a tool of "foreign" women, when it threatens to undermine the authority of the males of the community (Potiphar's wife, Delilah, the Strange Woman of the wisdom literature, the Corinthian female prophets, the Jezebel of 2 Kings and of Revelation, the Great Whore). This male fear of female wisdom understood as "feminine wiles" is so strong that the link between women's wisdom and their sexual unchastity is carried from and beyond the biblical texts to extend to wise women in Judaism like Beruriah, who according to rabbinic legend committed suicide after being seduced by one of her husband's students, and to women in Christianity like Mary of Magdala, who for centuries has been portrayed by the church as a repentant harlot, the "sinner" who anointed Jesus' feet and wiped them with her hair.[56] Thus, between the idealized "good woman" Wisdom of Proverbs and the monstrously evil Great Whore of Revelation is a borderland inhabited by the Strange Woman, the transgressor and trickster, the Adulteress and Adventuress who is beyond any but her own control. It is her story that illuminates those of her sisters—and our own. Therein lies its enduring power.

1

Adultery
and Other Sex Crimes

Indeed, the angel of the Lord told me and instructed me that women are more easily overcome
by the spirit of promiscuity than men.

—Testament of Reuben 5:3

SEXUALITY AND PROPERTY:
THE HISTORICAL SITUATION

The Jewish and Christian scriptures presuppose that the divine is revealed in human, linear history, thus sacralizing that history.[1] It is therefore
a difficult task to untangle externally verifiable events and persons from
their role in the biblical narrative of history as salvation. In other words, the
events of profane or ordinary history do not reach the biblical texts without already having been interpreted from a theological point of view: How
is the divine hand revealed in *this* particular event? How do *these* particular
social rules of conduct, let alone guidelines for ritual and statements of belief, define a relationship between God and the people who are called and
in effect "possessed" by God, whether they be "Israel" or the "church"?

It becomes necessary, therefore, when talking about biblical guidelines
for sexual conduct, including that of women, to examine those texts in
which regulation of sexual as well as other forms of communal behavior is
important. We must also recognize the possible historical situations that
both created the perceived necessity for such guidelines and dictated their
enshrining in sacred text. In the ancient world in which these texts were
written down, so much more than in our own, the act of writing itself was
one of privilege, practiced by an elite group of religious literates for the use
of a like group. Written texts, by their very nature, select from existing oral
narratives, lived experiences, and practices, and by this selection end up
ranking and privileging certain narratives, experiences, and practices,
sometimes to the near or total exclusion of others. Thus written texts, especially sacred texts, exhibit a narrowed range of vision. The creation of a
canon, a body of texts judged, again by an elite, as inspired and authorita-

tive because they support a particular view of the world, is an ultimate act of privilege, because these texts will now be regarded as revealing the divine nature, action, and will. As Sandra M. Schneiders wryly notes, "The text is not neutral," and more strongly, it is "ideologically biased," as is any interpretation of it.[2]

Such observations having been made, not even the most ideological nor the most fundamentalist interpreter of the Bible, however greatly they may disagree on the authorship and literal historicity of events as depicted in it, would deny that the biblical texts do contain information about the historical, political, and social contexts of the people for whom they had meaning. The problem arises when interpreters attempt to disentangle moral absolutes from culture-bound requirements. This problem is especially visible in the arena of sexual behavior. Only a few theorists of sexual politics would claim that the concept of adultery, like marriage laws and injunctions against homosexual behavior, belongs to culture-bound rules and customs about property and the continued fertility of a particular ethnic group, and therefore is not an essentially moral or religious issue.[3] The discussion that follows will pursue the link, even the tension, between mechanisms of social control, the historical situation, and the ideological perspective of the text.

In order to do this, however, something first needs to be said about the shape and the history of the texts themselves. The biblical laws are contained in that portion of the Tanakh known in Hebrew as the Torah (Teaching) and in Greek as the Pentateuch (Five Books). They are also known as the Five Books of Moses, since they have been attributed to the revelation by YHWH to Moses at Sinai. Although certain commandments and instructions are given by YHWH in the book of Genesis, the actual "revelation" begins with the Ten Commandments in Exodus 20 and continues, interspersed with historical narrative, through the books of Leviticus, concerning priestly purity; Numbers, composed mainly of genealogies and laws for the people of Israel; and Deuteronomy (the "Second Law"), a restatement of some of the preceding laws in the form of Moses' last words to the people of Israel before their entrance into Canaan. Jewish religious law has always begun with the Torah, with reinterpretations and expansions to apply biblical law to existing situations. This process led to the development of a second or "oral" Torah, which in turn, added to and expanded by religious sages, was written down as the Mishnah about 200 C.E.

Further interpretations, commentary, and expansions continued into late antiquity, resulting in the compilation of the collections of learned opinion known as the Palestinian (late fourth century C.E.) and Babylonian (beginning sixth century C.E.) Talmuds. The Gospels of the New Testament indicate that early Christians were also engaged in the process of interpreting and teaching the written and oral Torah (see Matthew 5—7, the

"Sermon on the Mount," for example). The "dual Torah" and its applicability (or nonapplicability) to new, formerly pagan members of the church was of great concern to missionaries like Paul (see Galatians 1—5, for example). For Christians, however, the books of what later became known as the New Testament which made up part of a Christian canon that also included the Tanakh in Greek and the Apocrypha in the late fourth century C.E., were themselves a reinterpretation as well as a continuation of the revealing of God's nature and divine will. Begun at Sinai, this revelation was regarded as definitive with Jesus and the apostles, passing from them through authoritative spiritual succession. The fourth century also marked the movement of Christianity in the Roman Empire from illegal to tolerated religion to the dominant religion in a state where the law of the land was also Christianized law.

The Torah itself, regarded as the word of God by Jews and Christians, was nevertheless always viewed by its exponents as needing interpretation according to the needs and concerns of communities widely separated by time and circumstance. According to Talmudic scholar Moshe David Herr, "The statutes of the Written Law could never have been fulfilled literally even in the generation in which they were given."[4] The question, however, is whether all the laws that appear in the written Torah were "given" in one generation. A nearly universal scholarly consensus says that they were not. The Torah itself reflects different periods of composition and different sources that in turn reflect perhaps centuries of oral tradition. Scholars of the Tanakh generally agree, however, that the first four books of the Torah (Genesis–Numbers) were compiled and edited, probably by scribal hands, in the sixth century B.C.E., during or after the Judean exile in Babylon.[5] The fifth book, Deuteronomy, is supposed to have been the "book of the law" that was "found" or recovered in the Temple during a religious reform headed by the Judean king Josiah in 621 B.C.E. (2 Kings 22:11). It too may belong to or possibly postdate the exile, since it reflects the postexilic "revisionist" hand also observed in the historical books from Joshua to Kings, known as the Deuteronomistic History.[6]

What we probably have in the five books of the Torah, therefore, are traditions and some materials reflecting a variety of historical periods from about 1250 B.C.E. to 500 B.C.E., written down, organized, and edited sometime during the sixth century B.C.E. by a scribal and priestly literate elite interested in reestablishing cultural and religious order in the face of the chaos that was caused by confused lines of authority, displacement, and dispossession from the land of settlement, and the threat of assimilation to another culture. Not coincidentally, this same elite expected to direct the reestablishment of order, as evidenced by the books of Ezra and Nehemiah, in which the first steps taken to "restore" Jerusalem are the demand to banish "foreign" wives and the rereading of the "book of the law."

All of the Torah and a good deal of the Tanakh thus may be seen to reflect a struggle between the forces of order and stability and those of disorder and uncontrollability. This battle is begun in scripture by YHWH in his creation of a cosmos, a defined world, out of chaos, the undifferentiated deep (Genesis 1). It culminates in his establishment of the covenant at Sinai as reenacted in the books of Exodus through Deuteronomy. The anxiety over the threat of overwhelming chaos, symbolized by the waters of the deep in the creation and flood narratives, appears in social terms as uncertainty over preserving ethnic integrity, controlling female fertility, and establishing and retaining lines of leadership and authority within a fragile nomadic tribal structure. In such situations, the greatest threats to the established order of a small and often marginal people are seen to come from the outside, from other groups who are rivals for the possession of land and women's reproductive capacity, and from the inside, from subgroups within the society, primarily women, whose compliance is critical to the maintenance of the establishment and the integrity of communal boundaries. Historian Gerda Lerner has pointed out that women, whose reproductive capacity is vital to the survival of the group, are sought after as a possession, not only by the group itself, but by any conquerors who seek to control or extinguish the distinct identity of the defeated.[7] In situations of a threat to group survival, prescribed ownership of women's sexuality and reproductivity is therefore deemed essential. Punishable offenses therefore are those in which men's rights to "their" women are violated.

Most of the laws relating to sexual offenses in the Torah are contained in the Ten Commandments (Ex. 20:1–7; cf. Deut. 5:1–21), the Covenant Code (Ex. 20:22–23:33), the Holiness Code (Leviticus 17—26), and the instructions to the people in Numbers (Num. 5:1–6:21), which include a complex test for a wife suspected of adultery (Num. 5:11–31). Similar assumptions about sexuality, however, inform other parts of the Torah, especially the stories of patriarchs and matriarchs in the book of Genesis, which link women's sexuality to the needs of the patriarchal family.[8] Consistent in both statute and narrative is the governing belief that a woman's status relates to her sexual potential and even more to the man who is entitled to its use. The only legally autonomous, free women in scripture are those whose sexuality has already been "owned" or enjoyed by a male. According to Judith Romney Wegner, these are interpreted in the Mishnah to include the daughter who is legally outside of her father's authority, having reached the age of twelve years, six months and a day without betrothal or marriage (a category more theoretical than actual); the divorced woman, no longer under marital authority (a potential adulteress in the New Testament); and the widow who has produced a legitimate male heir.[9] Adultery, whether committed by a man against his (male) neighbor by having intercourse with the neighbor's wife, or committed by a married woman

(*be'ulat ba'al*) against her *ba'al*, her "master" or husband, is "a crime deserv-
ing of the severest penalty," first as an "infringement of a husband's property rights," and later "as an offense against the moral sensibilities (and
structural concerns) of the society at large."[10]

WHOSE WOMB IS IT, ANYWAY?
THE "ENDANGERED ANCESTRESS"

The first passages that revolve around the possession of a woman's sexuality by the "appropriate" male occur in Genesis in the form of the
"wife/sister" or "ancestress in danger" stories of Genesis 12:10–20 and
Genesis 20, concerning Sarah and Abraham, and Genesis 26:6–11, concerning Isaac and Rebekah. In each of these stories, a Hebrew patriarch
(Abraham in the first two; Isaac, Abraham's son, in the second) resides in
Gentile territory as an "alien" (Heb., *ger*). In each, the patriarch's fear that
his liminal status will enable foreign males to kill him in order to possess
his wife is explicitly stated (Gen. 12:11–12; 20:11–12; 26:6–7). He therefore
alleges that she is his sister, protecting himself by offering her to be physically and presumably sexually possessed by another, more powerful male.
These stories are thus about power, played out in the guise of sexual authority over women. Their underlying assumption is that males who have
power will subdue other males through taking "their" women. Neither
Abraham nor Isaac is shown to be concerned about the possibility that their
wives will be forced to commit adultery, even less about the strong probability of their rape. Surrendering their sexual possessions will, in their view,
preserve their own lives.

As J. Cheryl Exum points out, these "endangered ancestress" stories are
more about danger to the ancestor/patriarch than to the ancestress/matri-
arch.[11] There is no suggestion in the narrative that either Abraham or Isaac
acted in a morally reprehensible fashion.[12] In only one of the stories is it
hinted that intercourse actually took place, when the pharaoh of Egypt
"takes" Sarah for his wife (Gen. 12:15–19), an act that results in dreadful
plagues, which expose the deception. In the other two stories, intercourse
is strenuously denied. In Genesis 20, God protects Abimelech of Gerar
from touching Sarah, even though both Abraham and she (in the only instance in these three stories where the woman is explicitly complicit in the
deception) allege that she is Abraham's sister. Further, Abraham insists that
he did not lie, because Sarah is indeed his sister—his half-sister, with not a
glance by the narrative at possible incest, which is forbidden in the later
Levitical code. Abimelech "redeems" Sarah by giving Abraham a thousand
pieces of silver, an act that is intended to vindicate her of any guilt (Gen.
20:16). The punishment for Abimelech's illegitimate possession of Sarah,

YHWH's "closing fast all the wombs" of the women of Abimelech's household (20:18) is reversed upon the restoration of Sarah to her rightful man. In Genesis 26: 6–11, the same king, Abimelech, is himself responsible for protecting Gerar by exposing the lie Isaac told "the men of the land" about his "sister" Rebekah. Considering the lack of expressed disapproval by any of the narratives over deception and sexual exploitation by the patriarchs, there is a suggestion of the trickster type of narrative, in which deceit by the underdog is viewed as necessary for survival, not only of the individual but of the group.[13] In this type of scenario, sexual trickery is a key ingredient and, like other forms of trickery against the more powerful outsider, is approved.

In each of these narratives—together with another narrative that revolves around the issues of sexual possession and deception, that of Lot and his daughters in Genesis 19, which immediately precedes the second wife/sister story in Genesis 20—not honor but survival is at stake. As Susan Niditch observes, "These motifs express deep concern about Israelite identity, and have ultimately to do with exogamy and endogamy," ways to differentiate the inside "us" from the foreign "them."[14] In establishing the boundaries between the two, women are once again vital pawns. According to Exum, "In patriarchal thought, women occupy a marginal position; they are at the boundary of the phallocentric symbolic order, the borderline between men and chaos."[15]

This borderline and its relationship to the possession of women's sexuality is nowhere clearer in the patriarchal narratives than in the story in Genesis 19 of Lot and his daughters during and after the destruction of Sodom. Like Abraham in Egypt and like Abraham and Isaac in Gerar, Abraham's nephew Lot lives in Sodom as a *ger*, an alien in a position of no authority and some danger (Gen. 19:9). The episode concerning Lot and his family opens with the impending destruction of the outsider (Canaanite) territory of Sodom because of its yet unspecified but "grave" sin, of which the "outcry" has reached YHWH (Gen. 18:20). When YHWH tells Abraham what he is about to do, Abraham persuades him to spare the city if there are "ten righteous" left in it (Gen. 18:32). Unbeknownst to Abraham and the reader, but implied at the beginning of chapter 19, YHWH has not found ten righteous and so decides to destroy the city except for the family of Lot. He sends his messengers to Sodom to tell Lot, but before they can get their message out, Lot's house, where they have been graciously invited to stay, is besieged by the "men of the city" of all ages (19:4), who demand to have the guests brought out "so that we may know them" (19:5). The Hebrew verb used here (*yd'*), "to know," has, as elsewhere, a dual meaning: in addition to its usual meaning, it serves as a euphemism for having intercourse with. That the Sodomite men are going to demonstrate their power over the strangers (and over Lot, unless he is able to protect them) by rape becomes clearer when Lot offers to appease them by offering his virgin daughters to be used by the Sodomites as they please. The men refuse the bait, showing that their intention is really to exercise their power, this time by crushing the *ger* Lot for attempting to assert his authority over them: " 'This fellow came here as an alien, and he would play the judge! Now we will deal worse with you than with them.' And they pressed hard against the man Lot" (19:9, NRSV). It is only after the danger is averted by the strangers' striking the Sodomites with blindness that they deliver their message, and it is only in this message—that Lot and his family, including sons-in-law, are to leave Sodom—that we find out Lot *has* sons-in-law, identified specifically as those "who were to marry his daughters." What the sons-in-law may have thought of Lot's offer to damage their brides we are not told; we are told, however, that the sons-in-law don't pay any attention to Lot because they think his tale of oncoming destruction is a joke (19:14).

The foolish sons-in-law are included, however, only to set up the remainder of the narrative. They and any sons (alluded to by the messengers in 19:12) Lot may have had perish in the destruction of Sodom, while Lot's wife is turned into a pillar of salt for looking back on it. Thus, the only reproductive potential of the family rests with Lot's daughters, who become the "endangered ancestresses" of this tale. Lot, another fearful patriarch, begs YHWH to be allowed to escape to the nearby city of Zoar and not to the hills, where he is afraid he will meet with disaster and die (19:19). Too timid to settle even in Zoar (perhaps he learned how precarious a position is that of the alien), he finally does flee to the hills, where he lives in a cave with his two daughters (19:30). At this point, the initiative passes to the daughters, with the older expressing her fear to the younger that there is "not a man on earth" who will have intercourse with them (19:31). That this is an exaggeration becomes immediately apparent from the following verse; the problem is not that potential mates do not exist, it is that their father is the only male left from their family line (19:32). Getting their father drunk, they have intercourse with him and in turn bear sons, the ancestors of the Moabites and Ammonites, relatives, though inimical ones, of the Israelites.

As often happens with such tales, the interpreter is left with more gaps than links. Interpreters have traditionally filled in the gaps with assumptions about ancient Israelite society that are based on their own social norms. Naïve modern readers, for example, who seldom encounter the whole of this text, suppose its point is that homosexual behavior is the "sin" for which God destroyed Sodom, totally missing the fact that the issue is *rape*. They are often appalled by the offer that Lot, a supposedly righteous man, makes of his virgin daughters, exposing them to gang rape as their first sexual experience, but they accept the frequent justification of commentators that one must understand the "law of oriental hospitality," in which male guests, whether heavenly or earthly ones, have rights that supersede those of the daughters of the house to bodily integrity.[16] They are quite aghast at the idea that the daughters subsequently manipulate their own father into having incestuous intercourse in order to preserve offspring for their family, but again tend to concentrate on modern preoccupations that are textual side issues at best. Several of my students, when first reading this passage, did not miss the point that the Moabites and the Ammonites, the ancestors of Israel's enemies, are the children of incest. They became preoccupied, however, with the idea that these offspring might have the defects modern science supposes to be the result of inbreeding, thence making them easy prey for the Israelites. They are rather chagrined when they find out that among all the Levitical laws prohibiting incest, father-daughter incest is not mentioned (Lev. 20:10–21). More suspicious readers have seen the seduction of Lot by his daughters as sexual vengeance, in which *they* overpower Lot and force him to do *their* sexual will.

This passage, like all of those about endangered ancestry, has to do with anxiety about offspring, the continuity of the clan line. In all four Genesis texts, the patriarch and his family occupy marginal situations, as minority aliens in lands controlled by "others," who have or could have power over them. This power is manifested from the outside, by the possibility that the "men of the land" may take the marginal group's women and kill the men (Gen. 12:11–13; Gen. 26:6–7), thus effectively ending the reproductive identity of the group, a technique recently practiced in the ethnic conflict in Bosnia-Herzegovina. Power is also demonstrated in the threatened rape of marginal men, whether travelers in strange places or strangers (aliens) in a strange land. In either case, authority is defined as sexual possession and the right to have sexual property at one's disposal. Having sexual property is usually understood in these texts as being able to direct and control reproductive capacity. The Jewish philosopher Philo (20 B.C.E.–50 C.E.), for example, enamored as he was of pagan Greek philosophy, heaped scorn upon the male homoerotic culture in which it was produced because he saw it as "unproductive" since no children resulted from homosexual relations.[17]

Similarly, endogamy—marriage, intercourse, and procreation within the tribe to continue tribal identity in situations where it is at risk, as critically demonstrated by the wife/sister stories, the story of Lot and his daughters, and later by Abraham's search for a "wife from his kindred" for Isaac (Gen. 24:3–4)—is of paramount concern in these texts. Female reproductivity is subordinated to the interests of those who create the order of the tribe, those whose identity is of paramount importance, the males. The patriarchs (fathers, husbands, and sometimes brothers) own the primary rights to the sexuality of their women (daughters, wives, concubines and slaves, sisters) to ensure the production of male heirs whose paternity is certain. They can even, perhaps foolishly, dispose or offer to dispose of this, their chief and often their only valuable possession in foreign territory, in order to save their own lives. If the patriarchs of Genesis own nothing else, they own their women, who may be exchanged, not only for the men's lives and continued security, but for more possessions (Gen. 12:16; 20:14–16; 26:11–16). Perhaps the primary lesson that is to be learned from the incest of Lot and his daughters in Gen. 19:31–38 is not that it is morally wrong, since father-daughter incest was never considered a violation of sexual ownership, nor that the daughters wish to continue the family line, a desire that in the context is perfectly appropriate. Instead the lesson is that the problem with the conception of the Moabites and Ammonites, who even though they are related to the Israelites are not regarded as "true" Israelites, stems from daughters taking the sexual initiative; it is they, and not their father, already established as their "owner" in Genesis 19:8, who control their father's sexuality and direct it toward their will, not he who ultimately controls and directs theirs. Lot is made drunk and is every bit as helpless as they were when he offered them to be gang-raped by the male citizens of Sodom. This illegitimate role reversal, the text implies, produces tainted and illegitimate offspring.

An endangered ancestress story of a slightly different type, one that presents the themes of the volatility of female sexuality as threat and as threatened, and the question of who owns women's bodies, is that of Hagar in Genesis 16 and 21:8–21. Hagar is a foreign slave among foreigners. She is the Egyptian slave of Sarah, who is herself the sexual property of the patriarch Abraham, a man who willingly used her as a sexual pawn to preserve his own life among the powerful Egyptians. As a slave woman, Hagar is a powerless Egyptian, but her presence still poses a threat to Sarah and Abraham. Although Abraham is understood as a man over against Sarah and Hagar as women, he is, with Sarah, in opposition to Hagar because the latter is "other" ethnically.[18] Sarah and Abraham, moreover, have the power to use Hagar sexually, and they employ it, Sarah because she is barren and must provide a surrogate womb, Abraham because he needs a male heir (Gen. 16:3). Hagar regards Sarah "lightly" when Hagar conceives Abraham's child (16:4). But Sarah still has power over Hagar, as Abraham allows his chief wife to abuse the foreign concubine so harshly that she runs away. Persuaded by YHWH to return, Hagar bears Ishmael, the son whose offspring will be as many as those of Isaac, son of the favored Sarah. Again there is conflict: Sarah will not allow the slave woman's son to compete with the sanctioned heir Isaac, and Hagar is sent into the wilderness because of Sarah's enmity and Abraham's consent (Gen. 21: 8–19).

Both Hagar and her son Ishmael, although preserved through YHWH's care, are forever threatening outsiders, Ishmael living on the fringes of Israelite territory and his descendants always at war with Isaac's descendants, his own kin (Gen. 16:12; 21:20–21). His descendants come from the Egyptian wife his mother obtains for him, and thus remain more Egyptian than

Israelite. The foreign woman, even though literally possessed, physically and sexually, by the Israelite chief couple, nevertheless has power to threaten the integrity of the line, to cause sexual and reproductive turbulence. The "strange woman" and her offspring must be exiled so that the true ancestress, Sarah; the chief of the clan, Abraham; and his sanctioned male heir are not imperiled in any way and legitimate descent is secured.

The story of Jacob and the women related to him also involves ownership of women and its relationship to the integrity of the family line and to property. The text implies that Jacob's mother Rebekah favors her second son over her first, the heir Esau, because of her "bitterness" toward her two foreign daughters-in-law, Esau's Hittite wives (Gen. 26:24–35; 27:46). Even when Esau realizes his Canaanite wives are not appropriate and marries a daughter of Ishmael, Mahalath, it does no good, for though related to the Israelites, as the tale of Ishmael shows, she is not one of them. Jacob, the favored son and heir through trickery, must search for a wife from the right kindred, from the daughters of his mother's brother Laban. But here the trickster himself is tricked: after serving seven years for his desired wife Rachel, the one he "goes into" on his wedding night is Leah, the elder daughter, and he is forced to serve another seven years for Rachel. As Laban's sons grow suspicious of Jacob's prosperity, achieved through their sisters, Jacob proposes flight back to Canaan with his wives. Rachel and Leah, indignant with their father and brothers, suggest that the time has come to get even:

> Is there any portion or inheritance left to us in our father's house? Are we not regarded by him as foreigners (lit., "foreign women," *nokriyyoth*)? For he has sold us (*mekerenu*), and he has been using up the money given for us. All the property that God has taken away from our father belongs to us and to our children. (Gen. 31:14b–16a, NRSV)

Rachel then takes her father's household gods, symbolic of the ownership of his property, and hides them in her tent under a camel saddle. Pointedly, when her father comes looking for them, she emphasizes the connection between her sexuality and the property, as she sits on the saddle, excusing her not rising because "the way of women is upon me" (Gen. 31:35).[19] Laban, who has acted upon the presumption that he owns the rights to his daughters' reproductivity, exclaims in exasperation, "The daughters are my daughters, the(ir) children are my children. . . . But what can I do today about these daughters of mine, and the children they have borne?" (Gen. 31:43, NRSV). What he does is make a covenant agreement with Jacob, whereby the daughters and their children pass out of Laban's ownership and protectorship into Jacob's. Once again, uncertainty over what man legitimately possesses the right to women and their sexual potential is a source of considerable conflict and anxiety.

In yet another text, the rights of possession of a woman's sexuality, and hence of her value (or honor) to her family and clan, are in dispute. This is the story of Jacob and Leah's only mentioned daughter, Dinah, in Genesis 34, which Niditch calls "a tale of would-be marital relations gone awry," since Dinah serves as "the potential link" between the native Shechemites and the nomadic Israelites, who view themselves here as the arbiters of appropriate sexual conduct even amongst strangers.[20] Again, a potential ancestress, or at least her reproductive value to her family, is endangered by a foreign power. Once again, the marginal situation of the Israelites is highlighted, this time quite literally, as Jacob and clan are camping on land purchased from the Shechemites outside of their city. Dinah ventures out of the camp, into presumably safe territory, although the reader suspects foreign territory cannot be safe, to visit the women of the region (Gen. 34:1). In a foreshadowing of the David-Bathsheba tale (2 Samuel 11), in which another royal male uses his power to achieve immediate gratification of his desires, the Hivite prince Shechem sees Dinah, lusts after her, and rapes her (34:2). In the next verse, however, he is shown to be in love with her and wishes to marry her. Although Jacob "holds his peace" when he learns of the rape, his sons are "indignant and very angry, because [Shechem] had committed an outrage in Israel . . . , for such a thing ought not to be done" (34:7, NRSV). Dinah, who says not a word in the entire chapter nor in the only other verses in Genesis that pertain to her, 30:21 (her birth) and 46:15 (her place in Jacob's genealogy), becomes the subject of negotiations between Jacob and Shechem's father Hamor, with the suggestion that this will be the first of many intermarriages. Her indignant brothers try another tack, alleging that they will not "give" their sister to one who is uncircumcised (regardless of the fact that they are not the ones who have the power to bestow their sister). Cheerfully, Hamor, Shechem, and all the men of the city submit to circumcision, only to be slaughtered "while in their pain" by Simeon and Levi, Dinah's full brothers, the Hivite wives and property becoming the possessions of the treacherous Israelites (Gen. 34:25–29).

To Jacob's remonstration that this attack has endangered him and his family, Simeon and Levi protest, "Shall our sister be treated like a whore?" (*zonah;* Gen. 34:31). This tale appears to be another inversion or perversion of the wife/sister stories, in that a real rather than feigned sister *does* provide both disaster for foreign powerful males and prosperity for her kin at the cost of her own sexual exploitation, but she never becomes a wife or a concubine, either of an Israelite or foreigner because she is "defiled." Although the laws of Exodus 22:15–16 and Deuteronomy 22:28–29 provide for compensation to the father (the owner of the minor daughter, as seen in the story of Lot), just as Hamor offers the bride-price to Jacob for Dinah, and for the rapist to marry the girl, Simeon and Levi will not permit even this to take place, even though Dinah, probably a minor daughter, is

Jacob's sexual property, and the decision is his. As Alice Ogden Bellis points out, there is no Hebrew word for rape: the closest is "shame" (*'innah*), and Dinah's brothers are shamed because their sister has been treated like the one "who can't be shamed," the whore who by social and sexual definition has no "shame."[21] The men "own" the disgrace as "theirs" because Dinah represents a sexual possession taken by a foreign and therefore illegitimate possessor. As in the other wife/sister stories, the focus is not on the woman's actions or feelings, but on relations between males, with women as the sexual property that is the locus of contention between them.[22]

In all of these stories, together with that of Tamar and Judah, which will be discussed later under a different category, women's honor is related to their sexual function and is always situational. In other words, the question of honor or shame does not apply primarily to the woman but to the man to whom she belongs as sexual property or, if she is unmarried, to the family that can benefit by her reproductive potential. Exum asks, "What is this [woman's] honor anyway but a male construct based on the double standard, with its insistence on the exclusive sexual rights to the woman by one man?"[23] Shame results only when the man who possesses her does not consent to the sexual use or exploitation of his daughter or wife. Jacob, for example, while initially indignant, is not "shamed" by Dinah's violation, when it appears to mean a potential marriage alliance, safety, and prosperity in Canaan. He is only outraged when Simeon and Levi, who do feel shame, avenge Dinah's rape, because he now feels the survival of the entire clan is endangered. When he blesses his other descendants in Genesis 49:5–7, he curses Simeon and Levi for murdering the men of Shechem, and presumably for losing a potential alliance, with the loss of their own ability to be patriarchs. The descendants of Simeon and Levi will be "divided" and "scattered" among Jacob's other offspring, as if *they* and not Shechem had damaged Dinah's value as sexual commodity, because they usurped Jacob's ownership rights to his daughter.

In these narratives, according to Sharon Ringe, women appear "as direct and indirect 'objects' and not as 'subjects.' "[24] Women are categorized by their status with regard to men in the religio-legal codes, which cover many centuries and situations of practice but are written from the date and from the standpoint of the exilic or postexilic periods. In the endangered ancestress stories, female sexual integrity is shown to be not a personal possession but a guarantee of the integrity of familial descent and thus of communal identity. As in the wife/sister stories, any woman outside of these corporate boundaries has the status, however temporary, of a foreigner and outsider, having the potential to disrupt sanctioned arrangements within the group and hence pose a threat to its identity. The surest way in which group identity is threatened and even destroyed is for its women to produce offspring whose status as heirs, members, and future leaders of the group is confused or in doubt. In these cases, the corporate boundaries, like the women themselves, are penetrated, leaving the community "open" to the outside, a situation that is deemed a particularly perilous one by those marginal groups, like the Israelites in the tales above, to whom the maintenance of a strong corporate identity is important. Maintenance of the "stability and health of the . . . social structure," observes Niditch, means that women "between categories," the use of whose sexual functions is open to question (the unmarried woman who has had intercourse, the barren wife or widow, the adulterous wife), must either be assigned to the appropriate category or "destroyed."[25] The woman who forfeits her sexual "integrity," read as "sexual rights exclusive to a family male," has seriously threatened the integrity of the group, which then sees itself responsible for righting their "wrong."

SEXUAL CATEGORIES
IN THE LAW

The books of Exodus through Deuteronomy, which represent the forging of Israelite identity through deliverance from slavery to a foreign power, also contain the core of biblical law in the form of utterances (*debarim*) from YHWH. Because it is YHWH, the voice from the burning bush, and no other deity, who redeems the people who belong to him from slavery to other, ultimately inferior masters, it is also he who defines what the people owe him in order to maintain this protective relationship. YHWH's ownership of the people Israel is described in various metaphors, but one of the most striking is that of the ownership of a wife by her husband. This metaphor is extensively employed in prophetic literature from the mid–eighth century onward, but it is present even in the Decalogue in Exodus 20:5 (cf. Deut. 5:9) in the form of YHWH's "jealous" demand for an exclusive relationship with Israel, the language of jealousy coming not from political covenant language but from the covenant language of marriage. The same "spirit of jealousy" that YHWH has toward Israel seizes the suspicious husband in Numbers 5:14, so that he makes his wife undergo the ordeal of the bitter water to clear herself.[26]

The relationship between YHWH and Israel is both covenantal and sexual.[27] A wife is described in biblical law as "*be'ulat ba'al*," a "woman laid by a master."[28] The eighth-century Israelite prophet Hosea, the first to exploit the relationship between YHWH and Israel as one of faithful husband to adulterous wife, uses this language in a pun on the name of the god Ba'al, with whom Israel has committed adultery, forsaking her true *ba'al*, her husband (*'iš*) YHWH (Hos. 2:16–17). YHWH is master of Israel, whether as protector-overlord or husband.

The story of the forging of the identity of the people Israel, the exodus from Egypt, the making of the covenant with YHWH at Sinai, and the anticipated settlement in Canaan occupies four books of the Torah, and good proportions of these books are concerned with legal codes that are represented as divinely commanded codes of conduct for the people of Israel, their leaders, and their religious authorities. As Drorah Setel points out, however, "Because the final editing of the text as we have it was in all probability the work of men with concerns specific to the priesthood," women are present only as they affect or are affected by these concerns.[29] Since the Priestly editors of the traditions represented in the text form an elite even among Jewish males, moreover, we have no way of knowing if their interests or practices reflect those of all males in their society, or if the laws and the penalties for their infringement were strictly followed. The death penalty for adultery, for example, is not recorded as ever having been exacted but is threatened several times, more often in the case of women (Tamar in Genesis 38, Susanna in the eponymous book of the Apocrypha, the Adulteress in John 7:53–8:11, for example) than that of men. The penalty for the woman's male partner, by the time of the writing of the book of Proverbs, is not death but public shaming in the assembly (*qahal*) of male Israelites, with loss of property to others, perhaps as appropriate compensation for his having stolen the sexual property of another male (Prov. 5:9–14).[30]

Women have significant roles in the exodus story largely as adjuncts to men, as preservers or threateners of male well-being. The Hebrew midwives Shiphrah and Puah rescue the valuable male babies of their tribe through typical underdog trickery (Ex. 1:15–21). The life of the most important male of the exodus, Moses, is protected by four women: his mother Jochebed, his sister Miriam, who later challenges Moses' authority and is severely punished by YHWH for it (Num. 12:10–15), the pharaoh's daughter who becomes his adoptive mother (Ex.2:1–10), and later his wife Zipporah, who saves his life even from YHWH (Ex. 4:24–26). Once again, the continuity and identity of the group, when threatened from the outside, are protected by women. When these women take authority away from men, as in Miriam's case, they are expelled until order—the appropriate male leadership—is restored. Miriam is stricken with leprosy and therefore put "outside of the camp" until she repents and is forgiven. As Setel notes, "The lineage, actions and title ('prophet') attributed to Miriam, as well as Zipporah's connections to a priestly household (2:16) and an apparently sacrificial act (4:25), point to a cultic status [for women] that was forgotten or repressed in the compilation of the text as it was handed down."[31]

Within the biblical laws themselves, women are largely defined by their sexual functions and by men's rights to and possible ritual "pollution" by those functions.[32] While YHWH's covenant is with the "people of Israel," it is apparent from Exodus 19:15 that these "people," whom YHWH tells to remain in a state of consecration by avoiding contact with women, are men. Indeed, the first conditions of YHWH's covenant, the "Ten Words" or Ten Commandments, are addressed to a male Israel, using the masculine singular "you."[33] It is this "you" that is enjoined, not only from committing adultery (Ex. 20:14; cf. Deut. 5:18) but from coveting a neighbor's wife, along with his other property, including his male and female slaves, ox, and donkey (Ex. 20:17; cf. Deut. 5:21).

Judith Romney Wegner summarizes the biblical laws about women as displaying "two distinct tendencies," one that deals with women as property, as in the Decalogue, the other that deals with their specific entitlements, as in the Covenant Code (Ex. 20:22–23:33). Female slaves are naturally regarded as property, but nonslave women are also regarded as possessions of men. These include minor daughters, wives, and widows without male children.[34] In the Covenant Code, a collection of religious law dating from various eras in Israel's history, not a great deal is said about wives as property, except for the law concerning compensation paid to a woman's husband when the pregnant woman miscarries because of an injury caused when others are fighting (Ex. 21:22–24). There are however several laws treating daughters as the property of their fathers. These include the law concerning a daughter sold into slavery (21:7–11) and that of a virgin not yet betrothed who is seduced (not raped), for whom her seducer owes her father the bride-price for virgins, defined in Deut. 22:29 as fifty shekels, whether her father allows her to marry him or not (22:16–17). When a daughter is sold into slavery, it is assumed that she consequently becomes the sexual property of her master, who, if she does not please him, must allow her to be purchased back, presumably by a relative, since he cannot sell her to "foreigners" (21:8). If the master gives her to his son as a concubine, he is to treat her as a daughter. If he himself takes "another wife" he is not to diminish the rights of the "first wife," his concubine, to food, clothing, or intercourse, or he will have to let her go free (21:11).

All three of these instances are exceptional, like other instances when women are specifically mentioned in the law[35] and all three assume that women are the sexual property of men. In the case of the miscarrying woman, both she and her fetus are assumed to belong to her husband. Consequently, he is the one who receives payment for the loss of a potential life belonging to him, according to the principle of *lex talionis*, the "law of retaliation," which fixes the limits of punitive damages. A daughter is a commodity that can be sold into slavery, where she becomes the sexual property of her master, who can in turn bestow her upon his son.[36] If she is intended for marriage but her virginity is "spoiled" by the man who seduces her, her father must be compensated for the loss of the price he would normally be paid for giving his daughter in marriage as a virgin.

Out of all the Torah and out of the Tanakh as a whole, it is in Leviticus, literally the "book of the priests," that the priestly elite's concern for the maintenance of order is paramount, shown in the establishment of categories of holiness and in the definition of group and personal boundaries between sacred and profane, "inside" and "outside," Israel and "the nations" (Gentiles). Whatever its importance to later Judaism (and its almost total lack of importance to emerging Christianity, with the principal exception of its rules on sexual conduct), Leviticus focuses on the worship of YHWH, centered physically in the Temple at Jerusalem but conceptually in the maintenance of an appropriate relationship. This relationship between YHWH and his people Leviticus defines as "holiness" (Lev. 19:2), an integrity manifested both in obedience to the divine will, expressed through YHWH's commandments, and in maintaining ritual purity.[37] The purity laws are designed to protect the community from "pollution," which is understood as a disturbance in inner stability, usually caused by a breach of boundaries. Many of the Levitical laws are concerned with bodily functions that are symbols of boundary transgression, such as intake by eating (kosher laws) and the emission of body fluids, especially semen, menstrual fluid, and other discharges.[38] Howard Eilberg-Schwartz observes that in Levitical law menstrual blood is especially surrounded by taboo, since it is an important boundary divider, "death over against life, the female over the male, and the involuntary over against the controllable [emission of semen]."[39] Further regulations surround life passages like birth, death, puberty, and marriage, and indeed all forms of sexual relations. Since these are the most vital to community integrity and survival, they are also potentially the most disruptive to the maintenance of communal, rather than strictly personal, identity and stability.

Leviticus also outlines a system of "redemption," of the religious repair of boundaries that ritually "undoes" the effect of their transgression. This is accomplished largely through blood-sacrifice, because "blood equals life" (cf. Gen. 9:4–5). The redemptive system also includes the monetary payment of vows to redeem persons from religious obligations, debts owed to YHWH, according to a "scale of values" found in Leviticus 27 (cf. Numbers 30). In this list, women even of presumably more "valuable" childbearing age (Lev. 27:4–7) are consistently valued lower than men in comparable age categories.[40]

Women are also valued lower than men in their exclusion from ritual and religious leadership by the law codes of the Torah. When they are mentioned at all, it is in regard to their relationships with men, which, given the general worldview reflected in these laws, are primarily but not exclusively sexual. The laws about "family purity" in the Holiness Code of Leviticus 17—26 are stricter and more detailed than those in the Covenant Code of Exodus 21—23, where adultery is not even mentioned.[41] Within the Holiness Code, Leviticus 18:6–20 deals with Israelite familial sexual practices by contrasting them with those of the two Gentile nations with whom the

Israelites have had the most contact, Egypt and Canaan, whose sexual practices are called "defilements" and "abominations."[42] Israelite males, to whom all of these prohibitions are addressed, are not to have sexual relations within twelve categories of female kindred, including any kinsman's wife (18:20). The practice of levirate marriage, the marriage of a widow who has not produced an heir to her husband's brother, is not specifically mentioned as an exception here. The one glaring omission from this category is a prohibition against sexual relations with one's own daughter, although granddaughters (daughter's daughters and son's daughters) are specifically mentioned (18:10). This omission is readily explained, as Wegner notes, by the fact that these prohibitions generally have to do with the ownership of women's sexual functions by specified male relations. While a father owns the sexuality of his minor daughter, in most cases he is bound not to use it in order to ensure her virginity for her husband.[43] In fact, a father is prohibited in Leviticus 19:29 from making his daughter into a prostitute (*zonah*). Other forbidden sexual acts include intercourse with any menstruating woman (18:1; cf. Lev. 15:19–30), male-male homosexual relations ("You shall not lie with a male as with a woman," 18:22, NRSV), and bestiality (prohibited for men, the "you" to whom this passage is addressed, and specifically also for women, 18:23).

What seems to drive all of the above laws is a concern for the regulation of reproduction within the kinship group. The prohibitions against intercourse with a menstruant, intercourse between males (intercourse between females is not mentioned, as the laws relate here only to males), and intercourse with animals, like the prohibition against offering one's children as sacrifices to pagan gods (18:22), most likely reflect a concern with directing sexual relations to their "appropriate" end, the reproduction of offspring. Intercourse with a menstruating woman, male homosexual intercourse, and intercourse with animals may be productive of pleasure, which after all is no concern of this text, but not of children, and certainly one would not go to all of this effort to channel reproductive potential only to sacrifice the offspring!

Leviticus 20:10–21 prohibits adultery, again prohibits bestiality and incest, and in addition prescribes penalties for all three. According to Leviticus 20:10: "If a man commits adultery with the wife of his neighbor, both the adulterer and the adulteress shall be put to death" (NRSV; Deut. 22:22 specifies *he* must be caught in the act; cf. John 8:4–5). The man is the one addressed, and he is the one assumed to be the initiator and therefore the responsible party. As in Exodus 20:17, the woman is assumed to be the property of another man. Adultery is therefore presupposed by these laws to be the stealing of one man's sexual property by another.[44] How much more fearful then, as will be apparent below in this chapter, is the initiation of the sexual act by the adulterous wife.

The death penalty is also prescribed for both partners when a man lies with his father's wife and with his son's wife, because "they have both committed perversion" (20:12, NRSV). For the same reason, both the active and passive partners in homosexual intercourse are to be put to death (20:13), while a man who has intercourse with a woman and her mother is to be burned along with both women (20:14), and men and women who have relations with animals are to be killed, along with the animals (20:15–16). In all of these legal executions, no bloodguilt is accrued by the executioners: "Their [the victims'] blood is upon them." In the case of bestiality particularly it cannot be assumed that the death penalty is applied to both partners because the responsibility for "committing perversion" is shared through consent. Neither mutual consent nor mutual responsibility is therefore implied in any of these penalties. It therefore seems rather inadequate to assert that "the severity of punishment is based on the conviction that Israel is to be a holy people, separated from others by its manner of life and worship."[45] These penalties, like the death penalty in several states of the United States, may be intended as and believed to be deterrents to behavior that is a grave threat to society. The matter for investigation, then, must be why sexual deviance is so great a threat, and who is defining what is deviant.

For purposes of comparison, let us examine the penalties for sexual transgressions prescribed in Leviticus 20:17–21. A man who commits incest with his sister is "subject to [unspecified] punishment" (20:17), while both he and she are "cut off in the sight of their people." Presumably this phrase means that they are now considered to be non-Israelites, people who have put themselves "beyond the pale," or to use the Exodus term, "outside the camp." A man and woman who have intercourse while the woman is menstruating are similarly "cut off" (20:18). The man who has intercourse with his aunt, his father's or mother's sister, will be, with her, "subject to [an unspecified] punishment," but if a man has intercourse with his uncle's wife, both shall be "subject to punishment," and die childless (20:20). A similar penalty is prescribed for the man who takes his brother's wife, presumably while the brother is living (20:21).

Perhaps if we translate these religio-social laws, intended to protect a community defined as a "holy" people, into the language of politico-social laws, we could say that some sexual crimes, including adultery, are in the category of capital offenses, tantamount to murder. Other sexual crimes belong to the felony-misdemeanor category. These are not worthy of punishment by death, but are serious enough that the offenders are either "cut off" from society or cursed with the failure to reproduce, so that their "line" is effectively cut off. Yet in both types of crime and their accompanying penalties, a disruption in the social order, the transgression of boundaries, threatens to occur from within, in the very locus of communal continuity, that is, sexual reproduction. The chaos is dealt with in a manner typical of

many early societies: identification of the source of disruption and its nul-
lification by ritual, expulsion, or death.

The social order reflected in Leviticus therefore may be seen as one in
which the boundaries are fragile and threatened. Continued emphasis on
the difference in the practices of the Israelites and those of outsiders like
the Canaanites and the Egyptians, both of whom at various times owned
the land in which the Israelites were residing, is evidence of a fear of more
powerful "others" by a group that regards itself as marginal, but that rhetorically construes that very marginality as chosenness. This fear of "other"
outsiders is translated into regulation of those defined as "other" in their
midst, those who have the potential to transgress the boundaries and thus
to violate or "defile" the group. These persons are labeled "deviants." Exercising rhetorical control (which in Israel and for other marginal groups is
often the only means of control) over these unruly elements preserves or
restores a sense of order and identity in face of the loss of identity and some
measure of control over the social order. The most unruly elements of
course are those of sexual relations, where the forces of desire and pleasure
must be harnessed in the interests of the production of legitimate offspring.
As Rachel Biale notes, "Judaism achieves its balance [between legitimation
of sexuality and ascetic regulation of the libidinal drive] primarily through
the legitimation of sexuality in the confines of [heterosexual] marriage,
which is the primary instrument for harnessing the 'constructive' side of the
sexual impulse and restraining its 'anarchic' aspect."[46]

Heterosexual marriage and its integrity are thus enshrined not only in
biblical law but in consequent Jewish and Christian teaching as well. Marriage is the touchstone for evaluating women's status and indeed their ability to act autonomously in Numbers and in Deuteronomy, the final two of
the four books of "Mosaic" law. In Numbers 30:2–16, an autonomous "person" is defined by the ability to fulfill a vow without its being annulled. According to Wegner, the rabbinic sages derive their teaching about women's
autonomy in the Mishnah (ca. 200 C.E.) from this "biblical law of vows." In
each case, a woman's autonomy, the ability to make and fulfill a vow to
YHWH without the possibility of its being annulled, depends upon her being free from sexual ownership by a male.[47] Numbers 30:3–15 covers
women who are under the authority of male kindred, the wife (be'ulat ba'al),
and the minor daughter (na'arah) living in her father's house and therefore
"under" his authority. Divorced or widowed women do not have a male authority over them and thus have the ability to make their own vows, which
are honored as binding (Num. 30:16).

Marriage in biblical law codes thus gives exclusive rights to a man to own
and possess one or more women sexually. Fathers also own their minor
daughters sexually, although they may not sexually possess them (cf. Lev.
18:6–20; Gen. 19:8); masters own and have the rights to possess female

slaves. Laws about rape, divorce, and adultery, like laws of incest, are therefore intimately related to these rights and the ability to preserve the sexual integrity of one's women, defined as virginity before marriage, chastity after it. Men have no obligations to preserve their own chastity, other than avoiding intercourse with a married woman. Prostitution is rarely mentioned, but passages like Leviticus 19:29, which prohibits Israelite fathers from prostituting their daughters assume that only "outsider" women will be prostitutes. Married women and women intended for marriage—betrothed women, minor daughters in their fathers' homes—have the fewest rights of any free women, and sometimes fewer rights than slave women (Deut. 15:17; 21:10–14).

The religio-legal codes of the book of Deuteronomy, which dates no earlier than the seventh century B.C.E. and probably comes from the sixth, restate, expand, and sometimes contradict the Covenant Code of Exodus and the Holiness Code represented by Leviticus. In these codes, there are extensive regulations of marriage, rape, divorce, and adultery.[48] Virginity is mentioned in the context of marriage in Deuteronomy 22:13–21, where the husband and the father are the two chief actors in the situation in which a man "dislikes" his wife after having intercourse with her and makes up a reason to divorce her without financial penalty (22:13–14). The husband therefore slanders her by alleging that she was not a virgin when he married her, thus aiming to get back the bride-price for a virgin that he paid her father.[49] The father and mother of the bride have to disprove the charge by publicly displaying before the guardians of the community's moral boundaries presiding symbolically at its physical boundary, the elders at the city gates, the *betulim*, her "tokens of virginity," presumably the bloody sheet of defloration from the wedding night. The husband is fined one hundred silver shekels, twice the bride-price of a virgin, because "he has slandered a virgin of Israel" (22:19) and is not permitted to divorce her. If the charge is proven true and the tokens are lacking, she is brought "out to the entrance of her father's house" and stoned "by the men of the town," because she has behaved like a "whore" (*zonah*) in her father's house (22:21), robbing both father and husband of their sexual rights to her. Thus the men of the community guard the violation of their boundaries by pollution: "So you shall purge the evil from your midst" (22:21, NRSV).[50] Divorce is also permitted if the husband finds some other objection to her (24:1–4) and gives her a divorce document (*get*). The wife is permitted to remarry (cf. Matt. 5:31–32, Mark 10:2–13, Luke 16:18; Matt. 19:3–9 *contra*), but if her second husband divorces her because he "dislikes" her or he dies, making her a widow, her first husband is not permitted to remarry her because she has been "defiled" by another man, even though he is also legally a husband.

Virgins deflowered by rape constitute three special cases that involve vi-

olation not of the woman so much as her future husband's marital rights
(Deut. 22:23–29). In the first and second cases, the status of a "betrothed
virgin" is at stake. If the betrothed virgin is met by a man "in the town" who
lies with her, it is considered adultery and both partners are stoned at the
city gate (cf. 22:22). Here the means of death and the place are more specific than in Leviticus 20:10, but they are applied not to a man and his
neighbor's wife, but to the latter's fiancée. Rape or dishonor (shame, *'innah*) is specified in the second case, where the man not only meets the engaged virgin in the "open country," but "seizes her and lies with her." In
this case, only the man shall be executed, because the woman's resistance is
assumed, her cries for help not being heard. In the third case, that of the
virgin not betrothed, as in the case of Dinah (Genesis 34), a man "seizes her
and lies with her," an act that implies rape. If they both are "caught in the
act," some kind of illicit intercourse is implied, but not adultery, since she
is not married or betrothed. The man gives the bride-price (fifty silver
shekels) to the woman's father and she becomes his wife, whom he may not
divorce. No provision is made for the woman who must marry her rapist.
A similar statute in Exodus 22:16 makes it clear that the woman has been
"seduced" rather than raped, and the father has the right to refuse to give
his daughter to the seducer in marriage. In none of the Deuteronomic laws
on marriage, divorce, adultery, and rape is the woman's consent an issue,
while male ownership of her as sexual property subject to damage is.[51] A related case is the prohibition of a man from marrying his father's wife. Although she is presumably not his mother and his father is dead, he
nonetheless is censured for violating his father's "rights" to her (Deut.
22:30).

The ownership of female sexuality by males within the kinship group is
made nowhere more evident than in the custom of levirate marriage (Deut.
25:5–10), one that is important to ensuring the continuity of the male familial and tribal line. Thus both patriliny (lineage coming through the male
line) and patrilocality (wife living with the husband's family), as well as endogamy ("When brothers reside together," 25:5), are presupposed. When
a male Israelite dies without a male heir, "the wife of the deceased shall not
be married outside the family to a stranger" (25:5, NRSV). The obligation
of the husband's brother is to "go in to" (have intercourse with) his dead
brother's wife so that she may bear a son to perpetuate the dead man's
"name" in Israel.[52] The seriousness of this obligation is reinforced by the
right of the widow to publicly shame the *levir* who will not perform this
duty; she may take her grievance to the elders at the gate, those whose
obligation it is to see that justice according to the law is performed. The
shaming ritual involves a public proclamation of the unwillingness of the
brother "to perpetuate his brother's name in Israel," spitting in his face, and
pulling off his sandal. Since "sandal" is sometimes a euphemism in the

Tanakh for the female genitals, as "foot" is for male genitals, this act may symbolize the unwillingness of the brother to "go in to" his brother's wife. The shame is also borne by his family, as they will be known as "the house of him whose sandal was pulled off." This practice clearly reflects andro-centric interests, in that the wife's willingness to be impregnated by her brother-in-law is not even questioned. Indeed this is regarded as her right, a right that she may actively pursue even to the sexual shaming of the brother-in-law or next-of-kin. The carrying on of the male line of one's dead husband appears to be so important a "right" of a widow that two tales in the Tanakh (Tamar and Judah in Genesis 38 and Ruth in the book of Ruth) and one controversy story in the New Testament (Mark 12:18–27) make use of it. The implied but not stated converse is that if the *levir* will not be shamed into or, in the case of Tamar and Judah, tricked into per-forming his duty, the widow also is free of her sexual obligations to her hus-band's family.[53] In the stories of Tamar and Ruth, neither makes use of the *levir*'s unwillingness to perform his duty in order to seek her own sexual freedom. Both are bent on securing the continuity of their husband's line by any means, including deception and seduction, and both receive not only the approval of the texts that feature them as heroines but praise by later generations (see the genealogy in Matt. 1:1–6). In the judgment of the so-cieties reflected in these texts, a rejected widow, like any woman capable of bearing an heir, who does not make use of her sexual freedom but instead subordinates it to the good of her husband's family, by finding another next-of-kin to continue his line, is a righteous woman (Gen. 38:26), a "woman of worth" (Ruth 3:11; 4:15).[54]

Throughout the codes of law in the Torah, as has been shown, the sex-ual functions of free women, especially their reproductivity, are treated as commodities with value to the males of their respective families. Slave women are usually treated as the property, economic and sexual, of their masters and the rights that they are given are related to their ability to please their masters sexually (cf. Ex. 21:7–11). Captive women are a special case. In the ancient world in general, the victorious army kills the males and rapes the females of the conquered, thus accomplishing both the humilia-tion of the conquered through the inability of its men to protect its women and the erasure of the identity of the conquered because their women will bear children for the victors. Such assumptions underlie many of the bibli-cal texts, especially those concerned with the struggle of Israel against its enemies (e.g., Judg. 5:28–30; 19:24; 20:5).[55] Deuteronomy also assumes that women will be acquired as possessions by the victors in battle (20:5–7; 21:10) but makes some provision for the feelings and rights of the captive woman even as it concentrates on the privilege of the victorious Israelite man (21:10–14). The Deuteronomist's usual harshly negative stance against intermarriage of Israelites and foreigners is mitigated in this case, perhaps because the foreign woman is not seeking the marriage or seducing the Israelite male, and she and their children will become Israelites. In this case, if an Israelite male wishes to marry a captive foreign woman, she is allowed to observe, unmolested, a period of mourning for her parents for a full month. After that, he is permitted to "go in to" her and make her his wife. As in the case of the concubine (cf. Ex. 21:7–11), if she fails to satisfy him, he cannot sell her but must give her her freedom. He cannot treat her as a slave because he has dishonored her, not merely by enjoying her sexually, but by doing so as a husband with a wife, thus according her a different sexual status.

2

Women on the Boundary

Sex and Subversion

For a prostitute is a deep pit; a strange woman a narrow well.

—Proverbs 23:27

PROSTITUTION:
SACRED AND PROFANE

Given the restrictions biblical law placed upon sexual relations, even of the privileged free Israelite men with the least privileged—captive women—it might seem as though the sexual energies of men, like those of free women, would be directed toward preserving and continuing the family line. Such is indeed the primary obligation for Israelite males, as it is for men in other ancient Near Eastern societies.[1] Men are therefore forbidden to violate the exclusive sexual rights to women owned by other men, but they are permitted intercourse with the slave women they own and unconditionally with prostitutes. A female prostitute (*zonah* in the Hebrew Bible, *porne* in the Greek Septuagint)[2] is a woman whose sexuality, under biblical law, is not owned by any one man and is not dedicated to reproduce heirs within a patrilineal family. Consequently, there are few laws in the biblical codes that govern the treatment or the behavior of female prostitutes, and most of these are mentioned in the context of a father's relationship to his daughter's sexuality. Only in the New Testament, with its relatively ascetic worldview and therefore narrower range of religiously permissible sexual behavior, is a man's patronizing a female prostitute (*porne*) considered morally wrong (1 Cor. 6:15–17).

In the Holiness Code of Leviticus, it is forbidden for a father to misuse his daughter's sexuality by making her into a prostitute (*zonah*), because the land will also be "prostituted" thereby (Lev. 19:29). This prohibition reflects the typical personification of the land itself as a female entity that can be defiled or prostituted by disobedience to the commandments of YHWH. Prostitutes are among those categories of "defiled" women that priests, the holiest of men, are forbidden to marry (Lev. 21:14), but it is not said that other men may not marry or enjoy the services of prostitutes.

However, the priest's daughter who defiles herself by becoming a prostitute also profanes her father's holiness and is thus sentenced to be burned
to death (Lev. 21:7). Deuteronomy prohibits the use of wages from a prostitute to pay an amount vowed to YHWH, because this profanes YHWH's
holiness (Deut. 23:18).

In the verse that precedes this passage in Deuteronomy it is also forbidden for any Israelite woman ("daughter of Israel") to become a *qedeshah*, as
it is forbidden for any Israelite male ("son of Israel") to become a *qadesh*. It
has usually been assumed, partly because this prohibition is followed by that
against using the wages of an ordinary prostitute (*zonah*) that a *qedeshah* was
a "temple prostitute" or "sacred prostitute," a woman attached to the temple of a fertility deity for purposes of sacred intercourse. Athalya Brenner
suggests that *zonah* and *qedeshah* are in fact two different categories of prostitutes, "the first tolerated" because she serves a secular purpose, commer-
cial sex work, but "the second not," since she serves a god other than
YHWH.[3] Mieke Bal asserts, conversely, that the *zonah* is "despised because
she is overtly sexual," but the "ritual 'prostitute' is respected."[4] Phyllis Bird
claims that the term *qedeshah*, or hierodoule (lit., "sacred female slave"), is
often used as another term for *zonah*.[5] Bird agrees with Tikva Frymer-Kensky, however, that there is no direct linguistic or conceptual evidence that
suggests the translation of *qedeshah* as "sacred prostitute."[6] It is more likely
that these "sacred women," like their male counterparts, were ritual servants
of other deities, and although that service was unspecified, they presented a
threat to the priesthood of the Temple in Jerusalem, which discredited them
by attaching to them a reputation of shameful sexual behavior. In the religious purge of the Temple conducted by Josiah of Judah, the "houses" of
the *qedeshim* (consecrated men) in the Temple are destroyed, and the women
who weave the robes for the goddess Asherah are driven out (2 Kings 23:7;
cf. Jer. 7:18). The NRSV translates *qedeshim* in Jeremiah 7:18 as "male prostitutes," but nothing in the context suggests that literal prostitution, homosexual or even heterosexual, is going on in the Temple.[7]

TAMAR AND RAHAB:
QEDESHOTH OR *ZONOTH*?

The confusion between the two terms is amplified by their apparently
interchangeable use in the story of Tamar and Judah in Genesis 38, a narrative that revolves around appearances of sanctioned and unsanctioned
sexual intercourse.[8] Tamar is acquired by the patriarch Judah as a wife for
his firstborn son and heir, Er. Because of some unspecified "wickedness,"
perhaps a practice inherited from his Canaanite mother Shua, Er is killed
by YHWH. Judah thence commands his second son, Onan, to perform his

duty as brother-in-law (38:8). Onan tries to hedge his bets by "going in to" the widow Tamar but "spilling his seed" on the ground to avoid impregnating her with children who will inherit in his stead, an act for which YHWH puts him to death also. Fearing for the life of his third son, Shelah, perhaps justifiably, Judah sends the levirate widow Tamar back to her father, ostensibly to wait until Shelah is old enough to perform his duty (38:11).[9] As Susan Niditch remarks, Judah thus turns Tamar into a social "misfit," a woman who has already left her father's house to become the sexual property of another "father's house," but who is returned, as neither unmarried virgin, disgraced wife, or true widow, without having received her sexual "right" to be able to produce an heir, a category the custom of levirate marriage was designed to avoid.[10] Tamar, however, who apparently suspects Judah of cheating her (38:12), makes use of her liminal position. Disguising herself, she sits along the roadside, where Judah waylays her, supposing by her outfit and veil that she is a prostitute (*zonah*, Gen. 38:15).[11] Because he does not have the payment with him, he promises her a kid from his flock. She wisely demands he give her a token in earnest of payment, and he gives her the ancient equivalent of proof of identity, his signet ring. When he sends his friend Hirah to recover the pledge, Hirah inquires the whereabouts of the *qedeshah* (translated "temple prostitute" by the NRSV) from the townsfolk, and they reply that there has been no such *qedeshah* there (translated "prostitute," NRSV 38:21). Why the interchange of terms?[12] Is Judah too embarrassed to have his friend ask for a common *zonah*? And if a *qedeshah* is truly the sexual servant of a fertility deity, would it not be an act of religious apostasy for a Hebrew patriarch to patronize her, whereas patronizing a common whore would be allowable?

Intriguing as they are, these questions must temporarily wait for answers. This portion of the narrative focuses not on Judah's sexual conduct but on that of Tamar. Even though he has sent her back to her father's house, Judah is still apparently the male with primary sexual authority over her, an authority that is paradoxically reinforced just at the point that it appears most threatened. Judah, not Tamar's father, is told that she has "prostituted herself" (*zanetah*, 38:24; NRSV has "played the whore") and as a consequence of her "prostitution(s)" (*zenunim*; LXX, *porneia*; NRSV has "whoredom") has become pregnant. Judah orders her to be "brought out" of her father's house and burned (38:24), as in the severe death penalty prescribed in Leviticus 21:9 for a priest's daughter who prostitutes herself, rather than in the stoning prescribed in Deuteronomy 22:21 and 24 for a nonvirgin bride. It is not clear whether, given the fact that Tamar's husband is dead, this is a question of adultery. The penalty for this is also death, but by unspecified means and one that includes the male partner (Lev. 20:10; Deut. 22:22). In any case, Tamar has "defiled" herself and therefore Judah's line. There may be a hint of irony in Judah's lack of awareness that

he, too, may be subject to execution as an adulterer, but it is not emphasized in the narrative. The severity of the penalty demanded by her father-
in-law makes more dramatic Tamar's production of the tokens identifying
him as the one who has impregnated the supposed "prostitute" (38:25). Judah acknowledges that Tamar is more "in the right" (*tzedeqah*, righteousness, justice) than he, because he tricked her out of her levirate rights in his
son Shelah.[13] Tamar thus survives the death of two husbands, the refusal of
a third, and a threatened execution in order to obtain her "right," the production of a male heir to her husband's house, and is rewarded for her per-
sistence by producing male twins, Perez and Zerah. Through Perez, Tamar
is linked to the case of another "borderline" widow, Ruth, who marries
Perez's descendant Boaz, and through Ruth to David, the descendant of
their son Obed. The glorious descent ensured first by Tamar and then by
Ruth is claimed for Jesus by Matthew, who specifically mentions both
Tamar and Ruth in his genealogy (Matt. 1:3–5).

The point of Tamar's story, as Niditch observes, is that it illuminates
"the question of the stability and health of Israelite social structure."[14]
Within this structure, as reflected here and elsewhere in biblical law codes,
the fertility of the woman is guarded, protected, and directed toward what
is deemed the appropriate social end, the continuity of the patrilineage.
Such is the emphasis on this end that it may include behavior on the part
of the woman that appears socially unacceptable. But this is only an appearance. Tamar is certainly no whore, since her "payment" is to receive
what she is already owed (a male heir) from the one who owes it to her (Judah). Further, she is only *disguised* as a prostitute and certainly does not
make it her profession, in that she only "plays the whore" once, despite the
multiple "whorings" (*zenunim*) with which she is charged. While she does
use sexual means to gain her ends, the narrative shows that these are not illicit, but legitimate ways to obtain her due, if not her obligation. Tamar's
dishonor is thus not the apparent shame that attends the discovery of unsanctioned sexual relations, but the dishonor of being put in a shadowy liminal position by Judah's shameful act of withholding from her the possibility
of producing a male heir. Judah, on the other hand, is not shamed by having intercourse with a prostitute (even a servant of a fertility god) or yet
with his daughter-in-law, but by having his treachery to her revealed.
"Playing" the prostitute, playing with the borderline between "acceptable"
and "unacceptable" sexual behavior thus serves to confirm where the
boundary is. Nevertheless, as Niditch has pointed out, maintaining the
proper categories is the responsibility of males: this is Judah's story more
than it is Tamar's.[15]

Still unanswered is the question about the *qedeshah* and her relationship
to the *zonah*, a relationship that has become even more muddled by the story
of Tamar. On the way to answering this question, let us examine the bibli-

cal story of a true *zonah*, one who is characteristically known by that epithet, *Rahab ha-zonah*, "Rahab the prostitute" (Josh. 6:17). As related in the book of Joshua, when the Israelites are about to invade Canaan, Moses' successor sends two spies to the great Canaanite city of Jericho (Josh. 2:1). Their first act on entering the city is to go to the house of a *zonah* named Rahab. They spend the night in Rahab's house, which is just within the walls. When the king of Jericho demands the whereabouts of the spies from Rahab, she shows her cleverness in not only feigning ignorance but hiding them, deluding their pursuers, and helping them to escape over the walls (Josh. 2:3–7, 15–21). Before their departure, however, she tells them that she knows (it is not specified how, perhaps by divinely communicated knowledge) that YHWH has given Canaan, including Jericho, to the Israelites, and asks only that she and her family be spared in the coming massacre (2:8–14). Not only are Rahab and her family, who live in a different house than her place of business, spared (Josh. 6:17, 22–23), but she comes down through biblical history in rabbinic literature as a repentant prostitute, an exemplary convert, the wife of Joshua and ancestress of prophets, in the Gospel of Matthew as an ancestress of the Messiah (Matt. 1:5), in James as one who is righteous by her action, and in the book of Hebrews, in which she even retains her epithet, *porne*, as a heroine of faith (Heb. 11:31).[16]

The status accorded Rahab in the biblical literature has been consistently pointed out as being all the more striking because of its contrast to her supposed marginal social status as a prostitute, but this contrast must be carefully examined.[17] First of all, Rahab is not a mere prostitute, but apparently the owner of a "house" of prostitution that the Israelite spies frankly patronize. There is no doubt about her profession—the sex trade—but no negative judgment of it either. Second, in the eyes of the narrators and editors of the text, who are Israelite males concerned with their separation from "others," Rahab is a foreign woman, a Canaanite woman at that, and therefore might reasonably be assumed to constitute some danger. The possibility of non-Israelite women seducing Israelite men and thence leading them into apostasy is alluded to in the text by the fact that the spies in Joshua start out from Shittim, the place where the Moabite women had "sexual relations" with the Israelites and thus induced them to serve Baal of Peor, an act terribly avenged on the women by Moses (Num. 25:1–9; 31:15–19).[18] The fact that Rahab is not once called *qedeshah*, however, may indicate that the text is very careful to confine her activities to secular "sex work," and not to suggest that Rahab serves any deity other than YHWH, of whose mighty acts she knows so well that she relates them at length (Josh. 2:9–11).

How "marginal" then is Rahab? From the perspective of the text, which is clearly that of Israelite males, Rahab, like Tamar, crosses margins and borders only temporarily and only to confirm them, being one of the proverbial exceptions that prove the rule. Rahab's "house" is on the border between "insider" territory (the Canaanites who occupy the land) and that of the "outsider" Israelites, who hope to penetrate and "take" Canaanite territory as they can expect to "take" foreign women. The Israelites are nonetheless considered to be "insiders" by the text, as the legitimate possessors of the land. Foreign women, especially sexually active ones, might pose the danger of betrayal to Israelites; Rahab, however, does not. Her borderline status helps her move to help the "outsider" Israelites and to move them "inside" Jericho and hence into Canaan, not because, as Bird and Danna Nolan Fewell both suggest, she is an "outsider" in her own community, since we are given no indication that the Canaanites thought her a member of a profession with a low social status.[19] Rather, her status comes from the fact that she is a woman who by Israelite definition occupies "no man's land," dwelling in a house headed by no man, not even her father (Josh. 6:22–23). She therefore might be expected to be "open" to all men, including "outsiders," which the Israelites are in Jericho. Such women are often doubly dangerous in biblical texts, as they answer to no male authority—in Rahab's case, not even to the king of Jericho. In Israelite society, women were usually under the protection of men; in this case, we have the reverse, men under the protection of a woman.

But we need to look at the end of Rahab's story to see whether it is indeed a tale that really reverses expectations either of prostitutes or of foreign women and find that it does not. Joshua and his troops succeed in capturing the city of Jericho and sacrifice every living thing in it to YHWH, including the women, effectively erasing the city's Canaanite identity.[20] Rahab and her family are spared because she has spared the Israelite spies, but they are still treated as a marginal group, literally "set outside the camp of Israel" (Josh. 6:23), and, while the text says that Rahab's descendants have lived "in Israel to this day" (Josh. 6:25), they are not spoken of as integrated into Israel in any part of the Tanakh, nor is Rahab herself mentioned again in it. Rabbinic commentators, feeling this lack, turned her into the exemplary convert to Judaism and married her to Joshua. Thus the potential threat of a foreign woman—of whose lack of sexual restriction there is no doubt—is dealt with by keeping her within and under the control of an Israel dominated by males whose interests women serve.

From these two stories, one about Tamar and one about Rahab, instances in which women's sexual freedom is praiseworthy, we can come to some conclusions about the definition of the *zonah* in Israelite premonarchic society. The three English translations for this term indicate its spectrum of meaning as used in these contexts: prostitute, harlot, and whore. The first two are virtually synonymous, although "harlot" has an old-fashioned and slightly more elevated tone to it. As translations for *zonah* (LXX, *porne*), both prostitute and harlot apply to women who accept money or goods in exchange for sexual relations of an impermanent kind and with multiple partners, those who are called "sex workers" in modern parlance. While "whore" may convey the same meaning, its use in English is more pejorative, applied as a term of opprobrium, usually by men, to any woman who is suspected of sexual promiscuity, and especially of marital infidelity. "Whore" may also be a verb in English, just as the Hebrew root *znh* (LXX, *porneuo*), "to engage in sexual relations outside of or apart from marriage," is also translated as "to play the whore (harlot)," "to whore."[21] This broader meaning naturally includes the more narrowly defined adultery (Heb., *n'p;* Gk., *moicheuo*) and is used as a synonym for it, particularly when applied to women or to entities such as "Israel," when described in feminine terms.[22]

The difference, moreover, between the professional "harlot" and the adulterous woman in biblical literature is that the prostitute's sexual freedom is acknowledged and, to a certain extent, sanctioned, since "the harlot's activity violates no man's rights or honor."[23] A woman who legally "belongs" to a man, however, as a betrothed woman, wife, or levirate widow, violates his rights and her own obligations if she assumes the freedom to have sexual relations with anyone else. This action puts her into a socially anomalous position that threatens the stability of recognized order, and she must either be "corrected," executed, or expelled. Prostitutes belong to every man and hence to no man; all other women belong to only one man. As Tamar's story demonstrates, even a levirate widow still technically belongs to one man, since it is the obligation of her brother-in-law to assume the role of his brother and to "build up his brother's house" through her.

This distinction leads us back to the problem of the *qedeshah*, who has traditionally been understood to be a woman attached to the temple or worship of a fertility deity, whose sexuality was also likewise dedicated. Because the worship of fertility deities was alleged to involve ritual intercourse, she is thus by implication a "sacred prostitute," a hierodoule.[24] Evidence for this kind of ritual sexual intercourse is scanty, often dubious, and its interpretation also flawed. The king of Babylon, standing in for the divine lover Dumuzi or Tammuz, enacted with the priestess of Ishtar, a stand-in for the goddess, the *hieros gamos* or sacred marriage that was a part of the symbolic world renewal celebrated in the Babylonian New Year's festival. Other "evidence" comes from decidedly biased or notably inaccurate sources, like the claim of the Greek historian Herodotus that the women of Babylon were required to have sex with male strangers at the temple of Aphrodite (Ishtar) prior to their marriage (*Histories* I. 199–200). It is, however, apparent from temple archives that there were several kinds of women who performed services for the Mesopotamian deities, among whom were female temple servants of a lower order called *qadishtum*, who may have provided sexual services.[25] The ready translation of *qedeshah*, consecrated woman, simply by *porne*, prostitute, in the Septuagint version of the Tamar story, and the interchangeability of *qedeshah* with *zonah* in the Hebrew, suggests that there may be some truth to the belief that the services of the consecrated women may have involved ritual intercourse. What is more likely, however, is that the Hebrew texts' bias against the worship of fertility deities, especially goddesses, leads to their definition of such worship as promiscuity.

The link in the biblical texts between female sexual activity, especially prostitution, and the worship of foreign deities, those other than YHWH, will be treated in more depth below in this chapter. For now, I would agree with Bird that priestly and prophetic texts of the Bible treat women who serve as priestesses or other servants "consecrated" to deities other than YHWH, like the Canaanite goddess Asherah (2 Kings 23:6–7), as "outsiders," foreign women who seduce Israelite men away from the worship of YHWH (cf. Num. 25:1–9). Similarly, Israel personified as female "plays the whore" by worshiping the fertility gods of Canaan instead of or alongside YHWH.[26] Frymer-Kensky further suggests that the lawgivers of Deuteronomy have joined the prohibition against making Israelite "daughters and sons" into *qedeshoth* and *qadeshim* to the prohibition against accepting the wages of a prostitute in payment of a vow, because the *qedeshah*, dedicated to a deity, and the *zonah*, belonging to no family, have the ability to "make their own sexual decisions" without father or husband, to have sex without being married.[27] Female sexual freedom from male control is thus once again portrayed as promiscuity, a metaphor that is continually used in the representation of the relationship between the "people of God" (meaning males, but symbolized by a female, whether Israel or the church) and a male God.

Foreign women, as members of communities that are themselves "consecrated" to foreign or "other" gods, are, like the *qedeshoth*, regarded as sexually promiscuous, threatening to import their deities and sexual practices across the borders of the bounded community to corrupt the order of the community by corrupting its males. Religious leaders' warnings against Israelite men having anything to do with foreign women appear throughout the Torah in the periods describing wandering and settlement, times at which the integrity of the community seems especially vulnerable. In the renewal of the covenant after the disaster of the golden calf in Exodus 34:10–28, YHWH reiterates the prohibition (Ex. 23:32–33) against making covenants with the people of Canaan but adds a prohibition against taking Canaanite daughters as wives for Israelite sons, because the daughters, who "prostitute themselves" to their gods, will cause their husbands to prostitute themselves also. When the men of Israel have sexual relations with the women of Moab (Num. 25:1), the verb that is used is *znh*, "to prostitute." The consequences are dire: the Iraelites are seduced into worshiping Baal (25:2–3), for which YHWH orders Moses to impale the leaders (25:4). Moses further orders the killing of any Israelites who worshiped Baal

(25:5). Moses issues one final warning against and later kills the women, whom he holds responsible for the crime of instigating the betrayal of YHWH (Num. 31:17–18). One reason that such heavy emphasis is placed on the fact that Rahab the foreign *zonah* in Joshua 2 and 6 helps the Israelite spies is that, despite her profession, she does not cause them to "whore" against YHWH because she herself is a believer in him. Once more, when a woman's sexual power is directed toward preserving the Israelite male community's stability under its god, it is a power for good. True "whoredom," however, is deviance from sanctioned religious authority, as it is from sexual authority.

STRANGE WOMEN WHO UNMAN MEN: THE STORIES OF JOSEPH AND SAMSON

As previously noted, the danger for men in Israel from foreign women appears greater when the community itself is perceived as a marginal group in the midst of another culture. It is then that the temptation to assimilate, represented by border transgressions from the inside and penetrations from the outside, is heightened in the narratives that show males of the community lured away from their ethnic and religious identity by seductive women from the "outside." In a double type of gender bending, the men of Israel are often described as "playing the whore (*znh*)" with foreign women and also with foreign gods (Num. 25:1–2; Ex. 23:32–33; Lev. 17:7; 20:5). This activity is portrayed as especially rampant in the critical period of the settlement described in Judges, in which the fragile existence of the Israelites as a scattered and relatively powerless people among the powerful cities of Canaan provides a sharp contrast to the blitzkrieg model in the book of Joshua, with its victorious warriors and its "good" foreign woman, Rahab (cf. Judg. 2:17; 8:27, 33).[28] The paradoxical double portrait of a male Israel that is prey to the wiles of sexually unrestrained foreign women, yet that is also symbolized by the wayward wife who betrays her divine husband, is accounted for, according to Howard Eilberg-Schwartz, by the construction of authority in Israel. Heterosexual males desire and visualize their being desired by an almost totally male deity. At the same time, while socially "homosocial," they are vehemently anti-homosexual. The "homoerotic tension" thus created is resolved rhetorically by envisioning the collective Israel as "she," making it possible for male authors to speak of themselves as women, while displacing their sexual anxiety onto actual women through rigid definitions of their status as sexual objects of males.[29] Self-control of one's own desires is thus written as sexual control of women's ability to enact their desires. The control of sexual relations and their impact upon male hegemony and sexual identity continues to be a source of anxiety. As women

are perceived to be more "open" to sexual penetration than men, so the female "body" of Israel is vulnerable to penetration (and therefore disruption)
from the outside.

Two examples of Israelite masculine behavior when faced with the
threatening sexual wiles of foreign women in the Tanakh are those of
Joseph and Potiphar's wife, a model of good male behavior, and of Samson
and Delilah, a model of bad male behavior and its consequences. Both stories reflect a special Israelite vulnerability to the influence of two foreign
cultures, that of the Egyptians (Joseph) from whom the Israelites were later
to escape, like Joseph fleeing from Potiphar's wife, and that of the
Philistines, a constant threat to Israelite viability in the land of the settlement, Canaan.

The story of the attempted seduction of the slave Joseph by his master
Potiphar's wife immediately follows that of Tamar's seduction of Judah. Although the Tamar story appears to be an interruption of the Joseph narrative, which begins in Genesis 37, it highlights the virtuous behavior of a
Hebrew woman (Tamar) in contrast to the scurrilous behavior of a foreign
Egyptian woman (Potiphar's wife). The upright sexual conduct of a Hebrew
man (Joseph) also contrasts with the sexual duplicity of his brother Judah.
As Genesis 39 opens, Joseph has been sold into Egypt at the instigation of
his brothers and is bought by Potiphar, an officer of the pharaoh. Impressed
by Joseph's management of his affairs, Potiphar leaves him in charge of his
house (39:5–6). Impressed by Joseph's good looks, Potiphar's wife, who is
not otherwise named or identified, a rhetorical strategy that heightens her
betrayal of him, boldly accosts Joseph and demands that he have intercourse
with her (39:7). He refuses, giving as his reason that Potiphar has entrusted
him with everything in his house, withholding nothing except his wife, and
that yielding to her would therefore be a "great evil," as well as a sin against
God (39:9–10). The woman persists, "day after day," but Joseph as stead-
fastly resists. Waiting until there is no one else in the house, Potiphar's wife
gets even bolder, seizing Joseph's garment and repeating her demand
(39:11–12). He runs away, leaving her in possession of nothing but his garment, which apparently gives her a clever if nasty means to avenge herself
for his refusal. She uses it as evidence as she accuses Joseph of trying to rape
her, implicating even Potiphar in her accusation, because he brought in that
"Hebrew" (39:13–18). Angry at the apparent insult to his wife and betrayal
of his trust, Potiphar has Joseph thrown into prison.

As in the story of Tamar and Judah, we have an apparent sex crime—
adultery—that is not actually committed, a righteous but wronged protagonist in a precarious position (note, however, that Joseph is merely thrown
into prison; Tamar is threatened with burning), and a deceptive antagonist
(Judah, who refuses Tamar her widow's rights; Potiphar's wife, who tries
to trick Joseph and then contrives a false accusation). But the pairing of

these stories also contrasts two women, both of whom pursue their aims actively through deceptive and cunning sexual strategies. Tamar's aim, that of securing her dead husband's lineage, even by disguising herself and "acting the whore," is approved by the narrative when Judah pronounces her "righteous"; it is he who has treated her like a whore and not she who actually is one. Potiphar's wife, on the other hand, is shown to have no motivation for soliciting Joseph save her own sexual satisfaction. If she gains her objective, she will betray her husband and make Joseph an adulterer. She likewise has no other motive for falsely accusing him of rape than the frustration of her desires, since he never intimates that he will tell Potiphar about his wife's bad conduct. But if we read the story of Potiphar's wife and Joseph from a different angle, if she were Potiphar and Joseph were a slave girl in his house, the sexual availability of the latter would incite no comment; it simply would be assumed (cf. Ex. 21:7–11). What makes her behavior subject to condemnation by the narrative is that, rather than being a powerful master, she is a powerful mistress who is nevertheless not entitled to use her position to treat a *male* slave as sexual property. As a wife, she is herself sexual property, and proposes to betray her husband's trust doubly by committing adultery with his trusted deputy.

Potiphar's wife, who has no name of her own, is a stock character in a cautionary tale, the classic foreign woman who can be counted on for obeying no law or rule, nothing other than her own sexual rapacity. As such, she is the "strange woman" who signals betrayal and danger to the upright man. As Niditch observes, Joseph is a typical "wisdom hero," who lives by the advice given young men in books like Proverbs, to beware the "strange woman" (*'iššah zarah*), the adulteress who, like the conniving wife of Potiphar, lures the unsuspecting youth into disgrace and doom (cf. Prov. 7:6–27).[30] It is by the lust and treachery of an Egyptian woman and not at the hand of any Egyptian man that Joseph meets the only reversal he suffers in that foreign country. Although he does come near disgrace and doom, his fidelity to YHWH is matched by YHWH's *ḥesed*, his steadfast love (39:21), which turns adversity into even more stunning success, and Joseph eventually gains a legitimate lover who is worthy of him. Because of Joseph's ability to interpret his dreams, the pharaoh himself confesses that there is no one wiser than Joseph (Gen. 41:39), and gives him Aseneth, the daughter of "Potiphera, priest of On," for a wife (41:45). Some traditions take up the similarity in names, suggesting that she is the daughter of the same Potiphar whose wife (Aseneth's mother?) was responsible for all of Joseph's trials, which come to a fitting closure when Aseneth presents him with two sons, Manasseh and Ephraim, eponymous ancestors of the "Joseph tribes" of Israel.[31]

If Joseph's story represents the prosperity to be gained, even by a marginal alien in a foreign land, by remaining faithful to YHWH and resisting

the wiles of the strange woman, who represents the lure of sexual temptation and cultural assimilation, Samson represents the opposite. The last of
the "deliverers" of Israel in the book of Judges, which tells the story of the
difficulty of Israelite settlement in and possession of Canaan, Samson consistently undercuts and betrays the expectations that the narrative raises of
him. Like Joseph, he is born with divine help to a woman considered barren (Judg. 13:2–3), and like Samuel, the last of the judges, Samson is consecrated to YHWH from his birth (and even within his mother's womb) as
a nazirite, one who may not take any wine or strong drink or cut his hair
(Num. 6:1–21; cf. 1 Sam. 1:11).

Although Samson's childhood passes with YHWH's blessing, and the
"spirit of YHWH" begins to "stir him up," in the pattern established in
Judges for those YHWH chooses as deliverers, his first act upon adulthood
is to seek to marry a Philistine woman from Timnah, despite his parents'
remonstration against taking a foreign wife, and despite the fact that the
Philistines are the foreign rulers of Israel (Judg. 14:1–3). He simply wants
her, as he says, because she "pleases him." According to the text, YHWH
is going to use the foreign wife as a catalyst for his campaign against the
Philistines (Judg. 14:4), but Samson is an unwitting tool, manipulated by
YHWH and deceived by his bride even during his wedding feast, an
episode that parallels and reinforces his later deception by Delilah. When
he proposes to the Philistine young men at his wedding feast that they solve
his riddle or pay him a price, they threaten the Timnite bride until she finally, through "weeping and nagging," coaxes the solution out of him and
tells it to them (14:11–17). When they taunt him with the solution to his
riddle, Samson immediately assumes that his wife has not only betrayed his
secret but betrayed him sexually (14:18), and, enraged, kills thirty men.
When his bride is given to another, Samson refuses to accept her younger
sister in her stead and sets fire to the Philistine fields, for which the
Philistines wreak a terrible vengeance upon the Timnite woman and her father, whom they judge responsible for Samson's wrath, by burning them
both (15:1–7). Samson however emerges victorious and is judge of Israel,
despite its domination by the Philistines, for twenty years (15:20).

In the above episode, the Timnite woman is an object, first of Samson's
jealous sexual desire, then of the rapacious Philistines, given to one of Samson's companions when he deserts her, and finally destroyed by the
Philistines as the cause of Samson's revenge. Although a feminist reader
like Fewell sees her as a "pawn in a larger conflict," who "cannot win" wher-
ever she turns,[32] the Timnite woman is portrayed through the androcentric lens of the text as an example of the way in which foreign women are
dangerous, sexually tempting but sexually treacherous, causing destruction
not only to Israelite men but to their own families and countrymen.

Samson, however, seems to have an irresistible attraction to Philistine women; whichever one he lays eyes on, he immediately and unthinkingly desires. Just as he first saw the Philistine woman at Timnah and at once demanded her in marriage (14:1), so he sees a *zonah* in Gaza and immediately has intercourse with her (16:1).[33] The danger of this rash act is also immediate: the Philistines of Gaza circle the prostitute's house, waiting until morning to kill Samson. Unexpectedly, however, he rises at midnight and escapes by pulling up the city gates and carrying them to Hebron. The story begins to read like a comic parody of the story of Rahab and the Israelite spies in another enemy walled city, Jericho. The prostitute has no speaking part, let alone a heroic role. The enemy stupidly waits for Samson to have his sexual fill, and Samson is merely given another opportunity to demonstrate his vast strength, showing he can enter and leave even an enemy city whenever he wants to by picking up the city gates and carrying them uphill for forty miles.[34]

This second encounter with a foreign woman, one sexually freer than the first, but one equally dangerous because of her nationality, sets up Samson's last and most tragic encounter with the seductive Delilah, the only named woman of the three and the only one with whom the text says he falls in love (Judg. 16:4). Although it is not clear whether she herself is a Philistine, she is amenable to the request from the Philistine chiefs to find out, for a fabulous sum, the source of Samson's strength so that they can overcome him (16:5). According to Fewell, if we see this story from Delilah's point of view, something that neither the narrator nor many centuries of interpretation has done, she is an independent woman, in charge of her own person and her own sexual and business choices, who may find wealth and alliance with the Philistine authorities a more solid base of security than the volatile and capricious love of a man like Samson.[35] Delilah may well be trying, without any male mediation, to make the wisest choices she can for her own survival.

Delilah's wisdom, in the form of cunning, is at first matched by Samson's. In a parody of the story of the Timnite bride, who tries to discover the solution of the riddle, Delilah attempts to coax from Samson the secret of his strength, and at first he matches her by deceiving her with his answers. Both women are portrayed by the narrative as nagging, pestering, and wheedling (16:16) until Samson, worn down, agrees to the request. Delilah, however, is much more in control than the Timnite bride: the Philistines do not threaten her but pay her, and unlike the Timnite, if she loses Samson she does not lose any security, but gains greater. Because of her greater power and her greater cleverness, Delilah is portrayed as much more dangerous than the Timnite, who pays with her own death for her presumed betrayal of Samson, whereas Delilah not only gets paid (16:18) but also suffers no penalty. Samson foolishly treats her cajoling as just another riddling game, despite the fact that the Philistines try to capture him three times

after Delilah thinks she has the secret of his strength. Finally put in a sexually vulnerable position, with his head on Delilah's lap (or "between her
knees"),[36] he is betrayed by her and overpowered at last by the Philistines
(16:19–22). They put out the eyes that were so attracted by foreign women
(14:1; 16:1) and force him to grind at the prison's mill, like a slave or an an-
imal (16:21). Whereas the Philistines were powerless to overcome Samson
in the house of the prostitute at Gaza, they are able to do so here. Intercourse
with the sexually cunning and powerful Delilah has drained Samson of his
manhood and outwitted him of his strength, so that he is powerless in the
hands of enemy males. Despite his flouting of the other aspects of his
nazirite vow through eating and drinking forbidden substances and having
contact with forbidden things,[37] Samson has had YHWH's support until a
woman in the service of the "uncircumcised" makes him break the final rule,
cutting his hair and thereby losing his strength and his last tie with YHWH.
In a last courageous act, Samson literally "brings down the house" when the
Philistines make him entertain them at the feast of their god Dagon, but he
kills his tormentors at the cost of his own life, while anarchy ensues in Israel
(16:23–31). Delilah, who disappears before the denouement, has the last
laugh.

Samson's story is the inverse of Joseph's. As an Israelite, Joseph is a
member of a possibly suspect and certainly alien group in a country far from
that of his birth. As an Israelite, Samson is a member of a minority group
currently under the domination of another people. Both encounter women
who are allied with a foreign male power structure, Potiphar's wife because
she is married to an Egyptian official, Delilah because she is hired by the
Philistine lords. Both women attempt to assert sexual dominance over the
vulnerable Israelite men. Yet Joseph's vulnerability is deceptive: Potiphar's
wife may use all her guile, but she cannot defeat Joseph because he stays
within the boundaries of the Israelite moral code, by which he knows that
her action is a "great evil, a sin," and by which the god of his fathers continues to protect him. Samson, despite his enormous strength, becomes
vulnerable and is defeated because he continually transgresses the boundaries even of his nazarite vocation because of his attraction to outsider
women, women who belong to the enemy men he is always fighting against,
but who are clearly his enemies. The women are more opaque to him,
blinded as he is by their sexual allure. In the end, the seductive power of one
of these women, Delilah, allows Samson to be violated, losing his male
strength and becoming prey, almost like a captured woman, to enemy
males. He is no longer "a man," the one in sexual control of himself and of
her; she assumes the man's role. The lesson is clear: Attraction to a foreign
culture, symbolized by the sexual seductivity, even aggressiveness, of its
women (cf. Judg. 3:6) is a fatal one. These women lurk on the borders of
the orderly but precarious Israelite society, threatening the introduction of

chaos and moral confusion through a different understanding of sexual norms. The women act like men, making sexual conquests and using sex to extend their power to dominate. The men become "women," passive objects who are used and often destroyed by the women's sexual aggression. No good can come from such women; instead men's social and sexual control is weakened. Foreign women, as the text constantly demonstrates, are the source of a lethal social disease; avoid them as you would the plagues that they cause (Num. 25:1–9).

THE FOREIGN WOMAN AS DEFENSIVE, DANGEROUS, AND DOMESTICATED: JAEL, JEZEBEL, AND RUTH

In Judges, the same book that tells the tragic tale of Samson, victim of a foreign woman's wiles, an earlier story tells of another victim of a foreign woman's wiles, the Canaanite commander Sisera. The book of Judges is part of the "revisionist" history of Israel and Judah called the Deuteronomistic History, written from the standpoint of those scribes who tried to make theological sense of the exile. The consistent pattern of this history, which includes the "historical" books from Joshua to 2 Kings, reflects the concern of this priestly and scribal elite with religious fidelity to YHWH, a fidelity that is often expressed through ethnic exclusivity called "purity." As previously observed, the recommended way of achieving the latter was through steadfast refusal of intermarriage or other connection with the non-Israelite "people of the land," the tribes of Canaan.

The story of Sisera therefore is one of an enemy, an enemy defeated not by the puny strength of the Israelite army, which after all had no iron chariots (Judg. 4:3, 13) and could not muster all twelve of its fractious tribes (5:16–18), but by "the hand of a woman," and ironically of a non-Israelite woman at that—Jael, wife of Heber the Kenite (4:17–22; 5:24). Although the battlefield leaders in this tale are men, Sisera on the Canaanite side and Barak on the Israelite side, the focus is rather on the actions and exploits of two women, Deborah the female prophet (*nebiyah*) and judge of Israel, and Jael. The Song of Deborah in Judges 5, a victory song that may be among the oldest parts of the Tanakh,[38] emphasizes women's roles as political and military actors (Deborah, Jael), but also as political and military victims (Sisera's mother and her "wise women," the female "spoil" that Sisera fails to bring home). The entire story, as told in prose in Judges 4 and in verse in Judges 5, is a tale of sexual politics par excellence,[39] a story in which the seductive wiles of a foreign woman and the consequent betrayal and death of her victim have the approval of YHWH and thus, from the perspective of the text, work for good, the good of a marginal people—Israel.

As the story begins in Judges 4, the people of Israel, in a pattern typical of the book of Judges, have been unfaithful to YHWH, who has punished them by "selling" them like slaves to the powerful King Jabin of Hazor, who through his superior military might, buttressed by the technological development of iron-shod chariots, "oppressed the Israelites cruelly for twenty years" (Judg. 4:3, NRSV). Because of the established theological pattern in Judges—the apostasy of the Israelites, the oppression at the hands of the foreigner with YHWH's consent, the Israelite "cry" for deliverance (cf. 2:16–23)—we expect the next event, the "raising up" of a deliverer (*mošiaʿ*) by YHWH. Unexpectedly, however, in a story that consistently raises and shatters expectations, the pattern is broken. It is Deborah herself, the judge of Israel, or at least part of Israel at the time, who summons the warrior Barak and gives him YHWH's instructions to fight the Canaanites under Sisera at Wadi Kishon, near Mount Tabor. Barak refuses to go unless Deborah goes with him, presumably so that he can be sure this woman who speaks for YHWH will bring YHWH's power. Deborah calms his fears by reassuring Barak that she will go, but that the victory will not be his, "for YHWH will sell Sisera into the hand of a woman" (4:9, NRSV).

At this point we expect that the woman's hand will be Deborah's, since she accompanies Barak to Mount Tabor and gives the battle cry, encouraging him by saying that YHWH has given Sisera into *his* hand. Perhaps forgetful of Deborah's taunt that YHWH would give victory to a woman, Barak and his "ten thousand" rush against Sisera's army, which panics and flees. (In the poetic version, they are swept away by the torrent of Kishon, in a scene reminiscent of the defeat of the Egyptians at the Reed Sea, Judg. 5:21; cf. Exodus 14.) Sisera, the powerful enemy commander, flees ignominiously on foot, his iron chariot abandoned.

The reversal of Sisera, from powerful warrior to war's victim, from man to violated woman, is not yet complete. Sisera flees to what he assumes is friendly territory, land belonging to the clan of Heber the Kenite, which is at peace with the king of Hazor (4:17). In this prose account of Jael's act (4:18–22), the readers are seduced, like Sisera, by certain assumptions about Heber's wife, assumptions that are countered by her subsequent actions. She comes out of her tent (note it is *hers*, not Heber's) to greet Sisera, asking him to "turn aside" to her, bidding him to have no fear, covering him with a rug as he enters, and treating him hospitably, even giving him milk rather than the water he asks for. Lulled by her soothing treatment, he asks her to keep watch at the entrance of the tent and to reply to any inquiries that no one is inside, just as the seductive adulteress offers to do for the young man she lures into her bed in Proverbs 7:19–20. As Danna Fewell and David Gunn point out, readers of this text are likewise lured by the patriarchal images of women serving male needs by alternately seductive and nurturing behavior, only, like Sisera, to be betrayed by them.[40] Jael "goes softly" to Sisera where he is lying asleep "from weariness," but, far from softly or gently, she drives a tent peg through his open mouth,[41] thus pinning his skull to the ground. Deborah's prophecy is fulfilled: the hand of YHWH is a woman's hand. "On that day," says the text, "God subdued King Jabin of Canaan before the Israelites" (4:23, NRSV).

In the poetic version of the tale, the victory song led by Deborah and Barak (Judges 5), in the same way as Miriam and Moses led victory songs after the defeat of the Egyptians at the Reed Sea (Exodus 15), both women, Deborah—and Jael—are praised for their efforts, and their names are associated with a hoped-for period of prosperity for Israel. "In the days of Jael," the people of Israel enjoy plunder, because Deborah has arisen, "a mother in Israel" (5:7). After those tribes that did not join Deborah are cursed, Jael is blessed, called even the "most blessed" among women (5:24). In the description of her triumph, however, the side of warfare that women usually experience is highlighted: waiting for news of the battle's outcome, rape and captivity if defeated. In contrast to the military activity of Deborah, Sisera's mother is envisioned as waiting for her son's return from battle. Her "wise" maids assure her, as indeed she reassures herself, that he and his troops are tarrying only to divide the spoil, a woman (lit., "a womb," *raham*)—or even two—"per head, per hero" (5:30), captured wombs to be enjoyed by the male victors as spoil, much as the women left at home enjoy embroidered and dyed finery, and with about as much consideration.[42] Instead, it is Sisera who belongs to an enemy defeated by an army led by a woman and whose death is described in terms of sexual violation caused by a woman. In the victory ode, Jael at first appears totally, even obsequiously, at Sisera's command (she brings him not only milk but curds when he asks for water; 5:25), but the roles are brutally reversed. In Fewell and Gunn's words, the "womb/woman has penetrated Sisera's 'head' [his 'parted lips'] with a phallic tent-peg," driven by a "workmen's mallet" (5:26).[43] Although he is described in the prose version as already lying down (4:21), in the poem Sisera is described in slow motion, sinking down, falling, and lying still at the feet of Jael, the victor (v. 27). This phrase, repeated in the parallelism often typical of Hebrew poetry that makes it more emphatic, may carry the sexual sense of Sisera's losing an erection (and hence his manhood) or may convey the idea that Jael and Sisera are standing face-to-face, head-to-head, and hence "man to man," in a single combat that has nothing to do with "women's wiles."[44] In either case, both the prose and to a greater extent the poetic versions of the death of Sisera at Jael's hand convey "the image of the defeated warrior as a seduced or raped woman," an image that is used over and over again by the prophets as a symbol of the defeated Israel. Here it is an image of Israel's emasculated enemy, vanquished "by the hand of a woman."[45]

The focus of the narrative and of the song, the victory of the powerless and their unexpected triumph over the powerful, tends to overshadow the grim vision of what would usually happen to the women of a defeated enemy (Judg. 5:29–30), indeed what may be happening even then to the Canaanite women at the hands of the victorious Israelites, in a victory that is achieved through the actions of two women. The victory ode alludes to the fate of the defeated women, if only to show how the gloating of the Canaanite women over their men's expected capture of Israelite women has been cruelly undercut, and we are not allowed to forget it. Perhaps it is mentioned as part of the relief felt by the Israelites over the fact that their victory means that "their" women do not have to suffer such a fate, that Israelite women are spared rape by Canaanite men and mockery by Canaanite mistresses by the action of two women, one a non-Israelite. After Jael's victory, Israel with her women consequently remains "intact" for forty years (5:31).

What are we to make of the character of Jael? From the perspective of the two texts that tell her story, Judges 4 and 5, she is clearly a praiseworthy woman, indeed "most blessed of all women." Her tactics are imitated and even improved upon, likewise to great praise, by another defender of the faith, the Judith of the apocryphal story that bears her name. If the character of Jael poses no problem in Judges or in Judith, why should we regard her as a problematic heroine? Perhaps it is because she deceives our expectations. First of all, Jael, unlike Deborah and unlike Judith, whose very name means "Jewish woman," is not a Jew. In fact, the clan of her husband, Heber the Kenite, is "at peace with" the Canaanite king of Hazor, meaning that they are neutral if not actually allied.[46] That makes Jael herself a foreign and almost a Canaanite woman, and we ought for that reason alone to suspect her of possible treachery, at least of sexual untrustworthiness. That suspicion is reinforced by the fact that Sisera flees, not to Heber's tent, but to a tent specifically mentioned as belonging to Jael (4:17), who not only is alone when he approaches, but even goes out to meet him and urges him to "turn aside" to her without fear (4:18). Her language lures him into her tent, where she covers him and tends to his needs, leading us to expect a sexual encounter (after all, he "goes in to" her) that turns lethal. But is the ending of the seduction scene all that unexpected? Surely behavior like this is what can be expected of foreign women, especially when their husbands are absent; after all, look at Potiphar's wife, look at Delilah! Jael does not simply betray Sisera into the hands of the enemy, is not merely responsible for his death, but is herself the direct instrument of it. Not only is the warrior's manhood damaged by his helplessness at a woman's hands, he is destroyed by her. So why is Jael, a foreign woman who uses seductive "women's wiles" to lure a man to his death, a heroic figure?

As we have seen, biblical literature draws a very fine line between women's using their supposed seductivity as an appropriate, even a wise weapon, to gain righteous ends, and women's using actual seduction to subvert those ends. As in the case of the biblical laws relating to marriage, those actions by women that contribute to saving the lives of the men of their households and of the minority ethnic group in general, not to satisfy their own desires, are praiseworthy. Jael, no less than Rahab and perhaps more so, since her tribe is at peace with Israel's enemies, is a foreign woman who saves the men and women of Israel, and possibly those of her own tribe, from defeat, abuse, and death. It may also be considered fitting by the compilers of the text of Judges that a foreign woman's wiles are the cause of defeat of a foreign man like Sisera rather than an Israelite man like Samson.

Jael's own motives are not revealed by the text, to which they are of no interest. Unlike Rahab, Jael says nothing about YHWH, although like Rahab she may know that the Israelites will be or have been victorious, and, like Rahab and the less praiseworthy Delilah, she may be casting her lot with the side of the victors for the sake of her personal and familial security and in order to avoid the fate of the defeated women delineated in Judges 5:30.[47] To avoid sexual violation, Jael uses sex as a lure to set up Sisera's own violation. Niditch sees in the victory of Jael, the foreign woman, the victory of Israel, the marginal "alien" people, against the "establishment."[48] But in this case again, an androcentric text has used a woman to promote its concerns, just as YHWH has used Jael and other women on other occasions, like the Timnite bride of Samson, to further his. Even marginal women can be good when they act on behalf of the "right" men, but they are not always good in themselves or when pursuing their own ends. Despite the flavor of sexual seduction in the Jael tale, there is no suggestion that Jael either satisfies or wants to satisfy her own sexual desires, a crucial distinction that differentiates her from Potiphar's wife. Her ends are once again subordinate to those of men, the same men who might sexually exploit or violate her if she were on the wrong side or to whom she might pose a threat. As Athalyah Brenner observes, foreign women like Jael are seen positively in the biblical text according to a "well-established intercultural tradition, that of a brave married or widowed woman who sacrifices, or seems to sacrifice, her virtue in order to save [the] people."[49]

Jael's tale is a violent one that is assigned by its editors to a confused time in the history of Israel in which expectations can be thwarted at the instigation of YHWH, in which foreign women are not always dangerous to Israelite men, and independent women among the Israelites themselves are not always adulterous or sexually rapacious, and, like Deborah, may even be married and have authority over other men without "unmanning" them. If anything, Deborah lends strength to the warrior Barak rather than vice versa. It seems, however, that the benign influence of the foreigner Jael is an exception rather than the rule. In the Deuteronomistic History's overall view of the history of Israel and of its monarchy in particular, foreign women (*nokriyyoth*) represent a threat to the Israelite community and its established hierarchical order.[50] These *nokriyyoth* are usually powerful women, of some stature in their own communities as well as in Israel; they often act independently of men or have authority over them, and they have their own religious affiliations that threaten the hegemony of the priestly and scribal elite. Therefore, they are often portrayed in the historical texts in a wearyingly familiar pattern, as devious and deviant, and as sexually promiscuous even when, like Jezebel, they are loyal to a fault to their husbands. The community must protect itself by avoiding these women, opposing them, or casting them out. Rarely are they integrated, into the community itself. The only example of such integration is Ruth, since Rahab's family remains circumscribed by Israel, not integrated, and Jael acts alone and disappears, presumably with her nomadic Kenite clan.

The pattern of powerful yet evil foreign women and their danger to the integrity of the people of Israel is established in the Deuteronomistic History as beginning in the time of Solomon. Solomon ascends the throne of his father David with the aid of his mother Bathsheba's intrigues, eliminates his chief rival and the heir, Adonijah, commits several judicious murders to shore up his position, and uses forced labor to build the Temple, his own palace, and other mammoth projects, creating a resentment among the ten northern tribes that splits the kingdom after his death. But nothing comes in for as direct and stern condemnation of Solomon by the text as his marriages to foreign women, in flagrant disobedience to the often-repeated warning of the Torah against intermarriage (1 Kings 11:1–2; cf. Ex. 23:23–33; 34:11–16; Deut. 7:1–6). According to the text, Solomon's wives and concubines, many of them royal women from traditional "enemy" nations—Egypt, Moab, Ammon, Edom, Sidon—"turn away his heart" from fidelity to YHWH to follow the "abominations" of foreign gods (1 Kings 11:3–8), seducing even Solomon, whose wisdom stunned the wise, wealthy, and powerful foreign queen of Sheba (1 Kings 10:1–13). For this reason, the offended and jealous YHWH vows to "tear away" the kingdom from Solomon's successor (1 Kings 11:31).

Throughout the rest of the Deuteronomistic History's account of the monarchy, powerful women, especially powerful foreign ("stranger") queens, are portrayed as a constant danger to the stability of the state. The paradigmatic evil foreign queen, whose name is even now (unjustly) synonymous with sexual vampirism, is Jezebel. This reputation is all the more astonishing when in the entire narrative (1 Kings 16:31–19:3; 21; 2 Kings 9:4–37), which is solidly against Jezebel, it is never suggested that she is anything other than aggressively loyal to her husband, Ahab of Israel, nor does she use overtly sexual wiles to gain control over him. Although perhaps her painting of her eyes in preparation for confronting the usurper Jehu has lent something to her vampish reputation, the legend of her promiscuity probably derives from the taunt Jehu hurls at her son, Ahab's heir Joram.

When the latter asks for peace, Jehu mockingly asks, "What peace can there be, as long as the many whoredoms and sorceries of your mother Jezebel continue?" (2 Kings 9:22, NRSV). The connection of whoredom to sorcery is a religious one, implying that the worship of any deities other than YHWH, including the worship disparaged as "sorcery," is "whoring."[51] Female practitioners of sorcery, like adulteresses, are to be put to death (Ex. 22:18). As we shall see, the use of the metaphor of adultery as apostasy and its connection with "whoring" or "harlotry" is made most strongly in the prophets, especially Hosea, Jeremiah, and Ezekiel, so it is no accident that Jezebel's chief opponents are the prophets Elijah and Elisha. The first prophesies and the latter instigates her grisly death. Jezebel is portrayed in the text as a "whore" because she is a worshiper of deities "other" than YHWH, and she influences Ahab and others in Israel to follow her example in "whoring after foreign gods." As Claudia V. Camp notes, Jezebel's narrative, like that of Solomon and his foreign wives, is one in which the themes of "gender, power, foreignness, and idolatry" are interwoven with the thread of sexuality.[52]

The very introduction of Jezebel's name in the text connects not only with foreignness, but with "lightness" of a religious and possibly sexual nature. Ahab is son of Omri, the king who is known in history as one of the most powerful and influential kings of the kingdom of Israel but is condemned by the biblical historian for doing unspecified "evil." His son considers it a "light thing" to commit the sins of the apostate first ruler, Jeroboam, by marrying Jezebel, "daughter of King Ethbaal of the Sidonians" (1 Kings 16:31). The narrative implies that the marriage itself is a form of apostasy because Ahab starts worshiping Jezebel's deities, Baal and Asherah, and may even have gone so far as to allow child sacrifice in the rebuilding of Jericho (1 Kings 16:34). Jezebel's religious corruption, as well as her power, are underlined by her stark contrast with another woman of Sidon, the poor widow to whom YHWH sends Jezebel's greatest rival, Elijah. The widow acknowledges both the power of YHWH and that of his prophet (1 Kings 17:8–24). In comparison, Jezebel, a powerful woman of Sidon, busies herself with killing off the prophets of YHWH (1 Kings 18:4, 13) and persecuting Elijah while supporting "at her table" four hundred and fifty prophets of Baal and four hundred of Asherah (1 Kings 18:19). The numbers are probably exaggerated by the narrator in order to reinforce Elijah's (and YHWH's) spectacular victory at Mount Carmel (18:20–46), but they also show that, despite the fact that Elijah addresses only Ahab throughout, Jezebel is Elijah's real—and more powerful—opponent. This becomes even clearer when she receives news from Ahab of Elijah's massacre of her prophets at Wadi Kishon (fittingly, the site of Barak's rout of Sisera's army [Judg. 4:12–16]). Jezebel herself sends word to Elijah that she will kill him in retaliation for the death of her prophets, and without resorting to appeals to Ahab, Elijah takes her threat seriously and flees for his life (19:1–3). The religious wars have begun.

The conflict, or, if we adopt the view of the historian, the abuse of power, continues in chapter 21, in which Jezebel acts to pacify the "sullen and resentful" Ahab, who has retired to his bed, by obtaining for him a plot of land that one of his subjects, Naboth, refuses to sell the king because it is the family's inheritance, to be preserved according to Levitical law (1 Kings 21:1–4). Impatient with Ahab's inaction, acting like a mother with a sulky child who is sure of her power to satisfy his wants, Jezebel declares, "I will give you the vineyard of Naboth the Jezreelite" (21:7). She proceeds to procure false witnesses who accuse Naboth of cursing God and the king, an act of religious and political treason (Ex. 22:28), for which the penalty is stoning (Lev. 24:13). Thus Jezebel violates a part of Israelite law, for which she clearly has no respect, by cunningly using that very law to entrap more scrupulous Israelites into executing Naboth and extending Ahab's power (1 Kings 21:15–16). Although Jezebel is clearly the actor here, Elijah instead confronts Ahab with the crime (21:17–24), declaring that disaster will come upon his house, and that the dogs will lick up Ahab's blood and will eat Jezebel "within the bounds of Jezreel," where the crime was committed. Perhaps, the text implies, Ahab should have had better control over his wife, or at least resisted her. But the historian lets us know, through a parenthetical comment, who the real villain is: "Indeed, there was no one like Ahab, who sold himself to do what was evil in the sight of YHWH, urged on by his wife Jezebel" (1 Kings 21:25, NRSV). Ahab is spared from immediate doom because he humbles himself and repents in front of Elijah (1 Kings 21:27–29). When Ahab, enticed by false prophecies of victory, is killed in battle against the king of Judah, the blood washed from his chariot is licked up by dogs, and the prostitutes (*zonoth*) wash themselves in it, the latter being a slight but fitting addition to the prophecy of Elijah, since Ahab has "prostituted" himself to serve Jezebel's foreign deities (1 Kings 22:38). They mingle together in the pollution of blood and death brought about by Ahab and his foreign queen.

Jezebel, who has caused Ahab to commit "whoredom," meets a like end, one that is instigated by Elijah's successor Elisha. Elisha sends a disciple to anoint Jehu king of Israel, passing over the seventy descendants of Ahab (2 Kings 10:1). The young man is instructed to tell Jehu, "Strike down the house of your master Ahab, so that I may avenge on Jezebel the blood of my servants the prophets, and the blood of all the servants of YHWH" (2 Kings 9:7, NRSV). Jehu refuses peace with Ahab's successor Joram, alleging that there can be no peace because of Jezebel's "whoredoms and sorceries" (9:22). Instead, Jehu kills not only Joram but Ahaziah, the king of the Southern Kingdom, Judah. Ahaziah's mother is Athaliah, the daughter of Ahab and Jezebel (2 Kings 8:18, 27). Another queen whose political ruthlessness and power to corrupt her royal husband and son are portrayed as equal to or surpassing those of her mother, Athaliah rules solo over Judah until her own assassination (2 Kings 11:1–16). Awaiting the news from battle, Jezebel, formally adorning eyes and head, confronts Jehu from her palace window with a taunt, "Is it peace, Zimri, murderer of your master?" referring to an earlier assassination in Israel (1 Kings 16:8–12). Like every other male in her story except for Ahab, Jehu does not answer Jezebel, but calls for support from within the palace by those who are on his side (2 Kings 9:32). Given Jezebel's reputation for sexual potency, it is ironic that only "two or three eunuchs" respond to Jehu's command to throw her down. (Perhaps there is mockery of Jehu's own flimsy political authority.) Jezebel is graphically trampled to death by horses, which are splattered with her blood. The brutal Jehu goes inside to "eat and drink," giving orders to bury Jezebel, who, even if a "cursed woman," is yet a king's daughter (9:34). The text delicately refrains from mentioning that she is also a king's widow and the mother of the just-slain king of Israel, but the fact that even Jehu is willing to give her an honorable burial is some recognition of her stature,[53] despite the fact that this recognition is immediately undercut by the observation that Elijah's prophecy (1 Kings 21:23) has been fulfilled: the dogs have left nothing of Jezebel fit to bury. Almost gloatingly, the text describes the once-powerful queen reduced to an unidentifiable collection of *disjecta membra*, a skull, soles of feet, palms of hands, "like dung on the field" (2 Kings 9:35–37). Her daughter Athaliah meets an end that echoes Jezebel's; she is dragged from the Temple in Jerusalem to the palace, where she is killed at the "horses' entrance" (2 Kings 9:15–16).

The stories of Jezebel and Athaliah show how dangerous the influence of foreign women—let alone powerful foreign women—can be. As these texts see it, the only form of power that women, even queens, possess comes through their manipulation of men—husbands and sons—and this power usually has sexual overtones. For women to have sexual power to manipulate men is somehow a betrayal of the proper order of things, where men should be in control of their women, as Ahab most clearly and to his own destruction is not. The power of women like Jezebel and Athaliah destroys the lives of men, who can only be protected if they resist and finally kill such women. Jezebel is lethal not only to the prophets of YHWH and to Naboth but also to her husband Ahab and her son Joram, whose deaths are indirectly attributed to her machinations, her "sorceries." Athaliah is likewise lethal, if not to her husband Jehoram, who is spared by YHWH's fidelity to the Judean house of David (2 Kings 8:19), nevertheless to her son Ahaziah, who is killed because of his relationship to the house of Ahab her father (2 Kings 9:16, 27–28), and most certainly to the remaining descendants of the royal house of Judah, including her own grandson Joash, whom she attempts to put to death (2 Kings 11:1–3). Only with the deaths of such voracious and deadly women, as with the execution of unfaithful wives, brides, and sorceresses, can the chaos be averted and sanctioned order restored. Only so can the community be purged of religious as well as political evil and the boundaries be "righted."

The Northern Kingdom, Israel, could not ultimately defend itself against invasion, possession, and the virtual erasure of its identity by the foreign power of Assyria, which prophets like Hosea describe as fitting punishment for "whoring" after foreign deities (Hosea 2). Its southern neighbor, described as Israel's promiscuous younger sister by the exilic prophet Ezekiel (Ezek. 16:46), also could not escape captivity and rape by a foreign power, Assyria's own conqueror Babylon. Since the prophecies of Hosea and Ezekiel, with those of other prophets who emphasize Israel's and Judah's "whoredom" against YHWH as a theme, will be discussed in chapter 3, it may suffice to say here that they, like the Deuteronomistic Historian(s), regard any contact of the people of YHWH with "foreigners" as fraught with potential disaster through shaking up the proper order of things. Foreign women sexually allure men's hearts away from their own women and from YHWH and cause them to become "whores." Because of their infidelity to YHWH, they lose their strength and become "unmanned," abandoned by their protector.

When the Judean exiles were allowed to return to Jerusalem by the decree of Cyrus the Great of Persia (538 B.C.E.), a small group of them led by a priestly and scribal elite did in fact come back, and their first concerns were recovering the land for its appropriate owners, reestablishing the Temple and its ritual in the appropriate hands, and redrawing the boundaries to assure ethnic and cultic integrity under the leadership of that elite. The postexilic books of Ezra and Nehemiah, like the Deuteronomistic History and the final edition of the Torah by priestly hands, vividly demonstrate how important the issue of what Niditch calls "self-definition and identity" was in the minds of the religious and cultural leaders of Jerusalem, with exogamy determining who was outside the community.[54] Beginning in the period after the exile, according to Léonie Archer, the regulation of sexual relations became part of a "rigorous code of conduct" that reinforced and reflected "the new social order and structure,"[55] a structure projected back by the text into the past and the institution of the law at Sinai. With this more rigorous structure and its accompanying anxiety about all matters sexual came the determination to reestablish male priestly authority through expelling the troublesome influence of foreign women. According to Ezra 7:25–26, as the priest and interpreter of the "laws of God" Ezra is entrusted by the Persian king Artaxerxes with ruling the province of "Judah and Jerusalem" according to the religious law of YHWH and the political law of the king of Persia. After setting up judges and priests, Ezra bemoans the pollution caused by intermingling of the "holy seed" of the people of

Israel, including priests and Levites, with that of the "peoples of the land" through marriage with foreign wives (Ezra 9:1–5). Ezra's solution to this "crisis" is to call a public assembly, where, shivering from fear and the heavy rain, the "people" (males) swear to separate themselves from the foreign women (*nokriyyoth*; Ezra 10:11). The foreign women themselves are given nothing to say, and the separation apparently does not apply to Jewish women who have married foreign men, thus implying that it is the women who are responsible for the religious fidelity or apostasy of their husbands, and for the purity of the line of descent.[56] In another version of the reestablishment of order, Nehemiah, a returned exile who is appointed governor of Jerusalem by the Persian king, makes it his first task to rebuild its walls, thus visibly and physically excluding others, to their distress and alarm. Nehemiah 8:2–3 recounts a reading of the Torah by Ezra to the assembly of all of the people, including women, in a rededication ceremony. After this reading from the "book of Moses" (13:1–3), the "people of Israel" separate themselves from "people of foreign (non-Israelite) descent." Nehemiah continues to berate the Judahites for violating the Mosaic law, but most vehemently and violently (by cursing, beating, and pulling out hair) berates them for intermarriage with foreign women, mentioning that they caused even the great Solomon to sin (13:23–27).

In the postexilic community that is reflected in the books of Ezra and Nehemiah, women are important, in that their reproductivity is essential to reestablish the family lines and structure on which this marginal community rests.[57] As in the patriarchal period, whenever patrilineal descent becomes important, the sexuality of the women of the group is important and needs to be channeled toward its building up. The belief that the presence of "outsider" or foreign women in the community after the exile has confused the lines of descent characterizes them as a threat to the community so great that their very presence within it causes the people of Israel to sin. Sin in this case is "pollution," a disease introduced by sexual contact with "stranger" women.

Not every voice in the postexilic community supported the reforms of Ezra and Nehemiah. The book of Ezra names four men, two of them Levites, who oppose Ezra and the rest of the assembly on the issue of divorcing foreign wives (Ezra 10:15). The female prophet Noadiah is mentioned as an opponent by Nehemiah as one of the prophets who tried to "frighten" him by political or religious intimidation (Neh. 6:14). Among the literary voices of opposition to the "Reformation" represented in the books of Ezra and Nehemiah is the book of Ruth, in which a woman of foreign and therefore suspicious origin—a Moabite—uses sexual wiles to secure for herself a second Israelite husband and thus to redeem the fortunes of her Israelite mother-in-law's house, proving "more valuable than seven sons" (Ruth 4:15), and eventually becoming the ancestress of King David

(Ruth 4:18–22). Although it is set in the time of the Judges, the book of Ruth may well belong to the period of the Ezrahite reforms and represent a negative response to the characterization of foreign women as dangerous and inimical to the faith and cultural stability of the people of Israel.[58]

The tale begins with a family—father, mother, and two sons—that has to leave their home in Israel for a fairly typical reason, because there is a "famine in the land." But unlike earlier Israelites like Abraham and Jacob, for example, they do not go to Egypt to obtain bread, but to Moab. The very name of the place conjures up danger, hostility, and sexual perversity, since the Moabites are the descendants of the incestuous intercourse between Lot and his daughter (Gen. 19:37) and are excluded from the assembly of Israel both because they have opposed their kinsmen the Israelites (Deut. 23:4) and because the "daughters of Moab" have had intercourse with the Israelite men in the Wilderness period, causing them to "whore" after foreign gods (Num. 25:1–5).[59] The element of danger to Israelite males through foreign women is heightened when the two sons, Mahlon and Chilion, actually marry Moabite women, Ruth and Orpah, and die leaving both of them childless widows. Their father's death leaves their mother Naomi also a childless widow, an exile in a foreign land. Clearly, marriage and settlement in a foreign land has not proven beneficial to the family of Elimelech.

In a move that has echoes of the Judahite return from exile in a foreign land (the Babylonian captivity, 587–538 B.C.E.), Naomi decides to return to Judah because she has heard that YHWH has "considered his people" and ended the famine (Ruth 1:6). Despite the fact that her daughters-in-law are Moabites, they seem to have won Naomi's approval by having shown the proper behavior toward the dead men and toward her (1:8). For this reason, she hopes that they will "find security" in the house of a husband, and, knowing that she cannot provide them with husbands, urges them to return, each to her "mother's house" (1:9). As A.-J. Levine points out, using this terminology instead of the more usual "father's house" evokes other situations (Gen. 24:28, the story of Rebekah's courtship; Song 3:4; 8:2, the place where the bride envisions intercourse with the bridegroom) in which it relates to "sexuality, marriage, and women who determine both their own destiny and that of others."[60] Perversely, Ruth does not heed Naomi's advice and sets out toward what appears to be a sexual and reproductive dead end, going to a foreign land with a foreign mother-in-law who describes herself as finished sexually (1:12–13). But Ruth "clings to" Naomi, as in a marital context a wife would cling to a husband (Gen. 2:24),[61] choosing her, her people, and her god in a beautiful poetic declaration of loyalty whose frequent (mis)usage at wedding ceremonies points out just how misguided it is in its own context (1:16–17), since Ruth is choosing reproductive death. At this point we may be reminded of Rahab, another suspect but unexpectedly righteous Gentile woman, who chooses to save the lives of the Israelites at the cost of her city because of her belief in their god.

Despite Ruth's devotion, however, Naomi considers herself "empty" and "bitter" when she returns to Bethlehem, scarcely recognized by its women, with no family, only "Ruth the Moabite, her daughter-in-law" (1:19–22). Ruth proves to be the resource Naomi needs to recoup her fortunes, even though the narrative suggests that Naomi is not as alone as she describes herself, for Elimelech, her late husband, has a wealthy and prominent kinsman, Boaz (2:1). The dispirited Naomi cannot take the initiative and ask Boaz for help; instead, Ruth goes into his barley fields to glean the remnants, the prerogative of the poor (Lev. 19:9–10), saying that she hopes she can find "someone in whose sight I may find favor" (2:2, NRSV). Her precarious sexual position is reinforced by the fact that when Boaz does notice her, and inquires whose "woman" she is, his servants answer that she "belongs" to no one; she is the Moabite who came back with Naomi (2:5). Recognizing her liminal and therefore precarious situation, Boaz at once adopts the role of male protector, urging Ruth to stay close to "his" young women, and ordering his young men not to molest her, as they might feel free to do with a "loose" woman (2:8–10, 15–16, 22). When Ruth falls prostrate with gratitude before him for having "spoken to her heart," even though she is a foreign woman (*nokriyyah*),[62] Boaz replies that it is because she has left father, mother, and native land for people she does not know, and prays that YHWH will reward her for her deeds (2:11).

When Naomi learns the name of the man whose favor Ruth has found, she conveniently remembers that not only is Boaz kin, but "next-of-kin" (*go'el*), the "redeemer," one whose responsibility it is to "redeem" (buy out) family members and property from destitution. It later turns out that Boaz does not actually have this position (3:12–14), a fact that heightens the sexual tension, for here the *go'el* is also apparently expected to fulfill the levirate obligation (4:1–11). Bent on providing security for her daughter-in-law, a security with a husband that she believed she could not provide in Moab (1:9), Naomi coaches Ruth on how to seduce Boaz (3:1–5). When he is lying asleep on the threshing floor ("threshing" being a metaphor for intercourse in many agricultural societies),[63] Ruth, as instructed, uncovers his feet (a Hebrew euphemism for the male genitals) and lies down (3:6–7). When Boaz "discovers" her, Ruth urges him to re-cover her with his cloak (*kanap*, another euphemism for genitals)[64] "for you are *go'el*." Boaz is once again overcome by this last instance of Ruth's loyalty (*hesed*), not because she is taking this risky action on Naomi's behalf, but because she has chosen him instead of younger men (3:10). He praises her, citing her reputation among his people as an *'ešet ḥayil*, a "woman of worth" (3:11). Our hopes are somewhat dashed when he claims that there is another *go'el*, but if he cannot be persuaded to fulfill his obligation, Boaz will act as redeemer (3:13). Boaz further protects Ruth's reputation (and his own?) by sending Ruth away before anyone knows that a woman came to the threshing floor (3:14), but he does not send her away before filling her cloak with grain, so that she does not go back "empty" to Naomi. Already Ruth begins to "fill" Naomi's inheritance, which is "empty" of male heirs.

Boaz himself is not above a little trickery to satisfy his own desires, for when he has the matter of relationship judged by the (male) elders in the gate, he represents the issue to the actual next-of-kin as one of redeeming "land" that belonged to Elimelech (4:3). When the *go'el* agrees to redeem it, Boaz adds, almost as an afterthought, that the widow Ruth goes along with it, and the *go'el* is expected to perform the obligation of the *levir* (4:5). When the *go'el* says that he cannot do this and still keep his own inheritance intact (4:6), the sandal-removing ceremony mentioned in Deuteronomy 25:5–12 is performed, and Boaz, now officially the next-of-kin, takes Ruth as his wife, in order to perpetuate her late husband's name and inheritance in Israel (4:10). The elders bless Boaz, expressing the hope that Ruth will be like Rachel and Leah and Tamar (4:11–12), all women associated with sexual trickery to secure a husband's issue and thus their own security. When Ruth has a son, thus securing the inheritance of her former husband's family, the women of Bethlehem, as those whom this most concerns, congratulate Naomi as the one to whom the son is born, since her fortunes have been restored by one who is "worth more than seven sons" (4:13–17).

Throughout this text, it is the "women who propose, men who dispose." The persons in positions of power are the rich Boaz, the unnamed male next-of-kin, and the elders of the city of Bethlehem. Ruth acts within a subservient and potentially exploitable position, and only with the counsel of Naomi. In this respect, as in others, the text defuses the threat of the *nokriyyah*, the foreign woman. Although she uses sexual wiles, she does not do so from a position of power but from one of vulnerability, since any of the "young men" of Boaz or Boaz himself could have raped her with impunity. The scene at the threshing floor, with its strong sexual aura, together with the emphasis on Ruth's being a levirate widow (although she really is not, since she has no living brother-in-law), recall the actions of another widow who uses sexual means to gain security, Tamar, to whom a direct and approving parallel is drawn by the elders of Bethlehem in 4:12.[65] The "foreign woman" Ruth is also linked by them to other revered matriarchs of Israel—Rachel and Leah.

Ruth's foreignness is also tempered by terms related to the Israelite worship of YHWH in the text. From the first, Ruth adopts Naomi's god as her own (1:16). On the first occasion that Boaz blesses her, he mentions that YHWH, the God of Israel, is the one under whose cloak (*kanap*) she has taken refuge (2:12), and it is under the *kanap* of Boaz that Ruth is to find true blessing, the blessing of economic and social security under male protection (3:9, 15). Much of the language in Ruth is that of "redemption," the quest for a "redeemer" (*go'el*) of the destroyed fortunes of Naomi's "house." Although the term comes from family law, and denotes, as here, the nearest male next-of-kin, it is often applied in the Tanakh to YHWH as the "redeemer" of the fortunes of Israel, whether from slavery in Egypt or captivity in Babylon. YHWH's *ḥesed* ("steadfast love," loyalty) is also a frequent theme in the Tanakh, especially in the prophets, who often refer to YHWH's *ḥesed* even toward the faithless and undeserving Israel. Although in this text it is Ruth who actually redeems the fortunes of Naomi's house, she does so by means of male "redeemers," first Boaz and then Obed, Naomi's *go'el*, whose lineage is prophesied to be glorious (4:14–15, 22). Ruth's chief quality, however, as the tale emphasizes over and over, is her *ḥesed*, her loving loyalty, to those like Naomi and Boaz who have no reason to expect or command it.

In the story of Ruth, then, we have a positive portrait of a woman from a foreign country that is known not only for its enmity to Israel but also for its "deviant" origins and sexual behavior (Gen. 20:37; Num. 25:1–5). Despite her apparently wanton behavior at the threshing floor, Ruth is never called a prostitute (*zonah*), because she does not cause Israelite men to "prostitute" themselves before alien deities (cf. Ex. 34:15–16). The story also goes to some pains to show that Ruth, although a foreign woman, is not a sexually "loose" or predatory woman. A measure of her worthiness and loyalty is that she has not gone after any man but the upright Boaz, who after all is close kin, and only after being directed to do so by her mother-in-law Naomi (3:10). A liminal figure like Rahab because she is a Gentile among Jews, in peril as Jews often are among Gentiles, Ruth is yet righteous; a liminal figure like Tamar because she is a childless widow whose *levir* is dead and whose next-of-kin will not perform his obligation, she does what she can to continue the line of her husband's "house" in Israel. Thus Ruth's sexuality, though that of a "strange woman," is directed toward the ends approved by this and other texts in the Tanakh, following the advice of Naomi to seek security with a husband. The young woman who belonged to no man in Israel (2:5) places herself under the protection of Boaz, a wealthy and prominent member of the Judahite community of Bethlehem, who is scrupulous about observing the law. The risk Ruth poses as a Moabite woman is nullified, as she herself is absorbed into the community of Bethlehem,[66] praised by the male authorities, the elders, who might otherwise have shut out the dangerous foreigner, and eventually taking her place as an Israelite ancestress comparable to Tamar (4:12), who herself has a place in Boaz's lineage (4:18). As Brenner notes, foreign women like Ruth were acceptable, "If and when they were prepared to forsake their previous ethnic, cultural, and religious ties, and to adopt the systems of values and beliefs prevalent in their new environment."[67]

"MY BELOVED IS MINE":
THE SONG OF SONGS

Like the book of Ruth, although to an even greater degree, the collection of love poetry attributed to Solomon, the lover of foreign women, is an anomalous text. It is the most fully and openly erotic book in the whole of the Tanakh—indeed, in the entire biblical canon. It is also "a text that offers a thoroughly nonsexist view of heterosexual love."[68] Like Ruth, the Song of Songs has a strong female protagonist and an erotic theme, but not as in Ruth, female desire in the Song of Songs is directed frankly and boldly toward its own satisfaction.[69] As Renita J. Weems has observed, "The protagonist in the Song is the only unmediated female voice in scripture."[70] So exotic is the Song of Songs that its acceptance into the canon, if its earliest interpretations are any indication, was largely occasioned by the belief that it is an allegory of the love between YHWH and Israel or between Christ and the church, the Virgin Mary (!), or the individual soul.[71] In addition, its attribution to Solomon seems to have included it among the wisdom texts. Both the rabbinic and Christian patristic views, which still affect readings of the Song, give the male rather than the female voice priority.

The Song itself is composed of several "songs" or love poems, whose speakers are only identifiable as female (sometimes called "the bride" or "the Shulammite") and male ("the bridegroom," Solomon). Both lovers praise each other erotically and long for the consummation of their desire, although the female voice is more often heard, more frank, and more often the initiator of the quest for sexual satisfaction than the male voice. The female lover begins the Song of Songs with her desire to be kissed openly and often by her beloved, expressing her satisfaction with her own color, the black that is "gazed on by the sun," and her disdain for being covered or veiled (Song 1:2–8). She envisions many places where they will make love: in the banqueting hall, in the vineyards, where he pastures his flock, in a garden, in the bedroom of her mother's house, in the "wilderness." She confesses to the "girls of Jerusalem" that she is "faint" and "sick because of love" (2:5; 5:6, 8; 8:4). In fantasies and dreams, she pursues "him whom my soul loves" through the streets of the city (3:1–5; 5:2–8), risking a beating by the city's watchmen (perhaps because they mistake her for a *zonah*; 5:7). She frequently praises her beloved's physical appearance, comparing him to symbols that often stand for male fertility: rams, young stags, and an "apple tree" in the woods, the latter presumably because it is the only tree there with fruit, and one of the fruits that the female lover wishes would revive her from her love sickness (2:3–5).

Although the male lover often seems to elude or vanish from the sight of the female, he too uses intensely sensual imagery to describe his beloved; he too calls and invites her to share her love with him. He attempts to enter the locked room, the enclosed garden (2:9; 4:12; 5:1). His physical descriptions of his beloved are as detailed as hers of him, but contain military imagery as well as the recognizably sensual imagery of animals, vineyards, fruits, spices, and fountains. He says that her neck is "like the tower of David," upon which hang the shields of a thousand warriors (4:4); she is "terrible as an army with banners" (6:30).[72] He likens her to "a mare among Pharaoh's chariots" (1:9, NRSV), a simile that conjures up a war strategem of sending a mare in heat among the chariots, which are pulled by stallions only, in order to throw the army into confusion.[73] She draws the gaze like a "dance before two armies" (6:13, NRSV).

The female beloved is thus to her male lover an object that attracts but is also dangerous. Perhaps that is why he so often eludes her embrace even as he invites it. Furthermore, she is a foreign or at least a "strange" woman. The "daughters of Jerusalem" initially stare at her because of her darkness (1:5). Her lover invites her to come from Lebanon, "from the peak of Amana, from the peak of Senir and Hermon, from the dens of lions, from the mountains of leopards," all foreign and wild places in comparison to Jerusalem, the city to which she must come and which proves inimical to the consummation of the lovers' desires.[74] In his commentary Michael D. Goulder, like Weems, suggests that the Song of Song's theology is "anti-particularist": its praise of the foreign bride belongs to the "literature of resistance" to Ezra's restoration.[75] The Shulammite is hence truly a "strange woman" to the women and the "watchmen" of Jerusalem, guardians of proper female behavior within the city. She, however, is not restrained, either in the expression of her desire for her male beloved or in her pursuit of him. As Weems observes, moreover, "The woman in touch with her sensuality . . . is a woman empowered."[76] The elements of danger are there: powerful female sexuality, pursuit of her male (Jerusalemite?) lover, the suggestion of other conquests. Their love, moreover, is "strong as death," their passion "fierce as the grave" (8:5, NRSV).

Why is this love—between a man of Jerusalem (who is called Solomon) and a foreign woman, a love that does not mention YHWH or theological matters directly even once—not destructive? At least on the surface, the erotic poems refer to an eventual marriage and the bride's desire is directed toward one man only, the bridegroom. The female lover seeks and wants the cooperation if not the approval of the young women of Jerusalem in her search for the one whom her "soul loves." It is she moreover who is "sick" and "faint" with love, not he. Hence, the love is one that is monogamous, love that yearns for only one beloved and will not be satisfied without him. Like Israel for YHWH or the soul for Christ in traditional Jewish and Christian interpretations of the Song of Songs, the lover seeks fulfillment of love for a single beloved. So single-minded is this passion, on both sides, that it can never become adultery: this is sanctioned love, a love contained fully within marriage. The book of Proverbs uses the lover's pursuit of the beloved in its portrait of Wisdom, who seeks and is sought by the wise man. But, as we shall also see, Proverbs shows how passion, when directed toward more than one "beloved," and especially in the hands of the Strange Woman, can be destructive and indeed deadly. The balance is a delicate one.

In conclusion, the "foreign woman" in the androcentric texts that have been discussed represents men's view of women's sexual "otherness," in both its alluring and its frightening strangeness. This otherness is portrayed as threatening and destructive if it is not controlled by men who wish to fulfill and also to master their own desires. The only exception is the portrayal of female and male desire in the Song of Songs, in which are depicted mutuality, not domination; interdependence, not enmity; sexual fulfillment, not mere procreation, and love that is as powerful as death but does not destroy.[77] Yet all women, even the Shulammite of the Song of Songs, are potential "outsiders," strange women who need to have their powerful sexuality eventually confined within a male-directed "house." Any female sexual activity that is outside of a heterosexual and patriarchal marriage that is directed toward securing the patriliny by producing male heirs, is thus liable to be called prostitution or "whoring" (znb). Even the independent female lover of the Song of Songs, who desires to make love to her beloved in her "mother's house" (a place presumably secure from patriarchal dominion) is caught, wounded, and chastised by the "watchmen of the city." When inside the border established by patriarchal control and thus "contained," women are considered "good"; when outside of that border and therefore "out of control," they are usually characterized as "evil" or at least dangerous.[78] Thus the bride whose virginity is not intact is to be brought out of her father's house, which she has dishonored through sexual betrayal, by "prostituting" herself (Deut. 22:20–21) and "purged" from the community by being put outside its boundaries and killed. The betrothed woman who lies with a man other than her intended husband is brought to the boundary of the town, the gates, and there killed by stoning, also to "purge" the evil from the community (Deut. 22:23–24). By using non-Israelite and non-Judahite women as the symbols of chaos and destruction, the male scribal elite, especially during and after the exile, reflect their anxiety about "otherness," their own marginality, their concern with the reestablishment of paternal lines, and their ability to maintain religious order under their leadership by defining tight boundaries for the community. Foreign women represent "difference" in lineage, custom, and religion, and their sexuality is therefore doubly dangerous. They should be kept, like prostitutes, on the margins of society, or even expelled from it. Foreign women can also *cause* prostitution, the "whoring" of Israelite and Judahite males after foreign deities (see Deut. 31:16). They also threaten to "unman" males, robbing them of sexual potency (Samson, Sisera), undermining the hegemony of the male political and religious elite and their claims to ownership of women's reproductive potential. Powerful foreign women (like Jezebel) are especially threatening and therefore all the more likely to be portrayed as sexual traitors, as "whores." When the people of Israel threaten to assimilate and abandon the cherished and carefully maintained cosmos of their religious leaders, Israel itself is described as a "whore," allying herself with foreign males, the Canaanite *ba'als*, instead of her legitimate *ba'al*, YHWH.[79] But the marital relationship between YHWH and Israel is the subject of chapter 3.

3

Jealous Husband
and Wayward Wife

Sexual Crime and Punishment

I have seen your abominations,
> your adulteries and neighings, your shameless
> prostitutions
on the hills of the countryside.
> —Jeremiah 13:27, NRSV

THE CONSTRUCTION
OF ISRAEL AS WIFE

One of the most striking anomalies of gender in the Tanakh, and to some degree in the New Testament as well, is that while God (YHWH) is portrayed almost exclusively as male, the people of God (the collective "Israel" of the Tanakh) are referred to as either male or female, but with notable differences in context. "Israel" is the name given to Jacob, the patriarch of the twelve tribes, and thus to his collective descendants (Gen. 35:9–12). When the Torah is given at Sinai, however, the "people" who await Moses' return from the mountain are male (Ex. 19:15), and their leaders, Moses, Aaron, and the elders, are also male (Ex. 19:24; 24:1–2, 9–11).[1] Most of the provisions of the Torah's law codes address free Israelite men and their concerns as the norm, defining women as exceptions to these norms or as objects of male interests, a method that continues in later interpretations of these codes like the Mishnah.[2] "Israel" is referred to in the prophetic literature as YHWH's "son" (Hos. 11:1; Mal. 1:6) but also as "daughter" (Jer.14:17; Isa. 37:22) and even as "rebellious children" (Isa. 30:1). In this context, YHWH is like the patriarch who is both responsible for and has *patria potestas* (the absolute power of the patriarch) over his sons and daughters. The firstborn son is of course the heir, and YHWH is often referred to in the Torah as "the god of our ancestors (fathers)," the god of "Abraham, Isaac, and Jacob."

But if YHWH has children (even metaphorical ones), who is his wife and their mother? In some contexts, YHWH is either the creator or the mother of Israel (e.g., Hos. 11:1–4) but has no mate and does not produce, as other gods do, through divine intercourse, *hieros gamos*. It is clear from the Deuteronomistic Historian and the prophets, who fiercely inveigh against the custom, that in actual practice, sometimes even in the Temple in Jerusalem, YHWH was assigned a female divine partner, usually Asherah/Astarte (perhaps the goddess to whom the *qedeshoth* were devoted; 2 Kings 21:7; 23:6–7; Jer. 7:16–20; 44:19). YHWH was at times also addressed in terms usually applied to Asherah's male partner, Ba'al (see Psalm 29).[3] For the priestly compilers and editors of the Torah, for the Deuteronomistic Historian, and for many of the prophets and their exilic and postexilic editors, the idea of YHWH as a fully sexual being was as abhorrent as that of YHWH having intercourse with a female divine being who was also fully sexual. Their problem was solved by the metaphorical representation of Israel, YHWH's possession, as YHWH's wife, just as in society a man's wife was his possession. Further, as one's wife was expected to be loyal to him and him alone, so Israel was expected to be loyal to YHWH, who not only had specifically chosen the collective "her" to be his exclusive possession (see Amos 3:2) but, unlike a mortal man, remained consistently faithful to her. This metaphor describing the relationship between YHWH and Israel, particularly in the prophetic literature where it is developed to the greatest extent, "is used more frequently and extensively than other personal metaphors."[4]

In the Torah, however, the preferred metaphors for the relationship between YHWH and Israel are those of overlord and vassal or father and son. As Howard Eilberg-Schwartz points out, even in Deuteronomy, which was probably written close to the time of the exile, Israel is only once personified as female and never as an adulteress (*ma'al*) or whore (*zonah*); the only time that the verb *znh* is used is to refer to the behavior of the people in worshiping foreign deities (Deut. 31:16).[5] In the account of the wilderness wandering (Lev. 20:5; Num. 25:1–5) and in the pattern of apostasy, slavery, and deliverance established in the account of the settlement in Canaan contained in Judges (Judg. 2:17; 8:27, 33), *znh*, "to whore," "to play the harlot," "to prostitute oneself," is used with masculine subjects, the men of Israel, with foreign women or foreign deities as objects.[6] How then does the term *znh*, with its related, narrower term, *n'p*, "to commit adultery," come to be applied as a metaphor dealing exclusively with the disobedience of a feminine Israel to a masculine god? As Phyllis Bird observes, both *znh* (the "general term for extramarital intercourse") and *n'p* (describes a specific extramarital act) are primarily applied to female subjects, "since it is only for women that marriage is the primary determinant of legal status and obligation." Women's sexual activity is judged by their status, and men's sexual activity is regulated by recognition and protection of the marital rights of other men.[7] According to Israelite theology, male Israelites cannot possess YHWH, who is also male, but they must conversely be his faithful possession. Given the emphasis in the Hebrew Bible on heterosexuality and reproduction, the exclusive erotic relationship between collective Israel and YHWH could have been imagined in no other way than as the relationship between wife and husband, the founders of a family.[8] As we have also seen in other contexts, male anxieties are often projected onto women as the "other," the more easily to examine and control them. Anxiety about Israel's infidelity to YHWH, with the potential loss of his affection and protection, can thus be "displaced" onto a female object.[9] The scribal elite brings home the horror of such infidelity and its consequences by using examples from social and familial life. An unfaithful wife, like a foreign or "outsider" woman, representing what is hoped to be a rare and unexpected occurrence, threatens to "unman" spousal authority and ultimately male hegemony, even the exclusive authority and hegemony of YHWH himself. As Renita J. Weems has observed, "It is not surprising that sexuality became a central metaphor for Israel's self-conception" in the prophetic writings especially, because of the profound anxiety aroused and characterized by sexual relations.[10]

Yet although the marital relationship is developed by the prophets as a dominant paradigm of the relationship of the masculine God and "his" feminized people, it is foreshadowed in the language of the Sinai covenant itself. In both versions of the Decalogue, Exodus 20:4–6 and Deuteronomy 5:9, YHWH demands exclusivity of worship because he is a "jealous" god. As Tikva Frymer-Kensky observes, "jealousy" (*qin'ah*) "is not a term found in the ancient political treaties," like the suzerainty (overlord to vassal) treaties on which the Decalogue is in part modeled. The word comes instead from terminology related to marriage, specifically from the long, detailed ritual trial of a woman who may be suspected of adultery because of nothing other than her husband's "spirit of jealousy" (*ruaḥqin'ah*; Num. 5:11–31).[11] Michael Fishbane points out that *qin'ah* may also be understood as "zeal" or "attention to honor."[12] Thus, as the husband is concerned lest his own honor, represented in his wife's exclusive sexual relationship with him, be impugned or lost, so YHWH is jealous/zealous for his own honor, embodied in Israel's total fidelity to him alone. Women are not really keepers of their own honor but emblems of male honor, an honor that is concentrated in exclusive sexual rights of a man to "his" women. The procedure of the *Soṭah*, which is conducted by the jealous husband in front of the priests, virtually assumes the wife's guilt as well as the husband's right to act on a mere whim. It subjects her to a terrifying ordeal[13] in which she drinks a potion believed to damage her in the area in which she is regarded socially as having most "value," her womb. She will suffer with "bitter pain, discharge, and drop," presumably making her unfit to bear any more children and perhaps causing her to lose the supposedly illegitimate one she carries (Num. 5:27–28). In addition to drinking the potion, the wife is also required to assent to the priest's ritual curse that will descend on her if she is guilty, making her an outcast (5:22). Even if she is innocent, no blame will attach to her husband for his unfounded suspicions (5:31): It is the nature of a husband to be "jealous."

In the period of the Mishnah, this passage becomes the focus of a debate among the rabbis about whether women should be taught Torah or are to be excluded from study, the debate revolving not around the issue of learning or of female intelligence but around honor and shame. According to Ben-Azzai, a father should teach his daughter Torah, or at least this passage, so that if she drinks the bitter water, she will know why, "For merit mitigates [her punishment]." Rabbi Eliezer, on the other hand, like many modern opponents of sex education, replies that any father who teaches his daughter Torah teaches her *tifluth*, "lightness," so he is really teaching her how to be "loose" rather than impressing upon her the grave consequences of light behavior. Rabbi Joshua's comment, that women take "more pleasure in one measure of lechery than nine of modesty," also leans in the direction of making all female sexuality suspect.[14]

This suspicion, already voiced in the Torah, is more sharply focused in the works of the prophets. There the marital metaphor for the relationship of YHWH and Israel, in a society in which the pivotal point of the honor/shame axis is male sexual authority, exemplifies male anxiety about female sexuality and its control writ large. As Frymer-Kensky observes, "This fear of women's sexual license arises in part from the male's fear of losing control over his wife. It is not sexuality that is the problem, but the fact that it is not directed towards the husband."[15] Female sexual freedom, the freedom from male sexual hegemony, becomes the apt metaphor for religious freedom from YHWH's exclusive rights to Israel's worship claimed on his behalf by the male priestly and scribal elite. The loss of political and religious control during two critical periods in the history of Israel and Judah—the divided kingdom in 922 B.C.E., followed two hundred years later by the fall of Israel (the Northern Kingdom) to Assyria; and the fall of Jerusalem and the Temple, together with the captivity of the Judahite (Southern Kingdom) elite in Babylon, in 586–538 B.C.E.—meant that their honor, linked as it was with that of their jealous and exclusive deity, YHWH, was seriously impaired. The triumph of the dangerous foreign "other" (Babylon and Assyria) and the realization of the feared loss of control and authority is displaced onto the female "other" at hand. As a wife betrays her husband, so Israel and Judah have betrayed their God. The prophets of the exile, then, like the Deuteronomistic Historian, are particularly jealous for the honor of YHWH, which becomes symbolic of their own, a point illustrated by the fact that by far the largest number of occurrences of the terminology of adultery (thirty-four) are found in the writings of the exilic prophet Ezekiel, who is also the prophet with the most graphic and violent imagery of sexual punishment.[16]

The representation of the covenant as a marriage contract between YHWH as husband and Israel as wife first occurs in the book of the prophet Hosea, where it is so prominent and powerful an image that it obscures the images that dominate the largest section of the work, chapters 4—11, where YHWH is often portrayed as a loving parent, even a mother (Hos. 11:3–4, 8), and Israel as a willful and erring son. The faithfulness of YHWH, whether patient parent or upright spouse, dominates the book, but the passages in which he is the wronged husband and Israel is the flagrantly adulterous, punished and redeemed wife (chapters 1—3; 12—14) serve as framework for the rest of the text.[17] It is these passages that have occasioned the greatest divergence in perspective between the traditional commentaries that reflect the androcentric view of the text and feminist/womanist commentaries that question it. The former emphasize the *ḥesed* (steadfast love) of YHWH toward errant Israel and his forgiveness and his willingness to renew the marriage contract despite the heinous actions of his adulterous wife (Hos. 2:14–20; 14:8). Dwight H. Small is typical of these commentators, pointing to Hosea as the biblical model for an alternative to divorce, even for reasons of infidelity (Deut. 24:1–4; Matt. 5:31–32; 19:3–12).[18] The Anchor Bible commentary on Hosea, by Francis I. Anderson and David Noel Freedman, sees even in the threats of terrible punishment for the errant wife "proof that the marriage continues" and that "punishment maintains the covenant."[19] Feminist/womanist commentators Gale A. Yee, T. Drorah Setel, Renita J. Weems, and Elisabeth Schüssler Fiorenza bring out the element of sexual violence in YHWH's punishment of Israel,[20] a violence that is seized upon and developed by later prophets, but that seems to be a missing element in the description of the personal relationship between the prophet Hosea and his "wife of whoring" (*'ešet zenunim;* Hos. 1:2), Gomer. Even if, as Phyllis Bird claims, Hosea's accusation is meant merely rhetorically, as an indictment of male Israel for its "cultic impropriety" by treating the male collective like a "fallen woman," the metaphor plays upon existing male anxieties about female sexual activities.[21] It "works" so well in that respect that the image of the faithless community as an adulterous wife, who Hosea first calls "whore," carries over as a dominant one, not only in the Prophets, where this extended "adultery vocabulary" occurs eighty-six times,[22] but into the New Testament as well, where it continues to be used as a metaphor for religious infidelity, an infidelity that is characterized in feminine rather than masculine terms (cf. Eph. 5:27; Jude 24; Rev. 5:1; 10:2, 11; 18:6–7; 21:2).

Hosea's characterization of the syncretistic religious practices of Israel as sexual license or "whoring" (*znh*) has, as we saw in chapter 2, a long history in the literature of the Tanakh, especially the Torah (cf. Ex. 34:15–16; Lev. 17:7; 20:5–6; Num. 25:1–5; 31:13–20; Deut. 31:11–16), in which sexual relations between male Israelites and female "foreigners" or "strangers" lead to the "whoring" of the former after the deities of the latter. Hosea, however, is the first to characterize Israel itself as a woman, a wife whose religious profligacy is analogous to sexual promiscuity. To put it another way, religious freedom in his discourse is identified with female sexual freedom, the latter being as unacceptable, given the exclusivity of male honor, as worship of other gods is unacceptable to the exclusive honor of YHWH. From the very beginning of the text of Hosea, YHWH's honor is personalized as the prophet's own, as YHWH tells Hosea to take for himself a "woman of whoring" (*zenunim*) and have "children of whoring" with her, for "the land (*ha'aretz*, fem. noun) has whored greatly" in turning away from the exclusive worship of YHWH (Hos. 1:2). Again, Hosea is commanded in 3:1–2, in more specific language, to love a woman (or wife,'*iššah*)' who has a lover and is an adulteress, because YHWH loves the people of Israel, although they turn to other gods and bring them offerings (i.e., they are adulterous). The prophet "buys" back his wife, an action perhaps symbolic of YHWH's redemption, or "buying out," of Israel from slavery, forbidding her either to "whore" with others or to have intercourse with him for a period of time (3:3). This act is explained in the text as symbolic of Israel's being without the symbols of any religion, either of YHWH (sacrifice or ephod, a priestly garment) or of the native religions (the pillar, a symbol of Asherah, the fertility goddess; or *teraphim*, household gods; 3:4).

The "human story" of Hosea and his God-given yet sexually uncommitted wife Gomer in chapters 1 and 3 frames and provides a commentary upon the "devine story" of YHWH and Israel in chapter 2 and initiates themes that will be picked up in the continuation of the divine story in chapters 4—11 and 12—14. Yet there are diffculties in reconciling these two versions of the prophet's symbolic action in marrying a "whore" wife, if they are indeed versions of the same episode. Since Hosea purchases the adulteress he is commanded to marry in 3:1–2, and since he is commanded to marry a "woman of whoring" in 1:2, it might and often has been assumed that both texts refer to Gomer, and that she is a prostitute (*zonah*).[23] The problem is that Gomer is never actually called a *zonah*.[24] Gomer is named as Hosea's wife in chapter 1, but the woman (or wife) in chapter 3 is not named. She is simply referred to as an adulteress (again, not a prostitute). Are these the same woman? Probably so: they are both unfaithful wives. The analogy being established here is that Hosea is to Gomer (or his unnamed unfaithful wife) as YHWH is to Israel, who is unfaithful to the covenant/marriage "she" has with him.

Both Hosea, a mere mouthpiece for the divine word, and Gomer, who does not have a speaking part in this drama, appear at first to be passive instruments of the divine will, just as Israel, who in the text both speaks and acts, ideally ought to be. But the truth is that neither the wife Gomer nor the wife Israel is passive; neither submits to being the *be'ulat ba 'al*, the wife mastered by the one *ba'al* (master-husband) who chose her "for himself" (see 1:2; 2:16–17; 3:1–2). Both "go after" other lovers. In the end, however, "whether he must threaten or seduce her . . . the husband/God will have the last word, not the wife/Israel."[25]

Little detail is given about Gomer's supposedly promiscuous behavior except that she has a lover (if Gomer is indeed the adulterous wife mentioned in chapter 3), has become alienated from Hosea, and is recovered by him through purchase, after which she must endure a period of enforced abstinence dictated by him (3:2–3). But the affairs of the promiscuous wife Israel, and the gifts she receives from her lovers, are vividly enumerated in the jealous imagination of YHWH (2:2, 5, 7, 10, 12, 13). The children of Gomer and Hosea, born in chapter 1, are given symbolic names because they represent the children of the whore-wife Israel, who are initially rejected by YHWH. The bulk of the material in chapter 2 is YHWH's threatened punishment of his "wife" because of her adulterous behavior that is called "whoring." Although some have pointed out that, unlike an Israelite husband, YHWH does not avail himself of the legal codes to punish his wife by divorce or death, he does resort to graphic threats of violent physical abuse as retaliation for her infidelity before he "restores" the erring wife to a monogamous exclusive relationship with him.[26] YHWH, the wronged husband, first threatens to "expose" and thereby shame his wife by stripping her naked and killing her with thirst (2:3). He then threatens to have no pity on her children because of her whoring, suggesting they are illegitimate and "not my people" (see 5:7). In an ironic and ugly parody of the marital imagery of the Song of Songs, which in many rabbinic interpretations also represents the marriage of YHWH and Israel, the wife is an "enclosed garden" (cf. Song 4:9–15) but is enclosed (and imprisoned) by a thorn hedge and a wall. The bride boldly seeks her lover in Song of Songs 3:2–4; the wife is restricted in Hosea by her husband so that she cannot go after her lovers, the objects of her wrongful desire (2:6; cf. 3:3–4).[27] At this point she is supposed to forsake her wanderings and direct her desire to her "first husband," in order to recover the well-being she mistakenly attributed to her lovers (2:7). YHWH, however, repeats his threats of stripping her naked, "uncovering her shame" (her genitals), and destroying her prosperity, taking away the fertility of the land (the fertility of Israel the woman) as punishment for her devotion to her "lovers," the *ba'alim*, and for her forgetfulness of her tie with YHWH (2:9–13).

Then, and only then, after Israel's dejection and humiliation in compensation for YHWH's loss of honor, the shaming of the husband whose wife actively pursues other partners,[28] YHWH "restores" the initial, youthful covenant between himself and Israel, a covenant forged in the exodus from Egypt and the wandering in the wilderness at Sinai (2:14–15). As Shechem did with Dinah, whom he shamed by rape, so YHWH "speaks to the heart" of the shamed yet also "beloved" Israel, and expects her to respond positively, calling him *'iš* (husband) instead of *ba'al* (master; 2:16). Thus the covenant will be renewed as a perpetual one of righteousness, justice, *ḥesed* (steadfast love), mercy, and fidelity (2:17–20). Israel's fertility will return, and the rejected children will be acknowledged, their transformation indicated by their change of name (2:21–23). YHWH's people will once again "belong" to him exclusively (2:23). As Weems points out, the structure of the narrative, with its fairy-tale ending of reconciliation and renewal, lulls us into accepting the theological point of the androcentric narrative: God, the accepting husband, forgives his flagrantly promiscuous ("disobedient") wife, "his" people, and restores them into his loving embrace. But that theological point requires us to ignore the human side of the narrative, the reliance of the text on "the physical and sexual abuse of a woman to develop its larger, presumably congenial, theological point about divine love and retribution."[29]

To be fair, and for the sake of the argument, however, the book of Hosea does not associate only women with sexual promiscuity, although Hosea certainly equates cultic with marital infidelity. In the *rib* (covenant lawsuit) that YHWH has against Israel in Hosea 4, he charges the people as a whole with committing adultery (4:2) among other crimes against the covenant, being led astray by a "spirit of whoring" (*ruaḥ zenunim*; 4:10–12). More specifically, he accuses the daughters of Israel of whoring and its daughters-in-law with adultery (4:13–14), acts that are equated with those of Israel's men, who consort with prostitutes (*zonoth*) and perform sacrifices with *qedeshoth* (women consecrated to other deities; 4:14). All of these practices are examples of how Israel itself (now again female) has "whored" (4:15; cf. 6:10b; 9:1; 10:11) and how Ephraim and Israel (characterized as male) have been imbued with a "spirit of whoring" (*ruaḥ zenunim*; 5:4) that prevents them from reconciling with YHWH. All the people of Ephraim/Israel are "adulterers" (7:4) and, like Samson and Solomon, have had their strength "devoured" by mixing with foreigners (7:8–9). Because of Israel's "whoring" (9:1) or worshiping foreign gods (9:10; apostasy with the Ba'al of Peor, cf. Num. 25:1–18), female Ephraim will be punished with "no birth, no conception, no pregnancy," no raising of children, "a miscarrying womb and dry breasts" (9:11–15, NRSV), and "she" will be driven out of the house, like a promiscuous daughter or erring wife, to have "the cherished offspring of their womb" killed (9:15–17, NRSV). In a change of tone in chapters 10—13, YHWH envisions Ephraim as a child who accepts the protection of its parent without really knowing where the protection comes from, crediting it to others (11:1–4; 13:4). In this section, although YHWH, here both mother and father, threatens to punish the wayward child, his/her parental love does not permit it (11:8–11). The note of anger over apostasy returns, however, and Samaria (capital of Israel, the Northern Kingdom) is cursed with bearing "her" guilt, the punishment for which will be the death of her children, even those still in the womb (13:16). A final reconciliation is urged in chapter 14, when Israel (characterized as male) will flourish after returning to YHWH, who will "love them freely" (14:4, NRSV). On balance, then, although the gender of "Israel" changes frequently here, the most frequent charges of "adultery" and "whoring" are brought against Israel as female.

It must further be admitted that the most graphic passages of violence in the book of Hosea have to do with women, and all are sexual. As Setel observes, the use of female sexual imagery in Hosea "can be seen as related to the intellectual and psychological disruptions caused by political events," such as the threat of the foreign power of Assyria to the Northern Kingdom.[30] In such a situation, the threat of loss of power, and hence manhood, is translated into terms of the loss of male heterosexual potency and domination by women. Although YHWH as angry parent threatens the wayward son Israel with punishment, punishment only becomes explicitly sexual and violent when Israel (as Ephraim, Samaria) is portrayed as a woman or when women are involved in men's apostasy against YHWH. At stake is power as played out on the arena of honor/shame. A powerful man or deity in this context is one who has the ability to prevent loss of honor and indeed to add to it. Sexual humiliation is symbolic of the most severe loss of honor: in fact, it is the means by which both women and the men of their families are shamed. The sexual humiliation of Hosea, which symbolizes YHWH's loss of honor, is avenged by the sexual humiliation of Gomer (3:3–4) and of Israel (2:3–13). Instead of being able to "pursue their lovers," that is, to be sexually autonomous, they are to be confined to (and often by) one male, who will dictate how their sexuality is to be directed, toward himself. Hosea's and YHWH's sexual fidelity to their spouses, far from being the norm or even the model for male Israel, is derived from the desired model for female Israel. Hence, the worst transgression of a male Israel in Hosea's view, that of apostasy from YHWH, is portrayed as acting like a sexually promiscuous wife. Weems notes that, of all the predominant metaphors in the prophetic books that describe the relationship between YHWH and Israel, "only the marriage metaphor was capable of signifying failure to obey and conform to the prevailing norms as a moral and social disgrace."[31]

By using the metaphor of monogamous heterosexual marriage to describe the ideal relationship between Israel and YHWH, Hosea "transforms the earlier, material understanding of nonmarital sexuality into an ethical transgression."[32] Female adultery (not male!) is portrayed as betrayal of God; men who betray the one God by keeping company with women dedicated to other gods (*qedeshoth*, who are in Hosea's opinion the same as whores, *zonoth*) or by simply "keeping company" with other gods, are portrayed as female adulteresses and whores. For Hosea, the worship of foreign deities thus "unmans" the male Israelites. As women are to have no choice of multiple sexual partners, so men are to have no choice of worshiping various deities, especially not those whose worship involves a sacralizing of sexuality, as with fertility deities like Ba'al and Asherah. Thus, even though the target of Hosea's warning and YHWH's wrath is male Israelites who worship foreign deities,[33] the community as a whole, directed as it is by heterosexual men, is nevertheless envisioned as a woman, the *only* appropriate heterosexual love-object and partner for a male god.[34] In fact, the only way in which "Israel" as a collective entity is perceived at all in a sexual manner is in terms of "her" marital fidelity or infidelity to YHWH, not in terms of her desire or yearning for "him." The danger posed by the idea of YHWH's sexuality is neutralized by projecting it onto a volatile female Israel, just as male Israelites projected their fear of losing sexual control over themselves or women onto the stereotypes of the sexually free adulteress or the sexually predatory "foreign woman." In the same way foreign or "stranger" women (who often represent these deities; cf. Hos. 4:14b) have unmanned Israelite heroes in the past.

THE WANTON WIFE AND
ANGRY HUSBAND: JEREMIAH AND EZEKIEL

The writings of the Judahite prophets of the exile, Jeremiah and Ezekiel, reflect the loss of city, Temple, and power for the religious elite they represent. The marital and sexual metaphors for the relationship of YHWH and Israel, first given shape by Hosea, become increasingly graphic and intense, as they evoke fears of aggression and betrayal that are cast in the form of men betrayed by "sexually aggressive women and sexually unsatisfiable adulterous wives."[35] In Ezekiel especially, but also in Jeremiah and to some extent in Deutero-Isaiah (Isaiah 40—55), "objectified female sexuality [is used] as a symbol of evil" for the first time, and the language of female sexuality and sexual violence against female characters becomes increasingly explicit, even pornographic.[36] The loss of power and control of Jerusalem by the elite of court and Temple, who were consequently humiliated by the destruction of their city and Temple and by deportation from "their" land and captivity in another, is portrayed paradoxically in the writings of these prophets as an actual assertion of YHWH's power as he deliberately humiliates and punishes his "wife" for her refusal to recognize his exclusive power over her.

The chaotic collection of writings attributed to the prophet Jeremiah

reflects the equally chaotic period from about 626 B.C.E., during the reign
of the Yahwistic reformer Josiah, through the Babylonian control over and
final destruction of Jerusalem in 587 B.C.E. Throughout the various oracles
and other texts that make up the book of Jeremiah, the helplessness and suffering of the people of Jerusalem and Judah are portrayed by using female
images (Jer. 4:31; 13:21; 15:8–9; 22:23; 30:6; 31:15–16). Cities and nations
are personified as women,[37] and the prophet himself, in one of his laments
over his helplessness and persecution, accuses YHWH of seduction and virtual rape (20:7–8). Nevertheless, Jeremiah's images of women are seldom
benign, portraying women as victims of a violence that is provoked and
merited by their own actions.[38] Jeremiah, son of a priest, is called and inspired by visions (Jeremiah 1) to proclaim YHWH's word to Jerusalem, not
as one of comfort but of indictment and blame for following "her" own
course and rejecting YHWH, the husband of her obedient youth (Jer.
2:1–6:30; cf. Ezek. 16:22, 43). This section opens with language that is reminiscent of Hosea 1—3, in that YHWH's covenant with the people Israel
at Sinai is compared to a wilderness honeymoon, in which the devoted bride
follows YHWH, her provider and protector (Jer. 2:1–3), the one who gave
her bridal adornment and attire (Jer. 2:32; cf. Ezek. 16:8–14).[39] Also reminiscent of Hosea (Hosea 4) is the *rib* or covenant lawsuit of Jeremiah
2:4–37, in which YHWH accuses priests, rulers, and people of having forsaken him and their trust in his protection to "dig their own cisterns" (2:13,
NRSV). Although this passage at first characterizes Israel (YHWH's people)
as having acted like a "slave" or "home-born servant" (male), it culminates
(2:20–25) in an indictment of Israel as the bride who "shakes off the yoke"
and "bursts her bonds," symbols both of the yoke and bond of Torah and
of marriage, to "go wild," as she plays the *zonah* on every hill and under
every tree, the probable sites of worship of Canaanite deities (2:20). She is
so "stained" with guilt that she cannot be washed clean with lye or strong
soap (2:22). Inhuman images are used to further characterize Israel's sexual
wildness:[40] she is not a vine planted and cultivated by YHWH but is an uncontrolled, "degenerate" wild vine (2:21). She is a restless she-camel or a
wild she-ass in heat, sniffing the wind with unrestrained lust (2:23–24).
Even in human form, Israel is wild, preferring to go unshod and thirsty in
the wilderness as she tracks her lovers, admitting that it is hopeless to stop
her pursuing "strangers" (*zarim;* 2:25), the foreign deities that are worshiped all over Judah (2:26–28). Judah, says the indictment, has refused to
repent even after YHWH struck down her children, and will not remember the bridal adornment and attire of her youth, or, presumably, the one
who adorned her or for whom she functioned as adornment (2:30–32).
Having had sexual experience, the bride no longer obeys her husband as her
master, but seeks sexual adventure. YHWH accuses Judah of going so far
in her promiscuity that she actually teaches it to "wicked" women (2:33),

staining her skirts with the blood of the innocent poor (2:34), an image that recalls the uncleanness of the whore in 2:22. Kathleen O'Connor observes that this latter image is "strangely twisted," since women normally were as powerless as and frequently made up the numbers of the poor.[41] Perhaps Jeremiah uses this image, which evokes the powerful but "wicked" queen Jezebel, also accused of "whoring" by the Deuteronomistic History (2 Kings 9:22), out of the conviction that women with power are always abusers of it, that the only power they really have is sexual, even when played out in the political arena. Because they are unable to handle power, they end up by becoming as capricious socially and politically as they are sexually. Punishment awaits the wicked Judah, however, as surely as it overtook Jezebel. In payment for the husband YHWH's "shaming," the wanton bride will be "shamed" by foreign nations, in imagery that plays once again on the humiliating reality of rape in warfare (2:36–37; cf. Gen. 34:2, 13). At the end of this indictment, the humiliated wife stands in a gesture of despair and mourning (hands on head) before YHWH (2:37).

But YHWH, judge as well as plaintiff, will not take her back. He does not have to. Jeremiah 3:1 says that this would "pollute the land," citing the law of Deuteronomy 24:1–4, concerning a husband who cannot remarry his wife after he has divorced her and she has become another man's wife (Jer. 3:1–2; Deut. 24:4). Judah has not even "remarried," but has left YHWH in order to pursue flagrant promiscuity, sitting by the wayside like a common prostitute (cf. Gen. 38:14–16), and even wandering the wilderness looking for lovers (3:2). She has no shame; she has the "forehead of a *zonah*" (3:3) and pollutes the land with "whoring and wickedness" (3:2, NRSV). Israel, the Northern Kingdom, which fell to the Assyrians in 722 B.C.E., is used as a bad example to her "false sister Judah" (3:6–10). Israel, says Jeremiah, was also faithless and "whored" in the same places Judah has (3:6). She refused to return to YHWH, so he divorced her as an adulterous wife (3:8). Judah, even more faithless and consequently more guilty than her "sister," continues to "play the whore" and to commit adultery, refusing to commit to YHWH alone (3:8–10). Already her "pollution" of the marriage covenant causes pollution of the land and failure of crops and herds (3:9, 24). In a plea apparently intended to be heard by Judah, the prophet says that even now the fallen Israel could return to YHWH, whom she has left as an unfaithful wife leaves a husband (3:20).

The fate of Judah and Jerusalem, however, if they persist in their present course of infidelities, will be like that of Israel (4:1–31). As Hosea envisioned YHWH enclosing Israel with thorns (Hos. 2:6), so Jeremiah sees YHWH sending an "evil from the north" to pen up the rebellious wife Judah as if she were their prey (Jer. 4:17). In 4:29–31, Jeremiah renews Hosea's image of the adulterous wife finding no help from her lovers: although the shamed one attempts to deck herself in crimson and gold and paints her eyes (more reminiscences of Jezebel), she will be rejected and killed by her lovers (4:30). In a jumble of feminine imagery, Jeremiah also compares Jerusalem ("daughter Zion") to a woman in labor and a woman helpless at the hands of her murderers (4:31). But Jerusalem will not be pardoned because her children have forsaken YHWH to go after foreign gods, a desertion that the prophet portrays as adultery. Zion's sons patronize the houses of prostitutes and act like bestial "lusty stallions, each neighing for his neighbor's wife" (5:7–8, NRSV). Jeremiah's enemies, the false prophets and priests, are also characterized as adulterers (9:2; 23:10, 14; 29:23). As in Hosea, however, the adulterous behavior of the males is the "shaming" not of themselves but of YHWH, the faithful god-husband, and so once again it is not the community as male but as female that brings dishonor and that will be dishonored. In Jeremiah 13, which apparently refers to the deposition of the king and queen mother of Judah (13:18), the prophet envisions the rape of Jerusalem (13:22, 26–27), in which YHWH himself will assist, by lifting her skirts and exposing her "shame" (genitals), because he has seen her "adulteries and neighings and shameless whorings" with other gods (13:27, NRSV; cf. Hos. 5:4; Lam. 1:8–9).[42] Jeremiah also attributes to women the responsibility for betraying of YHWH in chapter 44. The women who make the cakes for the goddess called "queen of heaven" (7:18; 44:19) not only shamelessly refuse to refrain from worshiping the goddess, even as refugees in Egypt, but have involved their husbands in the worship as well (44:15–19). For this act of defiance, warns Jeremiah, YHWH will withdraw his protection from the Judeans, men and women (44:24–30), for the same reason and in the same way that he allowed the destruction of Jerusalem and Judah (vv. 20–23). Blame for this destruction is thus placed on the women, who are the faithless ones who lure their husbands into being faithless to YHWH.

Against these depictions of women as wanton betrayers, Jeremiah offers little that is positive, and that occurs mainly in 30:1–31:40, where he prophesies the return of both Israelite and Judahite exiles to their land and the restoration of its prosperity.[43] "Virgin Israel," whom YHWH has loved with *hesed* and fidelity, will be restored, rejoicing in a victory song (Jer. 31:3–4), like that of Miriam at the Reed Sea (Ex. 15:21) or Deborah after the defeat and death of Sisera (Judges 5). When virgin Israel, the wavering "faithless daughter" returns, however, retracing the road of her exile, YHWH will not only renew and restore but create anew: "A woman (*neqebah*) surrounds a man (*geber*)" (31:22). It is hard to know what to make of this line, whose Hebrew meaning is uncertain. It has sometimes been translated as, "the woman encompasses the warrior," presumably because in the envisioned peace, not as in the terrible reality of warfare, women will have more power than male warriors, either to subdue ("surround") or to protect ("encompass") them.[44] This re-created world, with its dancing triumphant virgins (31:4, 13) its fertile, pregnant and birthing mothers (31:8), has been won at a great cost, the cost of women's suffering, much of which the prophet portrays as deserved. Even at the outset of his restorative vision, there is a cry of panic like that of a woman in labor—but it comes from men (30:5–6). The "delivery" will be that of the male Israel—Jacob—from bondage (30:7). The "yoke" and the "bonds" of obedience that tied the faithless female Israel to YHWH and which she herself broke (2:20) are here the yoke and bonds of slavery, which YHWH will break from the male Israel, his servant (30:8–9). Female Israel's desire to be free is characterized as sexual wantonness meriting correction; male Israel's desire to escape bondage is legitimate longing. The vision of restoration uses the image of the male Jacob (30:10–11), but when punishment is mentioned, the image changes to that of the wounded and deserted female Zion. The voice of YHWH taunts Zion, his forsaken wife, with the "incurable wound" that he himself has given her because of her guilt and sin (30:12–13, 14b, 15). She is now forgotten and abandoned by her lovers (30:14a), fulfilling the prophecy of 4:30 and 22:20–23. In an unexplained and equally capricious reversal of attitude, however, YHWH says that he will heal Zion and punish her enemies, to prove that he cares for her when they in turn mock her with her outcast state (30:17).

In another vision of restoration, the prophet exults over the return of the exiles, to whom YHWH has become a parent, whose "firstborn (son)" is Ephraim/Israel (31:9). The image of the parental YHWH with the male Israel as son is again balanced by a negative female image, one of the mother Rachel weeping for her dead children and refusing to be comforted (31:15). Once again Jeremiah counters the picture of female victimization and woe with unexpected male compassion: YHWH, who had used the death of her children to "correct" the errant Israel (Jer. 2:30; 15:8–9), will restore them to her (31:16–17). YHWH even takes on both parental roles in 31:18–20. The chastened "son" Ephraim speaks of the disciplining that brought repentance, disciplining usually belonging to the father's role (cf. Hos. 6:1–3), but the parental YHWH replies in terms of maternal compassion, a love that will not give up on Ephraim (cf. Hos. 11:8).[45] This reconciliation scene is followed by a final word to the "faithless" female Israel, encouraging her to retrace the steps of her wandering, this time not as the frenzied camel or lustful wild ass (2:23–25), but as the virgin daughter who has no rape to fear from the warrior any longer (31:21–22; cf. Lam. 5:11). The sexual reversal of the wayward bride is complete, from the sexually uncontrollable and insatiable wife back to the virgin daughter, who is sexually inexperienced and under the control and protection of a paternal male god as the minor daughter is in her father's house. The lesson has been taught: rape, wounding, and the death of children are the dangerous price of female sexual freedom.

In the writings of the prophet and priest Ezekiel, who was taken to Babylon with the first wave of elite deportees that included King Jehoiachin, in 597 B.C.E., the metaphors of the adulterous wife and the jealous and punishing husband are carried to their ghastly limit. Together with condemnations of specific non-Yahwistic religious practices of women (8:14–15; 13:17–23), they result in what Katheryn Darr calls "some of the Bible's most misogynistic texts."[46] The book of Ezekiel contains thrity-four occurrences of the adultery vocabulary, more than in any of the other prophetic books including Hosea and Jeremiah, although these are concentrated in two long chapters (16 and 23) of explicit sexual imagery, including those of incest and sexual mutilation.[47] The whore-wife image is multiplied as well. In Ezekiel 16, Jerusalem, the adulterous wife and "brazen whore," is joined by her elder sister, Samaria (who stands for Israel), and Sodom, the younger. Ezekiel 23 is a tale of two unfaithful sisters, Samaria/Israel (Oholah, "her tent") and Jerusalem/Judah (Oholibah, "my tent is in her"), both of whom are married to YHWH (23:3–4).

As a priest who was also a prophet, Ezekiel, much like the Priestly editors of the Tanakh, the Deuteronomistic Historian, and other prophets, seems to have adopted YHWH's honor as symbolic of his own. Religious syncretism that combined the worship of other deities with that of YHWH (Ezekiel 14), or toleration of polytheistic religions along with the worship of YHWH, resulting in a challenge to religious authorities like himself (Ezekiel 13) is—for Ezekiel—idolatry and apostasy, a religious betrayal and loss of honor equivalent to sexual betrayal and dishonor. As David Halperin points out, the book of Ezekiel reflects the experiences of a once-powerful exile who "could not have failed to contrast his own impotent misery and shame with the power and splendor of his captors."[48] His fury, the fury of a victim who has always been in control but now is under control of others, is turned against women, those whom he, like his audience, see as posing a threat to male honor and control.[49] Like a jealous and betrayed husband, YHWH is "crushed" by the "wanton heart" and "wanton eyes" of the people who have turned away from him to idols (Ezek. 6:9). Therefore, as Ezekiel portrays it, the ones who occasioned that loss of honor—the women representing Israel and Judah—must also be shamed.

Summoned to speak on behalf of a vengeful YHWH, whom he encounters both through striking, terrible visions and communications that result in symbolic actions (Ezek. 3:1), Ezekiel offers little comfort to the exiled leaders of Judah. In the first of his visions that relate to a still-standing Temple in Jerusalem, he encounters a terrifying being with "loins of fire," who sets the prophet in a "seat of the image of jealousy (*qin'ah*), which provokes to jealousy (*qin'ah*)" (Ezek. 8:3, NRSV). Although it has been suggested that this image refers to a statue of the goddess Asherah, who was often incorporated into the syncretistic worship of Israel as YHWH's female partner,[50] the image reminds us also of the implacably jealous god of Exodus 20:5 and Deuteronomy 5:9, and of the jealous husband of Numbers 5:14, whose "spirit of jealousy" forces his wife to undergo the trial of bitter waters in order to vindicate his own honor.[51] If Eilberg-Schwartz is correct, the figure Ezekiel sees is YHWH himself, and the emphasis in the text is on the fiery loins where other texts are remarkably reticent in speaking of YHWH's sexuality.[52] Here then is a god whose aggressive masculinity could easily become injured by any wayward behavior on the part of his "possession," Jerusalem, especially in the public and visible locus of his honor, the Temple. Halperin argues that the jealousy provoked by an image of "the rampantly sexual female" (symbolized by the fertility goddess Asherah) is "that of the excluded male—ostensibly Yahweh."[53] Among the various forms of worship of other deities castigated by Ezekiel and designated in the text by the now-familiar term, "abominations," there are women who are "weeping for Tammuz" (8:14). Tammuz, or Dumuzi, in the worship of the ancient Near East, is the dying and rising god of vegetation, and lover of Ishtar/Astarte, the same "queen of heaven" whose worship Jeremiah condemned (Jer. 7:18; 44). The ritual laments or "weeping" for Tammuz, composed for the death of vegetation in the heat of summer, often celebrate the love and longing of female lover for her male beloved.[54] Surely here is a male deity whose worship by women, involving as it does erotic and sensual devotion, can provoke YHWH's "fiery loins" to jealousy. YHWH's honor, according to Ezekiel, is also injured, as is his own, by women prophets and diviners (13:17–23; cf. Deut. 18:10). In a complicated passage, whose details are still unfortunately obscure, YHWH through Ezekiel condemns the women of Israel who, like the false male prophets (13:1–16), "prophesy out of their own imagination," that is, outside of the inspiration provided by YHWH. These women, according to Ezekiel, have a magical power over life and death that "profanes" YHWH (13:19) and challenges him to prove that he and not these sorcerers has the real power over the people (13:23).

YHWH's power as male sexual authority is the focus of the chapters on his adulterous wives, 16 and 23, which are filled with "pornographic fury."[55] In chapter 16, YHWH attributes the "abominations" of Jerusalem (who also stands for Judah) to her foreign parentage, as she is the child of an Amorite father and Hittite mother, "born in the land of the Canaanites" (Ezek. 16:3, NRSV). A consistent charge in the rhetoric of the Tanakh, contained even in the stories of the ancestors (cf. Gen. 9:20–27), is that the sexual practices of the indigenous peoples of Canaan, differing from those of the Israelites, were therefore "deviant" and made the Canaanites worthy of enslavement or extermination by the people of Israel. In the book of Ezekiel, moreover, Jerusalem, as the daughter of non-Israelite parents, is from birth a foreign woman, and thus doubly "deviant." The infant daughter Jerusalem is abandoned, like baby girls in many ancient societies, by parents who are unwilling to raise her. In chilling detail, Ezekiel describes how the baby is exposed ("thrown into an open field") with an uncut umbilical cord, unwashed, "unsalted" (a custom for newborns), and not wrapped in swaddling bands (16:4–5; cf. Hos. 2:3 for a much milder version). This "unpitied" daughter recalls the daughter of Gomer and Hosea, "Lo-Ruhamah," or "Not Pitied," the symbol of YHWH's lack of pity for Israel (Hos. 1:4). With no more than a word from YHWH ("Live!") the infant, who was helplessly writhing in the birth-blood (16:6), grows to mature womanhood, but remains exposed, to the gaze of the reader as well as YHWH, as the text describes her fully formed breasts, nakedness, and bareness (16:7).[56] Again, YHWH passes by and "looks on" Jerusalem, as Samson "looked on" the Timnite bride and the harlot of Gaza, with the inevitable consequence. Since Jerusalem is "at the age for love," YHWH spreads his cloak (*kanap*) over her, as Boaz did over Ruth, thus taking her under his protection and having intercourse with her. Thus YHWH enters into a marriage covenant by which Jerusalem becomes his (16:8). Then and only then does YHWH wash his bride, bathe off her blood, anoint her with oil and clothe her (16:9–10). There is a faint whiff of child pornography here: is the blood YHWH washes off the bride that of the torn hymen, the "tokens of virginity," or the blood of menstruation, or the birth-blood? Is the fine linen in which YHWH binds her the swaddling clothes she was not given? At any rate, YHWH seems oddly neglectful of the abandoned daughter until his gaze tells him she is sexually mature; she remains in the open field, naked and unwashed, until that moment. Throughout 16:3–14, the feminized Jerusalem has remained totally passive and mute, taking no action of her own, the inert object of attraction, first to YHWH, then to the nations after he has "adorned" her. What little action takes place is mainly looking (vv. 6–8, YHWH; vv. 13–14, "the nations") and touching through sexual contact, washing, bathing, clothing, adorning, and feeding (vv. 8–13).

As Halperin has shown, in the image of YHWH's "bloody bride" Ezekiel "conveys the fullness of . . . mingled desire and loathing."[57] Obviously, for YHWH as represented by Ezekiel, the "days of [Jerusalem's] youth" were idyllic, when she was totally "his" possession, a mute, beautiful, and sexually submissive bride, the plastic object of his desires (16:43). But then the bride becomes active—sexually active, in the feverishly jealous imagination of Ezekiel/ YHWH. In a long condemnatory passage (16:15–34), YHWH accuses her of whoring a total of sixteen times. Jerusalem/Judah has become for him a common whore who "lavishes" her favors on passersby (vv. 15, 25, 30–31); she makes her garments into shrines and platforms where she publicly whores (vv. 16, 24, 31), and uses her jewelry to make images of male gods which she apparently uses as sex-toys (v. 17). She is also inhumanly unmaternal; she sacrifices her children from

YHWH to these foreign male deities, "as if your whorings were not enough!" (v. 20, NRSV). The *zenunim* (acts of a whore) multiply and spread to other countries, as Ezekiel compares Judah's alliances with the Egyptians ("your neighbors big of phallus"),[58] the Assyrians, and the Chaldeans to sexual infidelities that are prompted by a sexual insatiability that causes even the daughters of the enemy Philistines to be ashamed (vv. 26–29; cf. v. 57). While denouncing Judah/Jerusalem as a whore, Ezekiel/YHWH points out the real difference between a whore and his bride: the former takes payment, while the latter, an adulterous wife, does it for nothing, exchanging strange men (*zarim*) for her husband (v. 32). The whore receives gifts, but the adulterous wife bestows the gifts her husband gave her on foreigners in order to entice them to her "whorings" (vv. 33–34).

Because she has forgotten the days of her youth, "naked and bare, flailing about in your blood" (v. 22, NRSV), and because the nakedness of abandonment and neglect is now the nakedness of abandoned sexuality (whoredom) and the birth-blood has become that of her sacrificed children (vv. 35–36), YHWH devises a plan to satisfy his "fury" and sexual jealousy upon the woman who has wronged him. First, he will publicly shame her by exposing her nakedness to all her lovers, even those whom she hated but still made love with (v. 37). He will judge her "as women who commit adultery and shed blood are judged, and bring blood upon you in wrath and jealousy" (v. 38, NRSV), judging her worthy of death for adultery and murder. Further, YHWH will get her lovers to perform her shaming and execution: they will strip her (again?) and leave her "naked and bare" (as in her infancy and youth), stone her, cut her to pieces with swords, and burn her houses (vv. 39–41). Even though, as Darr points out, the "metaphor slips a bit" at this point,[59] YHWH's intentions are clear: these judgments, executed "in the sight of many women," are to stop Jerusalem/Judah from playing the whore, and presumably to serve as an example to "her" women (cf. Ezek. 23:48). YHWH then will pronounce himself satisfied, his jealousy satiated, presumably by the mutilation and death of his faithless wife (v. 42).

Yet she is resurrected to witness the denunciation of the faithlessness of the bride's mother and her sisters, Samaria the elder and Sodom the younger (16:44–46), whom Jerusalem/Judah has imitated and surpassed in her own corruption and that of her "daughters," here the women of Jerusalem (vv. 47–48). Sodom, in Genesis 19 the site of threatened male-male rape and potential gang rape, is less guilty than Jerusalem, her chief sins being the nonsexual ones of pride and neglect of the poor (v. 49). Samaria (Israel) can't hold a candle to her sister in terms of transgression (v. 50); Jerusalem's sins make her appear righteous by comparison (vv. 51–52). Consequently, YHWH will judge Sodom and Samaria more leniently and restore their fortunes before he restores those of Jerusalem, after her public humiliation and merited punishment (vv. 53–58). YHWH promises a return to the days of Judah's youth and a renewal of the "everlasting covenant" (v. 60; cf. Hos. 2:14–18). But unlike the idyllic reconciliation between wife Israel and husband YHWH envisioned by Hosea, the reconciliation imagined by Ezekiel is punitive in itself. YHWH will take Jerusalem's "sisters," Samaria and Sodom, and give them to her as daughters, not for the sake of his covenant, but to further shame her (v. 61), to remind her of her sins and that he is YHWH. This final demonstration of his power over her (which the text calls "forgiveness") will render her perpetually mute because of her shame (vv. 62–63). Thus she becomes the perfect wife ("as in the days of her youth")—silent, passive, and ever mindful of "shame," that is, the public honor of her husband that is invested in his exclusive claim to and use of his wife's sexuality.

As if this were not enough, the "sexualized rage against females" in the form of a virulent denunciation of the sexual exploits of YHWH's "wives" continues in chapter 23, where the violent punishment for their "whoredom" is made a clear example and warning to actual women (23:48).[60] The long tale of two adulterous sisters, Oholah (Samaria = Israel) and Oholibah (Jerusalem = Judah) reprises many of the same themes and in the same pervivid tone of chapter 16. Because the names of both Oholah ("her tent") and Oholibah ("my tent is in her") are metaphors for female genitals, chapter 23 is another allegory of the exclusive worship of YHWH portrayed in terms of exclusive use of women's sexuality by a man.[61] In this story, "as told to" Ezekiel by YHWH (23:1), the sisters have played the whore from their youth in Egypt, where "their breasts were caressed . . . , their virgin bosoms were fondled" (23:3, NRSV). Fokkelien van Dijk-Hemmes suggests that the reference to the period of slavery in Egypt, when put in sexual terms, serves as a contradiction, since female Judah and Israel willingly submit to sexual abuse and thus are guilty of their own enslavement.[62] Ezekiel, the male voice of the text, treats the sex as consensual, evidence of the sisters' wayward inclination toward illicit sexual pleasure even before their "marriage" to YHWH (v. 4; cf. vv. 8, 21). Although marriage to sisters is forbidden in the Levitical code (Lev. 18:18), it is apparently permissible for YHWH, since he makes both sisters "his" (v. 4). Oholah (Samaria) immediately "plays the whore" (v. 5) with Assyrian warriors, whom Ezekiel imagines in some detail (vv. 6–8). Her fate, therefore, like that predicted for Jerusalem in 16:35–43, will be her delivery by her husband into humiliation at the hands of her lovers, who will "uncover her nakedness" (rape her), take her children captive, and kill her (vv. 9–10). She thus becomes another lesson to women (v. 10).

Oholibah (Jerusalem), who has witnessed the sexual humiliation and destruction of Samaria (722 B.C.E.), has learned nothing. She is still more of a whore than her sister, including the Assyrians and Babylonians among the lovers who "defile" her, in the sexual language used by Ezekiel to portray

Judah's alliances with those nations (vv. 11–17). He depicts Oholibah as enticing the Babylonians into "the bed of love," then turning from them in disgust after her lust is satisfied, probably a reference to the conflict between the pro- and anti-Babylonian parties in the Judahite court. "Flaunting her nakedness" and open adultery makes YHWH turn from her in disgust (v. 18), attributing her sexual insatiability to the memory of the "days of her youth," spent, not as a virgin object of YHWH's desire as in chapter 16, but lusting after the Egyptians, whose phalluses Ezekiel imagines are "like those of donkeys," and whose "emission was like that of stallions," longing for them to fondle her breasts (vv. 19–21, NRSV). Like a jealous husband, YHWH imagines that "others" (the "nations") are more potent than he.

YHWH's sexual jealousy vents itself in a long passage that predicts sexual violence against Oholibah (vv. 22–35). The consequences of her whoring, like those of Oholah's, will be terrible, but because Oholibah is even more shameless than Oholah, her punishment will be even more terrible. YHWH summons her former lovers, the "handsome young men" of Babylon, whom he has now made the instruments of his bidding, to execute his furious judgment (v. 25). These men, whose desire for Oholibah, like YHWH's, has turned into loathing (v. 29), will literally "deface" her, cutting off her nose and her ears; they will kill, burn, or capture her children (v. 25). Stripping her naked, they will expose her publicly (vv. 26–27). In this way, YHWH says, he will put a stop to Jerusalem's sexual waywardness that she brought from Egypt (v. 27), from a foreign land. Yet neither YHWH nor Ezekiel stop with Oholibah's sexual humiliation and mutilation. An oracle in verse (vv. 32–34) threatens Oholibah with being forced to drink from her "sister's cup," the destruction of Samaria, a cup that is filled with scorn, derision, drunkenness, and sorrow. Oholibah will not only drink but drain it, gnaw its broken pieces, and tear out her own breasts (v. 34), the breasts "pressed" so fondly by her quondam lovers. All this is retaliation for her "whorings" (v. 35).

As if even this grisly vision were not the final word, Ezekiel is compelled by YHWH to declare again the judgment of Oholah and Oholibah, this time emphasizing the more specific crime of adultery (v. 37), here defined as the worship of other deities, in which Ezekiel includes the sacrifice of children (vv. 37–39). Ezekiel envisions this worship as entertainment of foreigners and "rabble brought in drunken from the wilderness," summoned by the two sisters who, like the adulteress of Proverbs 9:13–18, have prepared a feast, and adorned themselves for it by bathing, painting their eyes and putting on their jewelry (vv. 40–42; cf. Jerusalem adorned by YHWH in 16:11–13; Jezebel in 2 Kings 9:30). Even then they are not "worn out with adulteries," but continue their behavior (vv. 43–44), for which they will be judged by the righteous as guilty of adultery and murder (v. 45), executed by stoning, and cut down with swords. Their children too will be killed (an irony, considering the fact that they themselves are accused of murdering their children in vv. 38–39), and their houses burned (v. 47). While some of these things—mutilation, rape, the murder of children, burnt houses—clearly happen to women in times of war at the hands of invading enemy troops, and in fact did happen during the destruction of Samaria (cf. vv. 22–34), Ezekiel introduces a disturbing variant here. These things happen as the result of judgment being pronounced, the judgment being executed, not by the enemies of Israel and Judah, but by an "assembly" (*qahal*) of their own men, summoned for the express purpose of making the two sisters "objects of terror and plunder," a warning to all women not to commit "lewdness" (vv. 46–48). There is no sense of restoration or resurrection, not even the one of shame in Ezekiel 16:60–63. Instead, the horrifying execution of women is viewed as justifiable and deserved by the male voice of the text. Consonant with the misogyny of this voice, in Ezekiel's visions of the eventual restoration of the people (chapters 40—48), female and marital imagery are conspicuously absent.[63] A "covenant of peace" is instead established with the "sheep" of Judah, under their shepherd, the king, and it is one of freedom and security, not shame and humiliation (34:25–31).

It is important to remember when reading these terrifying texts, with their images of animalistic female desire and the sadistic punishment of the female bodies supposed to contain that desire, that metaphors are never "simply" metaphors; they all "point to" objects and situations in real life. So it is not enough for the reader or interpreter to say that Ezekiel, who as a priest deplored the loss of the authority of Judah's religious leadership and Judah's own autonomy among the nations, was merely using terminology made familiar by Hosea and Jeremiah to voice his own explanation of this calamity, that the worship of deities "other" than or in addition to YHWH by the people brought it on. To hold this view is to deny the force and influence of Ezekiel's rhetoric, with its "fear and loathing of female sexuality."[64] Nor is it true that Ezekiel's condemnation of the "faithless" wives Judah and Israel is balanced by his condemnation of Jerusalem's male populace, which also commits acts of "adultery," either as idolatry or actual fornication, and other sins, including incest and the rape of menstruating women (Ezek. 22:1–16). It is not primarily for sexual crimes, but for forgetting the laws of YHWH that the men are judged, and their punishment is neither sexual nor (porno)graphic.[65]

It is one thing for a prophet, in typical prophetic fashion, to indict Judah and Israel for collective disobedience to YHWH, for worshiping other deities and failing to execute social justice, and to envision a judgment that will involve warfare and destruction as the result. It is quite another to turn

the terrible realities of warfare, with the inevitable humiliating consequences to the defeated—the murder of children and the rape of women—
into punishments that are deserved because of the unrestricted sexual
activity of women, however "symbolically" intended. This is not just blam-
ing the victim, it is taking the victim's abuse as evidence of her guilt. Most
modern readers concentrate on the cosmic visions and symbolic actions of
the book of Ezekiel and are unaware of chapters 16 and 23. I myself had
never really read these chapters until Howard Eilberg-Schwartz in his book
God's Phallus, mentioned their sexually explicit imagery. I would argue,
however, that the erotic attachment between YHWH (the husband) and Israel (the wife), while certainly problematic for a male-dominated community that envisions its deity as male and also the object of devotion that it
wants to call female, is equally problematic for the women of that community, who are thus always envisioned in male-centered terms.[66]

The ideal sexual relationship of YHWH and Israel in these texts, therefore, is the relationship between the initiator/actor, the husband, and the
passive/receptor, the wife. Israel (with the possible exception of the Song
of Songs, if one takes it allegorically to describe the marriage of YHWH
and Israel) never actively pursues YHWH. In the writings of the prophets
Hosea, Jeremiah, Ezekiel, and to a lesser extent Isaiah, Israel is only portrayed as taking the sexual initiative in a "wrong" direction, that is, one that
is not prompted by the desire for YHWH. When the people of God are envisioned as his "wife," it is primarily as an adulterous wife, thus making sexual initiative and the active pursuit of sexual pleasure inappropriate in a
female figure.

This concept approximately reflects the actual situation when these texts
were composed. Female figures, like real women, function in Ezekiel as
horrific object lessons of the right of men to possess and control their sexuality and autonomy.[67] When females are sexually passive, mute, and "possessed" by one male, they become "ornaments" of their husband's honor;
when sexually active and desirous of seeking pleasure with many males, they
are condemned as brazen whores and adulteresses, who not only have no
honor ("shame") of their own, but who destroy their husband's honor as
well. It is therefore only "fitting" that the man's honor and potency be restored through the collective male punishment of the sexually autonomous
woman. In Ezekiel 16 and 23, YHWH's power, humiliated through the
possession of Israel and Judah by "other" males (nations, deities), is re-
asserted and avenged by the sexual humiliation and punishment of his former possessions, symbols of his lost honor. When the situation is
envisioned this way, there can be no possibility of reconciliation or reci-
procity, as in Hosea's vision of the remarriage of Israel and YHWH (Hos.
2:14–20).

Understanding Ezekiel's historical and social situation, however, does not help us deal with his sexual imagery. Rather, it raises a further problem, not simply that such texts were and are used as justification for sexual and physical violence against women,[68] but why there is such consistency in the metaphorical language for describing the fall of either Israel or Judah in terms of jealous, dishonored husband and adulterous, wayward wife who needs to be violently "corrected." Metaphors of the type we find in the prophetic literature, as Weems notes, "teach us how to imagine what has previously remained unimaginable. In this case, the battered, promiscuous wife in the books of Hosea, Jeremiah, and Ezekiel makes rape, mutilation, and sexual humiliation defensible forms of retaliating against wives accused of sexual infidelity."[69]

THE FOREIGN WHORE

The portrayal of Israel or Judah as the sexually promiscuous wife of YHWH is also found in other prophets, but not to as great an extent as in the prophets of the exile. The eighth-century prophet Amos predicted that, because of the attempt of Amaziah, the priest of Bethel, to stifle his indictments of the priests, prophets, and rulers of that kingdom for their injustice to the poor, Amaziah's wife would become a "prostitute in the city" (7:17). Although he threatens Amaziah thereby with loss of public honor, Amos otherwise does not equate injustice with sexual infidelity. Isaiah of Jerusalem (mid–eighth century B.C.E.) uses the metaphor of whoring wife to express the turn of "the faithful city" to injustice (Isa. 1:21), and envisions "her" redemption as being accomplished by YHWH's harsh "cleansing with lye" (cf. Jer. 2:22), but the metaphor is a loose one, as only individual sinners, perhaps those who worship Asherah and Tammuz, will be shamed, not Zion itself (Isa. 1:29–30). Isaiah is much more concerned with Judah's infidelity to YHWH through social injustice than with religious apostasy, however, and is solidly in favor of Jerusalem, Temple, and Davidic monarchy, so that he does not dwell upon Judah's "whoring" with foreign deities. Isaiah's younger contemporary Micah interprets the fall of Samaria, capital of the northern kingdom, to the "idols and images" that were "the wages of a *zonah*" (Micah 1:7; cf. Ezek. 16:17). These give her an "incurable wound" (1:9; cf. Jer. 30:12, 15), but it is the prophet himself who goes naked in lamentation for Samaria's fall. In a section that may be postexilic or at least edited after the exile,[70] Micah pictures the "pangs" of "daughter Zion," like those of a woman in labor, as the nations who are her enemies call for her humiliation and exposure to their gaze (4:11). YHWH's plan in Micah is to have Zion instead vanquish her enemies, described in a passage where the metaphor of "threshing" is used to denote not sexual promiscuity but utter destruction (4:12–13; cf. Hos. 9:1; 10:11).

In the writings of the prophets of the postexilic period, only one, Third Isaiah (Isaiah 56—66), in a traditional attack on idolatry, characterizes Jerusalem as a whoring wife who deserts YHWH for Molech and other gods (Isa. 57:7–10). But the prophet reserves his main attack for those who are both idolatrous and unjust, indicting them for being "children of a sorceress, offspring of an adulterer and a whore" (Isa. 57:3, NRSV). The guilt of "whoring after foreign gods" once again seems to belong both to males and females, with only the guilty being punished, not the entire nation. Their penalty is not sexual humiliation, but to have their idols "blown away," as befits their insubstantial nature (57:13; 21). What few references there are in the postexilic prophets to the marriage of YHWH and Israel (or Judah) seem to portray the latter as the deserted and forsaken wife. Third Isaiah, for example, revives the image of the (re)marriage of YHWH and Israel used by Hosea (chapter 2) and Ezekiel (chapter 16) to describe the restoration of Jerusalem, but he does not dwell upon the punishment of Jerusalem as does Ezekiel. Instead, YHWH seems to be at fault for having abandoned her (62:4). Upon her restoration, Jerusalem will be addressed as "married" (be'ulah, mastered), the adorned bride of YHWH (62:4–5; cf. Isa. 49:18–21; 50:1). The prophet Malachi, whose orientation, like that of Ezekiel, is toward priestly purity in the worship of YHWH, refers briefly to the image of a female Judah as faithless (2:11a),[71] but he reproaches even more a faithless male Judah for having practiced idolatry by having married "the daughter of a foreign god" (2:11), thereby forsaking the marriage covenant with the bride of *his* youth (2:14–15; cf. Hos. 2:19; Jer. 2:2; Ezek. 16:8). Thus, according to Julia M. O'Brien, "Whatever actual practice the book is decrying, the prophetic discourse of idolatry as adultery has overwritten its own argument."[72]

The image of the sexually promiscuous woman, however, is applied by some of the prophets to foreign cities. Second Isaiah's message of comfort to the exiled Judah is also one of woe and humiliation to "virgin daughter Babylon" and "daughter Chaldea" (Isa. 47:1). Like a captive woman, Babylon will be enslaved and sexually shamed as part of YHWH's vengeance (47:2–3). As Ezekiel pictured a shamed and silenced Jerusalem (Ezek. 16:63), so Second Isaiah portrays a female Chaldea silenced (47:5). Her presumption of wisdom and knowledge, the Babylonian religion characterized by the writer as "sorcery and enchantment," is unable to save her from warrior YHWH's vengeance (47:9–13). The seventh-century prophet Nahum exults over the destruction in 612 B.C.E. of Nineveh, capital of the Assyrians who took Samaria a hundred years before. Nineveh is called "city of bloodshed" (3:1; cf. Ezek. 22:2, which applies it to Jerusalem) and is an utterly promiscuous, prostitute city, whose sexual wiles ("sorcery") lure the nations to become her allies (3:4). The invasion and downfall of Nineveh, led by the militant YHWH Sabaoth ("Lord of hosts"; 2:13; 3:5), is portrayed as

sexual shaming: YHWH will "lift up her skirts over her face" and expose
her nakedness to the nations she has enticed (3:5; cf. Jer. 13:22, 26–27).
From Zechariah in the early sixth century B.C.E. comes an image transformed by the New Testament apocalyptic author John into the Whore of
Babylon. The woman called "Wickedness" is carried in an ephah basket out
of Jerusalem to Babylon, thereby ridding the land of idolatry (and of foreign women) and leaving its "faithful" women (Zech. 5:5–11).[73] The predatory and wicked "strange woman" goes back where she belongs.

In a two- or three-hundred-year span of prophetic writings, most of
which were probably either edited or composed during or after the exile of
the Judahite elite to Babylon (597–538 B.C.E.), whenever the covenantal relationship between YHWH and his people is metaphorically represented
as the relationship between a husband and the wife who belongs exclusively
to him, the relationship of YHWH's people with any other deities is
harshly portrayed as adultery, synonymous with "whoring." The exile itself
is depicted as a betrayal of the honor of a jealous YHWH by his chosen but
sexually promiscuous "wife," who pursues her own lovers as she pursues her
own destiny with no thought of her "husband's" authority. To recover his
honor, which is also that of the male priestly and scribal elite, YHWH must
reassert his rights over his wife after sexually humiliating and physically
abusing her, often with the assistance of her "foreign" lovers, who are now
at his command (Hosea, Jeremiah, Ezekiel).

In the writings of other prophets, the fall of Samaria (Israel) and of Jerusalem (Judah), are the work, either of a deserting husband (YHWH or Judah) or, more often, the conniving of a foreign city-state (Nineveh,
Babylon). Characterized as female, the foreigner's attempts to seduce other
nations to insult YHWH's honor are foiled by the male warrior- and
avenger-god YHWH, who recovers his temporarily maltreated possession
by sexually shaming the evil "foreign woman" in turn and thus exposing her
wiles. Sexual degradation and restriction, capture, and silencing of the female, whether the sexually unrestricted Oholah and Oholibah or the seductive foreign Nineveh and Babylon, are the means by which male power
and hegemony are recovered. The fear of loss of authority by the elite of
Israel and Judah, especially the latter, is translated into the fear of loss of
exclusive male control of female sexuality.[74] Male fear of female sexuality
and male desire to direct and control its power also find expression in the
wisdom literature of the Tanakh, where female sexual desire is portrayed
from a male perspective as both protective and dangerous, creative and protective, and as dangerous and destructive, through the mirror-figures of female Wisdom (*Hokhmah*) and the "strange (outsider) woman" ('*iššah*'
zarah). To the delineation and exploration of these we now turn.

4

The Whore and the Holy One

Mirror Images of Wisdom

I am the whore and the holy one.
—*The Thunder, Perfect Mind*

INTIMATE KNOWLEDGE:
WOMEN, WISDOM, AND SEXUALITY

In the ancient Mesopotamian *Epic of Gilgamesh*, the tyrannous and sexually voracious Gilgamesh, semi-divine king of Uruk, distresses the elders of his city. At their request, the deities develop a strategem to "tame" Gilgamesh through the offices of a wild man, Enkidu, who becomes the only partner fit for him. In order for Enkidu to fulfill this office, however, he must first be tamed himself, separated from the wild animals that are his associates. For this purpose, a "harlot" (*harimtu*), perhaps a hierodoule, is hired by the local shepherds to teach the wild man her "woman's art."[1] Intercourse is the first step in Enkidu's initiation into the arts of civilization, cultivated food, liquor, clothing, and association with other humans. This knowledge is a mixed benefit, as Enkidu later is forced to acknowledge. Although he wins the companion of a lifetime, Gilgamesh, it is through the association with the human world, first begun by the harlot, that Enkidu loses his companionship with the natural world and indirectly meets his death. As he is dying, he both curses and blesses the harlot and the knowledge she gave him. Through his association with Enkidu, Gilgamesh also faces and comes to fear death and thereby the limits of his own humanity.

When the Hebrew nomads left Mesopotamia to wander and later to settle in Palestine, as the ancestral tale of Abraham narrates, they brought such stories with them, stories that resurface in the primal history of Genesis 1—11. In the older of the two creation narratives in Genesis 2—3, a woman is also responsible for teaching a man the knowledge that is even more of a mixed experience than it is in *Gilgamesh*. Once more, it is a woman who possesses the knowledge that separates the "natural man," the "man of earth" (*'adam;* from *'adamah,* earth), from his close communion with the natural world (Gen. 3:17–19), that imparts the necessity of clothing (3:7, 11) and cultivation of food, including grain for bread (3:18–19), and that ultimately makes him face death (3:20, 22–24). The woman herself is blamed, both by the man (3:12), as in the *Gilgamesh* epic, and by YHWH, the deity who created them (3:16). Part of YHWH's curse is that the woman (later named Hawwah or "Eve," the "mother of the living") will have sexual desire for the man, who will "rule" over her (3:16). She will desire the man despite the painful childbirth that will be the result of intercourse.

After their wild natural existence in Eden is barred to them, Adam "knows" the woman Eve sexually, and she conceives and bears a child, the "production" of which she attributes to the help, not of Adam but of YHWH (4:1). As Howard Eilberg-Schwartz points out, in both of these ancient Near Eastern tales, "Sexual knowledge is thus the key to . . . transformation from a wild thing into a human being. Like Adam and Eve, this knowledge makes Enkidu more like the gods. In both cases, a woman initiates the transformation."[2] However, this divine sexual knowledge proves costly, in the Genesis story especially to the woman, and is also portrayed as a source of danger to her partner. The satisfaction of the desire for intimate knowledge of the divine mysteries, especially those of creation and reproduction, is shown to be deadly. Thus it is "necessary," according to the Genesis story, to restrict such knowledge and its purveyors. Nel Noddings observes that the story of Eve, connected as she is with the sexual power, wisdom, and autonomy that are also aspects of the ancient Near Eastern goddesses like Ishtar in *Gilgamesh*, whose sexual power is also destructive to mortal men, is "domesticated" in Genesis by "turning her great natural gifts into mortal evils and [justifying] her subordination to man." Women's views on moral matters in Judaism and Christianity alike are silenced by placing "undue emphasis on sexuality in moral discussion."[3]

That sex and intimate knowledge are connected is indicated by the frequent use of the Hebrew verb *yd'*, "to know," to signify "to have intercourse with." Throughout the Tanakh, especially in the ancestral narratives of Genesis, it usually applies to a man's "knowing" his wife and producing children or to virgins who have yet to "know" a man.[4] The metaphor of intercourse as intimate knowledge carries over into the prophetic descriptions of the sexual relationship between Israel and YHWH, as we have seen in the previous chapter. Israel's lack of commitment to YHWH is described both in terms of adultery and wantonness and in her failure to achieve "knowledge," true knowledge of "her" husband. Intimate knowledge is given, not to female Israel, but to YHWH alone. As Hosea envisions the remarriage of YHWH and Israel, punished for her forgetfulness, it is consummated by a renewed covenant through which Israel, taken again as YHWH's wife and bedded in safety, "shall know YHWH" (Hos. 2:16–20).[5] Jeremiah, who also envisions the broken covenant between Israel and Judah and YHWH as a violated marriage contract, sees the restoration of the marriage as a renewal of the intimate knowledge of YHWH that Israel has lacked (Jer. 31:31–34). Even Ezekiel, caught up as he is in nightmarish visions of the sexual humiliation of Israel and Judah, sees their punishment as a type of painfully intimate and exclusive "knowledge" of the vengeful husband YHWH (Ezek. 23:49). As Ilana Pardes observes, "Erotic power . . . is too great a power to eliminate entirely from the realm of faith. Even the prophets . . . couldn't resist appropriating sexual desire, developing it, and returning it to their audience in a different form," as the sacred intercourse, not of pagan deities, but of YHWH and Israel.[6]

Thus a connection is established between female sexuality and secret, intimate—and potentially intimidating—knowledge. If men are able to possess and "master" this female knowledge, they can channel and control it to their benefit, along with female sexuality, as the two are often equated. If not, female knowledge, "knowing women" as well as "women's knowing" is portrayed, like women's sexuality, as an uncontrollable, dangerous "outside" force that can be deadly to men. Women throughout the Tanakh and Apocrypha and in the book of Revelation in the New Testament are shown using sexual wiles as strategic moves, which appear clever and cunning when they serve the interests of the male authorities in family, clan, and community, conniving and destructive when they serve other interests, or even their own. Men often appear unable to perceive that they are being deceived or manipulated by the wiles that play on their own desires. Such women are manifestations of the "trickster" figure, inhabiting the borders of the community, causing both disruption and restoration of communal values.[7]

Tamar of Genesis 38 deliberately transgresses the border of acceptable behavior for a levirate widow in Israel, playacting the prostitute by the wayside to gain sexual security for herself and to perpetuate Judah's own lineage, finally and ironically proving herself "more righteous" than he. Ruth, as a Moabite woman from beyond the borders of the Judahite community of Bethlehem, manages to penetrate its borders and become part of it by seducing one of its leading members, Boaz. Rahab and Jael are both literally "on the borders," Rahab as a potential enemy to Israel but living just inside the boundary wall of Jericho and occupying, as a prostitute, a liminal position in society; Jael because the tents of her Kenite clan are pitched on the border between Israelite and Canaanite territory. Rahab's cleverness in concealing the spies results in the destruction of her own community but the salvation of her own family and the success of the Israelites. Jael's seduction and murder of the enemy general Sisera certainly helps the Israelite cause and probably that of her own clan, even as it results in the destruction of the power of the Philistine army and the hopes of Sisera's family.[8]

Similarly, in the apocryphal tale of Judith, composed during the Hellenistic period of Judaism (fourth to first century B.C.E.), the pious and beautiful widow Judith (lit., "the Jewess") defends the city of Bethulia ("the virgin") against a Gentile army outside the walls and against the craven inclinations of its own elders, by leaving the city and entering the enemy camp. Casting off her modest widow's garb, Judith adorns and beautifies herself to seduce the enemy general, Holofernes, but she also arms herself with seductive speech (9:10, 13; 11:21, 23). In a probably deliberate reprise of the story of Jael and Sisera, Holofernes is deceived and betrayed; Judith decapitates him as he sleeps off a drunken banquet. In the book of Esther, composed in Hebrew with Greek additions in the Jewish Diaspora during the same period, the heroine accomplishes her purpose—the salvation of her entire people—by using less spectacular and more traditional feminine wiles. The clever Esther, who heeds the voice of her cousin, the wise but stubborn Mordecai, completely disguises her "outsider" ethnic identity and allows herself to be taken into the Persian king's harem. She first wins the respect of the influential royal eunuch Hegai and finally charms King Ahasuerus himself.[9] Esther neither resists nor protests openly even the most foolish and destructive actions of the easily swayed king, but using her physical attractions, she manages both to maneuver the hated vizier Haman into humiliation and finally destruction and to manipulate the king into achieving her ends. In this way, she not only maintains herself and her Jewish people, but is able to do so openly and with the king's favor (8:2), thus proving that she is wiser than the stiff-necked Mordecai (4:1) and the "foolish" Queen Vashti, her predecessor, who refuses to be exposed in front of the king's drunken friends, thus publicly dishonoring the king and threatening the dominance of men over their wives (1:1–22).[10]

Ruth, Rahab, and Jael are examples of "good" and therefore "wise" foreign women because they, like Tamar, Judith, and Esther, allow the boundaries of the communities they have saved to enclose and contain them once their extraordinary actions, "beyond the pale" but on behalf of sanctioned goals, are completed. As Athalya Brenner notes, stories of "foreign" or "outsider" women in the Tanakh, even those of "good" women, emphasize their sexuality, embodied in their "powers of seduction," and as we saw in chapter 2, such women "overpower" hapless males to their harm, as Delilah did Samson (Judges 16).[11] The sexual independents use their power to benefit themselves, and men may become sexually dependent on them. Foreign queens are especially dangerous in this regard, since they breach the borders of the native society and are the sexual intimates and often counselors of men who hold near-absolute power. Such is the case with Jezebel (1 Kings 16—19; 21; 2 Kings 9) and with the foreign princesses to whom Solomon "clings in love," who seduce his heart away from fidelity to YHWH (1 Kings 11:1–8). The one wise, powerful, and independent foreign queen who does no harm is the Queen of Sheba (1 Kings 10:1–13). Coming to test (and possibly best) Solomon and his wisdom with her "hard questions," she is nevertheless vanquished by his splendor, so that she is literally "breathless" (1 Kings 10:5). In the "erotic subtext" of this story, Solomon can satisfy the foreign queen's every desire (1 Kings 10:13), which may be sexual fulfillment as well as other forms of knowledge. Satisfied, she departs for her own country, having failed to entrap or defeat Solomon with her foreign wiles, but properly awed by his potency, having showered a number of valuable and costly gifts upon him, as Wisdom adorns the wise man with riches (Prov. 3:16, 22).[12] This sexually independent and clever queen, "mastered" by Solomon, cannot control him and therefore poses no further threat. Or it may be that he is wise enough to realize that the foreign woman cannot be domesticated, that a "strange woman" in the house will only destroy it.

The "Shulammite" of the Song of Songs is a problematic figure because her desire for her lover causes her to transgress the norms of "acceptable" behavior in her search to satisfy their love. Her quest seems always to be foiled by his elusiveness, interruption by the women of Jerusalem, or opposition from the watchmen of the city of Jerusalem. Consequently, the lovers seek places that are "wild" and therefore fit for a love that is not to be restricted. Their desire is tacitly approved as acceptable because it is "properly" monogamous, but it is not certain whether that desire is ever fulfilled. The Song of Songs, despite its inclusion in the canon, remains highly ambiguous, as witnessed by its extensive allegorizing. Its ambiguous nature may be due to its explicit and positive portrayal of the desire of a woman who is an outsider, one who initiates pursuit of the beloved to satisfy her sexual longing.

MIRROR IMAGES:
FEMALE WISDOM AND FEMALE DECEPTION

The simultaneous attraction to and fear of the "otherness" of female sexuality, symbolized in the biblical texts by outsider, foreign, or "strange" (zar) women, finds its most distinct expression in the parallel figures of feminized Wisdom and feminized Anti-Wisdom (Illusion, Folly) in the book of Proverbs. These two figures embody the positive qualities of the woman possessed by a man (Wisdom as wife) and the negative qualities of the woman incapable of being mastered by any man (Folly as the adulteress). Both women vie for the attention of the young man who is the subject of the various pieces of advice in the book of Proverbs, and both are portrayed as seductive. The perspective of the text is in most cases that of the sagacious elder, a male teacher, and more rarely a mother as instructor, or the sage taking on the role of mother (Proverbs 7; 30) to give advice to a young man on the proper social behavior. From this perspective, Wisdom, like a good wife, helps him succeed and take his appropriate place in society. Anti-Wisdom, the "strange woman," like the adulteress, threatens a youth's position in society because, being "outside the family structure," she represents "unlicensed, unauthorized, and basically antisocial adulterous love."[13] The strange woman is portrayed as adulteress rather than prostitute in this text because the latter does not present this kind of threat to the family structure but rather a confirmation of it by her permanent liminality. No man will be injured by another man's moving outside of the confines of the family to consort with a prostitute.

The society presupposed by this advice is, as might be expected, one in which heterosexual males and their interests are dominant. The book of Proverbs consists of several collections of sayings that convey the "common sense" insights of elders to their juniors. The emphasis within the text as a whole is on the transmission and preservation of conventional morality. As a book of "wisdom" in the ancient Near Eastern tradition of Mesopotamia and Egypt, it includes both folk sayings and scribal teaching, but is dominated by the elite perspective of the latter, as indicated by the ascription of the entire book to Solomon (Prov. 1:1) although only three of its collections may have come from his court.[14] The cosmopolitan flavor of the book is indicated by the fact that neither history nor covenant is the way in which YHWH relates to people, but rather through intimate knowledge of the created world.[15] Persons who are "wise," therefore, have a close communion with YHWH. Further, although the conventional saying, "The fear (awe) of YHWH is the beginning of wisdom," is reiterated throughout the book (Prov. 1:7; 9:10; 15:33), wisdom in Proverbs is more often characterized as accessible, as a loving and intimate partner, with emphasis placed on the sexual dimension of knowledge (Prov. 4:5–9; 7:4–5), rather than as an inaccessible and fearful mystery, as in Job (28:28). YHWH intends and is meant to be known, and therefore creates the mediating, appealing, and accessible female figure of Wisdom (*Hokhmah*), who actually enjoys and solicits contact with humanity (Prov. 8:22–31; 1:20–22; 9:1–12).

If it is in fact the case that, whatever the provenance of its collections, the book of Proverbs was probably put together in the early postexilic period, questions of the ideal construction of familial and communal identity, possibly with a view to their reconstruction, can be expected to be prominent, if not paramount, in the text.[16] As in the ancestral narratives, the ideal family is one in which stability and order are necessary for the continuance of life. It is thus no accident that both Wisdom and the *'ešet ḥayil*, the "woman of worth" or ideal wife described in the acrostic poem of Proverbs 31:10–31, which closes the book, are described as "far more precious than jewels" (Prov. 31:10; cf. 3:14–15; 8:10), giving the man who possesses them public honor and long life. The most disruptive and chaotic figure, Anti-Wisdom, is a woman who is both foolish (*'ešet kešilut*) and adulterous, publicly shaming her husband with her loud and lewd behavior (Prov. 9:13–15; 7:10–12) and bringing her sexual partners public shame and death (Prov. 5:14; 6:26; 7:21–27; 9:18). If Joseph Blenkinsopp is correct, the figure of Anti-Wisdom, the "strange woman" (*'iššah zarah*), also incorporates post-exilic warnings against the "foreign woman" (*nokriyyah*), whose "association with non-Yahwistic cults," perhaps especially involving worship of fertility gods and goddesses, figures in the prohibitions against exogamy found in Ezra and Nehemiah and at various places in the Deuteronomistic History.[17]

But there is more to the figure of Anti-Wisdom, evil personified in seductive feminine guise, than simply the fear of "pollution" of the community socially by exogamy and religiously by worship of foreign deities. Anti-Wisdom also represents the adulterous Israel, faithless to the husband of her youth and to the marriage covenant (Prov. 2:17), whose image so dominated the writings of the prophets of the exile.[18] Thus, the Strange Woman is not so foreign after all, but is rather frighteningly close, a traitor from within, as her characterization as adulterous wife implies. Camp observes that the figure of the Strange Woman in Proverbs exists both outside society and "very much within" its boundaries."[19] An alternative to Wisdom, the Good Wife, Anti-Wisdom as the Adulterous Wife shares many of the same characteristics: actively seeking the society of men, calling out to them, beguiling them with speech, inviting them to her house, sharing her secret knowledge with them. Both Wisdom, as an attribute of an omnipresent deity, and Anti-Wisdom, as a woman attached to no one man, are "available" to more than one man. Camp suggests that these dual figures as one "literary unity" embody the "necessary complementarity of human experience."[20] That experience is, however, portrayed as a male experience, the fear of women's sexual "knowledge."

The figure of Wisdom may represent a "mastered" (married) and thus controlled version of the wilder, sexually uncontrolled Strange Woman. Given the existing literary type of the dangerous and seductive foreign woman (Delilah, Jezebel), Athalya Brenner observes that "It seems possible that the prototypical description of the Foreign Woman serves as a literary model for the personified figure of Wisdom . . . , a well-known but negative type . . . utilized to create a new, original and positive type." [21]

In light of this assertion, it would be fruitful to examine first the Strange Woman, Anti-Wisdom, of Proverbs, as do both Brenner and Gale Yee, to see where her "evil" lies and how it is made positive in the characterization of Wisdom as the Woman of Worth. She first appears in the admonition of an elder or parent to a son or male pupil (2:1; *beniy*, "my son") to seek wisdom, understanding, knowledge, and prudence (not personified) actively and diligently, because they will save him from the path of evil, which is crooked, and from those who are also "crooked" in their ways and speech

(2:12–15). Among them is specifically mentioned the *'iššah zarah*, who is also the *nokriyyah* with her "smooth" words (2:16). So far, we seem simply to have a typical warning against foreign (*zar, nokri*) women. But this woman also forsakes the "companion of her youth" and the "covenant of her God" (2:17), reminding us of the prophets' images of Israel as the adulterous wife (Hos. 2:15; Jer. 2:1–3; Ezek. 16:22, 43). Her house is on the way to death, and those who "go [in] to her" do not regain the paths of life (2:19).

In a second admonition, specifically from a father to a son, the father repeats advice his own father gave him, to pursue, love, and "embrace" Wisdom (this time personified; 4:4–9; cf. 3:13–18), who will protect him against evildoers and their evil ways and speech, among whom again is the *zarah*, with her sweet, smooth speech (5:3). Again she proves deceptive, because she actually is bitter and sharp rather than sweet and smooth (5:4), and her path is the way of death, since with her wandering ways she does not keep "straight" on the paths of life (5:5–6). The young man who even goes near the door of her house will lose his honor (5:9) and his wealth (5:10) and experience a painful end of life (5:11) after he is ruined in the public assembly (*qahal*, 5:14). In 5:15–20, it is clear that his ruin is the result of seduction by the *zarah*. He has embraced the breasts of the *nokriyyah* rather than those of "the wife of his youth." While it is the husband who is not only faithless but foolish here, since his youthful bride is beautiful (5:18–19) and should be sexually satisfying, even "intoxicating," he is apparently powerless to resist the Strange Woman's wiles, even though he knows better (5:12–13). The penalty for adultery—death—is not literally exacted here, implying that the unwitting youth is beguiled rather than actively guilty (cf. 6:24–35).[22]

Even more clearly, the son is warned to follow both father's and mother's counsel (6:20), to be preserved from the "evil woman" (*'ešet ra'*), the smooth-talking *nokriyyah* (6:24),[23] who captures him with her beauty and her eyelashes. As in the Song of Songs (4:9; 6:10), here again it is the female glance that is responsible for attracting the male gaze. Intercourse with a prostitute (*zonah*) is preferable, because her price is not costly, whereas adultery with another man's wife costs the lover his life, although the ultimate penalty is not death but dishonor, permanent disgrace, and the fury of the jealous husband (6:33–35). Perhaps the fact that the latter turns on the adulterer rather than upon his own wife is intended to emphasize the helplessness and senselessness of the young man (6:32), or it may imply that even a jealous husband is powerless to control his prowling wife, who cannot be mastered.

The actual seduction scene is played out in Proverbs 7, again following an admonition to the "son" to be exclusively intimate with the woman Wisdom (7:4; cf. Song 4:9–12) so that she may protect him from the *zarah*, the *nokriyyah* with her smooth speech (v. 5). To reinforce this fourth warning, the teacher (perhaps the mother this time, looking out through the lattice of her house; 7:6; cf. Judg. 5:28; Prov. 31:1–3)[24] sees a young man "without sense" walking to the house of the *zarah* as darkness is falling (vv. 8–9), a time when "normal (decent) people" are usually, like the teacher, at home.[25] But the *zarah* does not even wait at home; she comes seeking him, dressed like a *zonah* (v. 10), and acting like one, behaving loudly in the public streets and squares, her feet refusing to stay at home (vv. 11–12).[26] She accosts the young man and boldly kisses him, mentioning her eager search, describing her perfumed and decorated bed, and inviting him to make love until morning (vv. 13–18). As Yee has pointed out, this activity is fully appropriate when undertaken by the eager bride of the Song of Songs 3:1–4,[27] but is not appropriate here, since an already-married woman describes her husband's absence as the occasion for the rendezvous (vv. 19–20). With this "seductive speech," "smooth talk," and more she persuades the hapless young man (v. 21), unmanning and dehumanizing him, trapping him like an ox, a stag, a bird (vv. 22–23). Her victims are many (v. 26), her house a way to Sheol, her chambers, death (v. 27). Sex with the Strange Woman is intimacy that kills. If the fruit of the tree of knowledge is both good and evil, she is the evil knowledge. As David Halperin has noted, the Strange Woman's Sheol, "into which her victims disappear forever, will have been inside her body."[28]

The Strange Woman appears one last time in Proverbs as a fully developed persona, in chapter 9, where she is directly contrasted with Wisdom (9:1–6). Here she is characterized as the *'ešet kešilut*, the Foolish Woman (9:13), but in actuality she represents the Folly (Anti-Wisdom) that the foolish choose instead of Wisdom, as the senseless young man chose the Strange Woman (7:10–27). Indeed, although she is not called *zarah* or *nokriyyah* here, the behavior of Folly is exactly like that of the Strange Woman, loud and publicly shameless (9:13–15; cf. 7:11–12). She solicits young men to come into her house and share a secret, "stolen" banquet (9:16–17; cf. 7:14–20). But her house is likewise full of the dead, a route to Sheol (9:18; cf. 7:25–27). Although uniquely in this passage this female character is called "ignorant," "foolish," "knowing nothing" (9:13), it is not Anti-Wisdom who lacks knowledge, but the "simple" and the "senseless" men who do not "know" death is the result of following her invitation.

Throughout the rest of the book of Proverbs, the figure of the Strange Woman persists, not as a full personification but in the persons of bad or foolish women, usually in contrast with good or wise women. She is a shameless wife (12:4), a foolish woman who destroys her house by her "own hands" (14:1); her mouth (speech) is a "deep pit" (like the *zonah* in 23:27) into which those at whom YHWH is angry fall (22:14); she is a "narrow well," who "lies in wait like a robber" and multiplies the number of the faithless (23:27–28, NRSV), an adulterous wife who takes her fill and claims to have done nothing wrong (30:20). The symbols of a deep pit and a well that seeks to be filled are heavily sexual: the foolish young man will "enter" such a woman only to find a *vagina dentata*, a vagina with emasculating teeth. The oracle taught King Lemuel by his mother, herself a wisdom-teacher (31:1–9), contains a blanket warning against giving one's "strength" to any woman (31:3).

The negative portrait of the Evil Woman, despite her characterization as "strange" and "foreign," nevertheless seems to strike uncomfortably close to home. An adulteress is after all someone's wife; her house is accessible to all; she roams the streets and appears in public places within the community itself, enclosed by its gates. Perhaps by projecting the fear of female sexual freedom onto a figure that is not really "one of us," the androcentric text of Proverbs can thus create a female ideal that *is* "one of us," a "domesticated" partner and helpmate, the Good Woman Wisdom, the prototype of the Victorian "angel in the home." This character possesses many of the traits of the Strange Woman, but they are trained toward the building up of the family and the community, not the accomplishment of "unproductive" sexual pleasure. To possess Wisdom is to possess at the same time the ideal *'iššah* (woman/wife) and the secret, divinely given knowledge she represents. Because Wisdom is an ideal, like the wife whose value is "far above jewels," she is both a universal and a unique possession, something that is impossible for Anti-Wisdom, who possesses many but is possessed by no one, to be.

Just as marital imagery is an important element in the depiction of the independent Anti-Wisdom, and in the prophets' portrayal of the relationship between YHWH and Israel, it is important in the depiction of domesticated Wisdom.[29] After all, the first step in domesticating a woman is to marry her, to make her a *be'ulat ba'al*, a woman mastered sexually. At first, however, this appears a difficult step to take with *Hokhmah*, Wisdom, as she, like the Strange Woman, cries out loudly in very public places—in the squares, the most frequented street corner, the entrance to the city (Prov. 1:20–21; cf. 8:1–3; 9:3; and 7:10–12; 9:14–15, describing the *zarah*). She chides those who do not listen to her and therefore reject her invitation, and threatens them with calamity (1:26–33). This too has resonances of the lament of the rejected *zonah*, to whom Jeremiah compares Jerusalem (Jer. 4:30–31). Regarded in another light, however, the voice of Wisdom is itself that of a prophet, a wise woman who is not one of the despised soothsayers decried, for example, by Ezekiel (Ezek. 13:18–19) but is one whose words echo those of male prophets, who are also rejected (Jer. 7:13, 24–27).[30] The desexualizing, as well as defeminizing, of this voice of female Wisdom is further accomplished by the paraphrase of her warning in chapter 2, where the male voice (supposedly Solomon's) warns the son to listen to the voice of Wisdom, the gift of YHWH, which will keep him from the Strange Woman and her smooth words (2:16).

The male voice goes on to emphasize the desirable nature of Wisdom: "She is more precious than jewels, and nothing you desire can compare with her" (3:15, NRSV). Thus she is like the good wife, the woman of worth ('ešet ḥayil), who in the acrostic poem of 31:10–31 is also described as "more precious than jewels." Like the valuable wife, moreover, Wisdom once attained brings long life, wealth, happiness, and honor to the one who "gets" her as his (3:16–18; cf. 31:11–31). The elder's transmission of instruction from his own father to his children is rife with bridal imagery (4:1–9). The youth is instructed once more to "get" Wisdom and not to forsake her, to keep her, love her, prize her, and embrace her, just as he is instructed to be satisfied by the breasts of the wife of his youth and to avoid the embrace of the foreigner in 5:18–20.[31] Once more, the elder man enjoins the younger to love Wisdom as "sister" and "intimate friend," terms used in heterosexual love poetry and in poetry celebrating marriage (7:4; cf. Song 4:9–12), so that the youth may avoid the blandishments of the Strange Woman (7:5), who solicits fools to their ruin (7:10–27). In contrast, while Wisdom, like Anti-Wisdom, walks the streets (8:1–3), her speech is not "crooked" like the seductive speech of the adulteress, and her insight is true. Instead of offering the foolish youth a night of sexual fulfillment (7:18), the end of which is entrapment and death (7:21–27), Wisdom offers what is more precious than jewels (8:11), the way to long life and prosperity. Wisdom is a delight, both to YHWH, who created her (8:30), and to the human race, in whom she also rejoices (8:31). Those who love her are successful and happy (8:21, 32); those who reject her are in love with death (8:36).

Wisdom and Anti-Wisdom (the Woman of Folly) are pitted directly against each other in chapter 9, where they use words and actions that are similar, but with subtle differences in phrasing and great differences in result. From her house, which she has built firmly on seven pillars, Wisdom sends out an invitation to a feast (9:1–2). Folly likewise invites guests to a feast (9:14–17). The language of invitation they use is identical, addressed to those who pass by, those who "are simple!" and "those without sense" (9:4; 9:16, NRSV), and they issue their invitations in the same places, "from the highest places in the town" (9:3; 9:14, NRSV).[32] The menu of their respective banquets as well as the outcome, however, is far different. While Wisdom offers bread and (temperately) mixed wine (9:5), with the possible luxurious addition of sacrificial meat (9:2), reminding us of the adulterous woman who has just "paid her vows" (7:14), Anti-Wisdom offers bread and water that are supposedly sweetened by their clandestine nature (9:17). In the sayings sandwiched between the descriptions of the two faces of Wisdom, the warning voice of the elder defines Wisdom once more as "the fear of YHWH" (9:10), and promises long life as the reward for following her; the result of accepting the invitation of Anti-Wisdom is, conversely, death and Sheol (9:18).

What can we make of the close similarity between these two female characters, especially with regard to publicly seductive activities, usually deemed inappropriate for real women?[33] Both Wisdom and Anti-Wisdom, the Strange Woman, attract and pursue young men. But although the youth is instructed to give in to the attraction of Wisdom, in fact to make her his wife, he is vehemently warned by his elders not to give in to the wiles of the Strange Woman, one who is already the wife of another, one who will not build up his status within the community but will actually cause his exclusion from it (5:7–14). Wisdom, however seductive, is not characterized by the aggressive sexuality with which the Strange Woman is invested (7:10–20).[34] The former is thus more of an ideal, a female figure who may share traits with real women, but the sum of whose traits are not found in any one woman. Just so the ʾešet ḥayil of Proverbs 31:10–31, who appears to be the embodiment of Wisdom, represents a collection of wifely virtues valued by the men of the community, especially the elders who are its rulers. Yee points out that, while "erotic imagery" is employed to describe both Wisdom and the Strange Woman, "only man pursues Wisdom [the ideal] like a lover, and it is a woman [the far-from-ideal] who seduces him away from her."[35] "Real women," with the exception of brides, who are pictured as pursuing their bridegrooms (Prov. 9:1–6; Song 3:2–4), are not to direct their erotic desires toward more than one male object. Their aim should be marriage, marriage that is also offered as a satisfactory channel for male desire (Prov. 5:15–20; 12:4; 18:22), or at least one that will keep a man away from his neighbor's wife (6:24–35).

Thus the aim of the elders' advice in Proverbs is to "domesticate" sexuality, to enable young men to restrain their own desires within heterosexual and patriarchal marriage and to confine women's sexual knowledge within the family. Further, it must be acknowledged that in Proverbs, unlike Genesis, female Wisdom is not only a creation of YHWH (as was Eve in Genesis 2) but her sharing of divine knowledge through marital intercourse with a wise man is a positive thing (Prov. 8:30–31). Since "Wisdom is not conceptualized totally independently of God," according to Eilberg-Schwartz, she is not portrayed as sexually autonomous; instead, because YHWH is not portrayed as a male sexual being in Proverbs, Wisdom cannot be YHWH's consort, but provides an acceptable (i.e., heteroerotic) way for male Israelites to be erotically intimate with YHWH, to "know" him in the biblical sense.[36] Wisdom thus symbolizes desire controlled, restrained, and directed from above by YHWH as a gift to the male sage (cf. Sirach 1:1–10), and from below by the sage for whom knowledge of YHWH, like sex in marriage, is an appropriate object of desire.[37] Although she may appear to solicit and seduce men in the same way the Strange Woman does, Wisdom does so for an entirely different purpose, not to satisfy her own sexual desire, but to fulfill male desire for intimacy with YHWH. Ultimately, Wisdom lacks the Strange Woman's sexual power and autonomy.

The Strange Woman conversely remains "strange"; that is, she cannot be "known" other than sexually, her secrets cannot be possessed, she herself cannot be confined to one man. At some points, the text seems to rob her of this mysterious erotic power by characterizing her as ignorant of what she is doing (5:6; 9:13), but more often she is portrayed as knowing it well, with her "smooth words" and her sweet, "seductive speech" (2:16; 5:3; 6:24; 7:5, 21). The foolish young men who are her prey are the ones who are "without sense" (7:7; 9:16). There is a hint that these do in fact obtain the "knowledge" they seek, but it is a sexual mystery that is emphatically disapproved of by the text, the way to death, not life (7:24–27; 9:18). Like Wisdom in the book of Job, which is hidden from the living, but of which "Abaddon and Death" have heard (Job 28:21–22; 11:7–8), so the Strange Woman's inner chambers are the depths of Sheol and Death, a deep sexual knowledge that has no benefit for males, or perhaps a knowledge that is unattainable, that cannot be legitimately possessed.

It is interesting to note that throughout the book of Proverbs, unlike the writings of the prophets, the sexually unrestrained woman herself never receives punishment. Indeed, even when she is specifically characterized as an adulterous wife (Prov. 6:24–35), it is her partner in adultery, ensnared by her eyelashes (6:25), who is punished, wounded, dishonored, and disgraced by her jealous husband's fury (6:32–35). The Strange Woman is thus a fearful figure who disrupts the ideal balance of society envisioned by the writers of Proverbs, a woman who is not under male sexual hegemony. "Sexual interactions," as feminist theorist Laurie Shrage observes, "represent social texts that call for interpretation," and in societies where men's entitlement to sexual pleasure and satisfaction is assumed over women's, women are held "uniquely blamable" for adultery, both if wives fail to give the husband sexual satisfaction or if they seek it for themselves elsewhere than in marriage.[38] Both the initiative and priority in sexual satisfaction are assumed to be the male's, an assumption fully endorsed by the book of Proverbs. Thus, a man who cannot "control" his wife's sexuality is shamed, and her partner is also seen as a "victim" for succumbing to her aggressive eroticism despite its danger.

In the other wisdom books of the Tanakh, Job and Qoheleth (Ecclesiastes), both of which, like Proverbs, are probably postexilic, Wisdom is not personified as feminine, nor is evil Anti-Wisdom personified as the Strange Woman. These, however, are books of "pessimistic" or "negative" wisdom, in which the encounter with the divine being is mysterious, and knowledge of the world is either inaccessible to human understanding (Job) or incapable of transforming one's life (Qoheleth). Women in any role are almost completely absent from Qoheleth, whose author, purporting to be Solomon (Eccl. 1:1), includes "many concubines" among the "delights of the flesh" he experienced (2:8), with no allusion to the foreign concubines and princesses as the cause of Solomon's downfall (1 Kings 11:8). In Job, the title character exemplifies the ideal that is held up for young men by the elders of Proverbs, one who does not follow "crooked" paths, who "fears God" (Job 1:1), and, in protesting his own righteousness, swears that he has "covenanted with his eyes" not even to look at a virgin (31:1, NRSV) and that he has not been "enticed by a woman" into committing adultery, a crime for which the fitting punishment would have been for his own wife to become the sexual property of other men (31:9–12). In short, Job exemplifies the type of conventional morality so praised in Proverbs. Job's wife, however, counsels him early in the book that in the face of such terrible adversity, insisting on his integrity is the wrong strategy; rather, he should blame the one who caused the calamity, God, and then die (2:9). To this advice, which in the Greek translation is lengthened to six lines, in which Job's wife mentions her suffering at the loss of the sons and daughters she bore with such labor, as well as his own pain,[39] Job replies that she speaks like "any foolish woman" and rejects her advice, refusing to "sin with his lips" (2:11, NRSV). Here we have an echo of the speech of the Foolish Woman in Proverbs which leads to sin and death, but without the element of sexual temptation. Job's wife's advice sets the tone for that of his "comforters," who offer him essentially the same "foolish" advice, which comes from their ignorance that is proffered as knowledge of YHWH (Job 42:7–9). The only other women in the book, Job's daughters, lost (1:5) and restored (42:13), have no speaking parts, but unlike their mother (who apparently survives her indiscretion), they have names and descriptions that indicate their surpassing beauty (42:14–15). They are also presumably desirable for the inheritance Job gives them (42:15), which in the *Testament of Job*, a pseudepigraphical tale of the first century B.C.E., is said to be greater than that of their seven brothers. Three multicolored "cords" or sashes give the women the ability to know "heavenly things," to have the strength given by God, and to speak ecstatically, composing hymns of praise (*Testament of Job* 46—50). The *Testament of Job* stands alone among other pseudepigraphical "testaments" that convey the idea that women are sexual beings whose only power over men is seduction and whose intercourse with angels is adulterous and evil (e.g., *Testament of Reuben* 5:1, 5–6). As Rebecca Lesses points out, works like the *Testament of Job* celebrate women as beings capable of spiritual insight rather than beings limited by their sexuality, and form a minor but distinctive strain in formative Judaism.[40]

In the so-called apocryphal wisdom texts—Baruch, Sirach (Ecclesiasticus), and the Wisdom of Solomon—that appear in the Greek version of the Hebrew Bible, the Septuagint, but not in the Hebrew canon, Wisdom personified as female reappears, perhaps as the result of the challenge offered to intellectual Jews by Hellenistic "wisdom"—philosophy and other Greek ideas—during the period from the third century to the first century B.C.E. One of the ways in which that challenge was answered was to claim that

Wisdom (Gk., *Sophia*) was a creature of the God of the Jews, and that Jews, by following the precepts of that God, were the original "lovers" of Sophia (philosophers). "Sophia," claims Silvia Schroer, "shows the way to a just Jewish life amid a pluralistic world."[41] For Baruch, as for Sirach, while Wisdom still appears as distinctly female (Bar. 3:9–4:4; Sirach 24; cf. Proverbs 8), she is embodied not merely in the teaching of the elders (Sirach 39:1–11; 50:27; 51:23) but in the Torah, "the book of the commandments of God, the law that endures forever" (Bar. 4:1, NRSV; Sirach 24:23), and in the emerging tripartite canon of Law, Prophets, Writings (Prologue to Sirach). For the writer of the Wisdom of Solomon, who considers bodies earthly, perishable, and a burden to the soul (Wisd. Sol. 9:15; 8:19–20), Wisdom is disembodied, "pure spirit" and intellect, a "breath," emanation, reflection, and manifestation of the divine in the world (Wisd. Sol. 7:26; cf. John 1:1–14; Heb. 1:1–3; Col. 1:15–19 in the New Testament). Using language reminiscent of that in Proverbs, the writer, called "Solomon," describes how he has loved and sought Wisdom from his youth (8:2; cf. Prov. 5:18) and how he has fallen in love with "her" beauty and desired her for his bride, since she is a restful companion and, like the good wife, creates a home full of peace (8:16). It is nonetheless clear that this metaphorical language is conventional, subordinated to the concept of a spiritual Wisdom who is a "mystic" (*mystis*) in the knowledge of God, a sharer (*hairetis*) in his works (8:4), and an instructor in the four cardinal virtues known to Greek philosophy: self-control, prudence, justice, and courage (8:7). Consequently, it is Wisdom, the gift of God (8:21), who has been the guide and savior throughout Israel's experience of history (10:1–21). Knowledge of God is thus intellectual and historical rather than sexual, although the author does say that the making of idols results from a mistaken idea of the divine and is the beginning of "fornication" (*porneia*) and other forms of sexual "perversion" (14:12, 26; cf. Rom. 1:18–32).

The most conventional of the Hellenistic Jewish wisdom books, and consciously so, is the Teachings of Jesus Ben Sira, known in Greek as "Sirach" and referred to in the English translations of the Apocrypha as "Ecclesiasticus." The praises of Wisdom in 1:1–20; 4:11–19; 14:20–27; 15:1–10, the youth's pursuit of Wisdom in 51:13–22, and the extensive aretalogy (self-praise) of Wisdom in the heavenly assembly in chapter 24 incorporate images already found in Proverbs, especially of Wisdom as the creation of God, "lavished" upon those who love and revere him (Prov. 8:22–31, Sirach 1:10). She is the desirable and hotly pursued bride (14:23–24; 15:2b; 51:20–21), a fruitful mother (4:11; 15:2a), a bountiful field (6:18–37; cf. Prov. 4:10), and, again, the Torah (15:1; 24:23). In fact, Sirach declares that Wisdom's praise can be found entirely in the "book of the commandments of God" (24:23). Wisdom is for Sirach completely the possession of God, to be bestowed like a daughter as a bride upon his favorites, those who study his commandments, the male sages. Like the elders of Proverbs, Sirach recommends that a young man get and keep a good wife (7:19, 26; 26:1–4, 22), who is a "good possession" (36:29). If sensible, she is better than any other companion (40:23). Her husband is not to be jealous of her, lest he learn an "evil lesson" (9:1). Sirach does not, however, adopt the demonic character of the Strange Woman as one from whom Wisdom and a good wife will protect the wise man, and the only "prey" to be hunted and captured is Wisdom herself (14:20). He nevertheless condemns women in general for being the cause of sin and death (25:24), of being responsible for wickedness worse than any other (25:13, 19), and of bringing such shame and disgrace that a man's wickedness is better than a woman's goodness (42:14). He also lists entire categories of women that men should avoid, especially prostitutes, promiscuous women, and one's neighbor's wife (9:2–9; 19:2; 41:20–22). He compares "bad" and "good" women (26:1–9, 19–27), the "bad" generally being characterized as shameless, talkative, headstrong, and promiscuous, the "good" as modest in behavior, silent, domestically skilled, and chaste. Adultery, both male and female, will be punished (23:16–27), but Sirach says that while the adulterer commits a sin only against his own marriage bed (23:18), the adulteress commits three crimes, crimes against God, her husband, and her children (23:22–23). The adulteress not only will be condemned by the public assembly (23:24) but will leave behind forever a shamed and disgraced memory (23:26). Daughters are uniformly a "loss" and a "worry" for their fathers, because they must be continually watched for signs of sexual independence that Sirach labels "impudence" or shamelessness (26:3–5; 42:9–12). They must be kept away from married (sexually experienced) women, whose wickedness is lack of shame and emerges like corrupting moths from garments (42:13–14). Hence, danger for a man still comes from the sexual desires of and for women, who in Sirach are a collective evil. Wisdom, the "bride" sought by the young man in the erotic language of 51:13–22, because she can be completely possessed or "mastered" by him, is a positive good. But once possessed, Wisdom seems to lose any separate and distinctly female characteristics: she is absorbed by the man. As Torah, Wisdom is even more completely "possessed" by men, and in the long history of Torah scholarship, the sages pronounced largely negatively on women's learning as promoting female promiscuity.[42]

In an apocryphal text that is not counted as part of wisdom literature but nevertheless shares some important imagery and themes with it, a wise young man vindicates the honor of a beautiful but tempting wife and confounds his elders, who have ignored the conventional advice voiced by Sirach not to gaze at female beauty that belongs to another (Sirach 9:9). This is the story of Susanna, in which even a woman who behaves with sexual propriety may, like Bathsheba, become an occasion of dishonor by provok-

ing the volatile desire of men who are not her husband.[43] This is not to say
that Susanna (or Bathsheba) exemplifies the Strange Woman, because she
is not foreign and does not appear outside the confines of her garden. Nevertheless, her story is, like that of Bathsheba (who also takes a ritual bath on
the roof of her house), an example of the androcentric preoccupation with
the power of attraction of female sexuality unless it is totally confined
"within" the house (domestic sphere). Set in Babylon, which symbolizes the
Jewish Diaspora, the story of Susanna tests both conventional wisdom and
those who dispense it (the elders) and resets the boundaries of good conduct for the Jewish community. From the beginning, Susanna is both desirable in appearance and God-fearing (Sus. 2, 31–32), so it is no wonder
that the elders, who ought to be wise, desire to attain her for their own, just
as in the conventional wisdom literature they advise the young man to pursue and obtain Wisdom. The bridal imagery often associated with Wisdom
is further reinforced by the fact that Susanna walks about and bathes within
an enclosed garden (Sus. 7, 15–18), echoing the portrayal of the bride in
Song of Songs as an "enclosed garden" (Song 4:12; cf. Prov. 5:18). The
problem, however, is that Susanna, however beautiful, desirable, and God-
fearing, is not an appropriate object for the elders' gaze and pursuit, since
she is a real woman and wife of the judge Joakim. In a stratagem made familiar in the episode of Potiphar's wife (Genesis 39), the elders, overcome
by their desire, press Susanna to yield or be accused of adultery. Susanna is
"completely trapped" (v. 22), as the foolish young man is by the Strange
Woman. Unlike Joseph, she cannot escape, although the elders claim that
her fictitious young lover flees on discovery (v. 39). When she "cries out
with a loud voice" (like Wisdom; Prov. 1:20), she is not believed and her
predicament even shames her servants (v. 27). She is accused of being an
adulterous wife before a public assembly, like the punitive *qahal* in Ezekiel
23:46–47, with her relatives and her children present, and is condemned to
death (vv. 28–43). Apparently Joakim, who has no speaking part, does not
avail himself of the trial of "bitter waters" (Numbers 5), but trusts that the
elders have caught Susanna "in the very act" (cf. John 7:53–8:11). Crying
out loudly once more to God, who knows what is "hidden" (v. 42; cf. Prov.
15:11), Susanna is finally heard, and a wise young man, Daniel, uses a
Solomonic stratagem to get at the truth (Sus. 52–59; cf. 1 Kings 3:16–27).
Daniel condemns the elders as foreigners, as "children of Canaan" who are
known for their deviant sexual practices, and they are put to death "according to the Law of Moses" for bearing false witness (v. 62; Deut.
19:16–21). Thus the tale of Susanna reemphasizes the importance of the
law, the tempting aspect of female sexuality, however virtuous, and the reputation of the wise man in being able to discern the truth, especially in matters of sexual misconduct (Sus. 63–64). Further, it is Wisdom in the guise
of a learned male that rescues a female trapped by male lust. Men accuse,

men judge, wise men deliver. Susanna, despite her virtue and perhaps because of it, has a beauty that attracts the volatile male gaze (cf. Sirach 9:8) and therefore generates male desire. After all, beauty is what makes both Wisdom and the Strange Woman desirable (Prov. 5:15–20; cf. Song 1:9–17; 4:1–15), and the wise youth is the one who can discern in what direction his attraction will lead. Like Wisdom and the Strange Woman, Susanna does "expose" her beauty to a semi-public gaze, since the elders, who are meeting with other men at Joakim's house, see her "walking about" in her husband's garden (Sus. 7–8). Clearly, however, the onus is not on Susanna but on the foolish, lustful elders, who pervert the good, both of Wisdom and the law. Susanna, like Wisdom, is merely the object of desire, not the subject, as is the Strange Woman.

What then can we make of the relationship between female sexuality and knowledge, as portrayed in the Tanakh and in the Apocrypha? First of all, women's wisdom, as portrayed by men, is mysterious, deep, and often full of guile. Females "know" how to persuade, either by speech or by appearance. Their attraction for male desire because of their perceived difference is depicted as "strangeness" and "foreignness," and it threatens male hegemony because males fear loss of control. The female figure who can be pursued, "taken," and domesticated as a mate, a helper yet a subordinate, who enforces rather than undermines male sexual, familial, and political dominance, is a benign intimate (cf. Prov. 31:10–31; Sirach 36:29–30). As Wisdom, she is the creation and gift of God for those men who love him, providing a kind of sexual satisfaction and mastery by knowing God's will (Sirach 51:13–22). Wisdom is the erotic divine, desire for whom by a largely heterosexual but homosocial male community is acceptable,[44] modeled as it is on her human counterpart, the wife whose own study is to provide for her husband's comfort and honor, and the building up of the household (Sirach 26:3, 13, 26). The Strange Woman, on the other hand, is identified with female sexual autonomy, defined as "shamelessness" and dishonor to males, "folly" to those males who choose her because they do not know that she is inimical to male domination and hence an "outsider" to the family structure.

Wisdom and Folly, like women, are for these texts seductive, alluring in appearance and smooth in speech. Both are sources of mysterious knowledge that is hidden from all but the discerning man, as the story of Daniel and Susanna shows. This "wise man" will know which of these women will direct her wisdom, her sexuality, and her desire toward him and him alone. He may possess Wisdom as he possesses a wife, with intimacy and completeness that are symbolized by marital intercourse. She becomes the *be'ulat ba'al*, the "mastered woman."

The Strange Woman is the one who, even though married, will never be completely mastered, and never belong completely within the boundary of the family and patriarchal community. As such, she is called *zarah* and *nokriyyah*, terms that indicate her outsider status. She herself may however possess many men in her quest for the satisfaction of her own desire, and her sexual "looseness" or lack of restriction is conveyed by the term *zonah*, prostitute, harlot, whore. Men who accept the invitation of this woman are merely her "victims," her "prey," and if she has a husband, he has no control over her, becoming himself her victim as she unmans him through public dishonor (cf. Prov. 6:24–35; 7:6–27; Sirach 25:13–26). Such a woman is anathema to male heterosexual and social hegemony and must be avoided or "cut off" (Sirach 25:26), kept outside the boundary of the bonded group. The curious absence of the mention of the punishment or even death of the Adulteress/Strange Woman in the wisdom literature (except of course for its being threatened but prevented in the case of the "insider" woman, Susanna) is perhaps an indication of the terrible power this figure has in this androcentric literature. Noddings interprets the contrast between "good" (restricted) and "evil" (autonomous) women in the literature influenced by Jewish and Christian models: "Confined to the home and subject to men's rule, the obedient woman has been an angel in the house [cf. Prov. 31:10–31; Sirach 26:1–4]; loose in the world or rebellious against male domination, she becomes 'the devil's gateway,' an ambiguous evil indeed."[45]

But if we in fact regard the Strange or "Wild" (undomesticated) Woman as the original and "Lady" Wisdom as her tamed or domesticated counterpart, what might we uncover of positive value? Enkidu, the Wild Man of *Gilgamesh*, is tamed and mastered by the sexual wisdom of the harlot, learning the art of belonging to a human community as a balance of positives and negatives, including the final negative of death. So also the Wild, or "outsider," Woman, once she surrenders her sexual wisdom to one "master" (*ba'al*), is corralled within the structure of male domination and becomes "Lady" Wisdom, the Good Woman/Wife. The "outsider" does indeed bring death (Prov. 7:27; 9:18; Sirach 25:24), but it is death to binding and confining structures, death to the idea that sexual pleasure, if actively sought by women, is inappropriate and women's sexual wisdom is suspect (cf. Gen. 18:12–15; Song 5:7). Camp notes that Wisdom and the Strange Woman together can be regarded as aspects of one trickster paradigm, and by paying attention to the Strange Woman especially, we might achieve "a positive valuation of women's power as anti-structural, regenerative [of the social order] because of its liminality."[46] Women might thus perceive themselves as both wise and sexually "loose," that is, freed from the exclusive confines of the male heterosexual hegemony that attempts to define and therefore confine their life choices. That such "Wild" women have been perceived in the literature under discussion as immoral is hardly surprising.

5

Spirituality and Sexuality in the Body of Christ

It is a good thing for a person not to touch a woman.

—1 Corinthians 7:1

THE SCHEMA OF THIS WORLD

As in the Tanakh and Apocrypha, there are distinct "voices" within the New Testament. The two most powerful are the voice of Jesus of Nazareth, known as the Christ (messiah) in the "common" (*koine*) Greek that is the language of the New Testament and quite possibly of Jesus' earliest followers as well, and the voice of Paul of Tarsus, the most prominent interpreter of Jesus as the Christ. What distinguishes these two, however, is that Jesus' voice is always mediated, known not through his own writings but through traditions orally transmitted for nearly a generation following his death and shaped by different sorts of believers. Although Paul's writing is subject to editing, interpolation, and pseudepigraphical extension, he is more immediately known through the letters he wrote to congregations of converts in the urban centers of the Jewish Diaspora than is Jesus in the Gospels. Paul's writings are supposedly the earliest literature of the New Testament canon, his first letter to the congregation at Thessalonica dating from perhaps mid-first century C.E., but they show little continuity with, or knowledge of, the teachings of the Galilean master. At times Paul seems deliberately conscious and reverential of the Judean tradition (1 Cor. 11:23–26; 15:3–8) and at other times scornful of it (Gal. 1:11–12, 16–17; 2 Cor. 5:16). What unites both Jews, Jesus and Paul, as far as we can discern from the canon, is the desire to reform religious practice (not belief) in society with an eye to the eventual reformation of that society according to the divine will through divine intervention. Whoever the rulers of this present age may be, God is the ruler of the universe and hence of all ages.

Like the written composition of the Torah, most of the Prophets, and some of the Writings, the writing of the New Testament Gospels and the collection, editing, and embellishment of Paul's letters were initiated by political and social crises that had an impact on the marginal group that was known by many names before it was called "Christian" (Acts 11:26; late first century C.E.). The first crisis was that of the First Jewish War (66–70 C.E.) and its aftermath, the destruction of the Second Temple at Jerusalem and the dispersion and persecution of various Jewish sects. Other rebellions that followed were the uprisings against Trajan (114–117 C.E.), during whose reign "Christians" appear in Bithynia as a distinct group; and the Second Jewish War (132–135 C.E.), the messianic rebellion of Bar Kochba during the reign of the emperor Hadrian, which occasioned the execution of some prominent rabbis and the leveling of the Temple remains and renaming of Jerusalem. Perhaps it is not surprising that around this latter period we get the first controversies over the formation of a distinctly Christian canon, consisting of one or more written Gospels and ten or so letters of Paul, around 150 C.E.

Part of the debate over the Christian canon for two centuries was how much continuity it was to have with the Hebrew Bible (which for most Christians meant its Greek translation, the Septuagint) and the continuing authority of the patriarchs of the church (the twelve apostles) and their disciples. Increasingly, the structure of Christianity mirrored the structures of the Roman society that continued to produce the literate elite of the churches. Thus, in its final form, the canon of the Christian Bible (Septuagint and New Testament) reflected the interests and concerns of this literate male clerical elite. Christianity went on to become the dominant religion and instrument of the ruling class of the empire. No longer marginal (at least not after 311 C.E.), Christianity was eventually able to dictate what classes and categories of persons were themselves to be considered marginal or even "outside" the borders of the social order. The only comparable events in Judaism were the restoration of a religious elite in Jerusalem following the Babylonian exile and the patronage of the Pharisees by the Hasmonean rulers of the mid–second to mid–first centuries B.C.E., admittedly short-lived.

Coincidental with the rise and eventual triumph of so-called orthodox Christianity as a powerful religion within a widespread empire was, naturally, a reexamination of the social order and with it a reexamination of sexual relations, definitions of gender, and sexual interactions as part of that order. Within the past couple of decades, feminist scholarship in particular, though not exclusively, has sought to characterize the Jesus movement as one in which gender hierarchies, along with other socially constructed orders, either did not obtain or were in flux.[1] What little can be established about very early Christian understandings of sexual and gender relations, and that with a relative degree of certainty, is that sexuality, especially that involving marriage and parenthood, was problematic. Whether the result of a later impulse toward freedom from sexuality as part of "this world" (not to be understood as sexual freedom) or from the avoidance of sexual relations that were held to impede the rapid spreading of the gospel before the eventual transformation of the world, Christian literature of many varieties seems to have depicted Jesus as celibate, if not asexual (cf. Matt. 19:11–12). Paul seems to have preferred celibacy, both for himself and for others who were unmarried (1 Cor. 7: 6–7). He never refers to raising children or children as the products of marriage, speaking only of his converts as "children" (cf. 1 Thess. 2:7, 12). Jesus' celebrated blessing of the children can be viewed as a prophetic action that commends an attitude of dependent and obedient trust on a parent as that of the believer toward God rather than an endorsement of family life (Matt. 19:13–15; Mark 10:13–16; Luke 9:46–48; 18:15–17; cf. Mark 9:42; Matt. 18:6, 10; cf. *Gospel of Thomas* 21; 22; 37; 46).[2]

Jesus is depicted rather consistently throughout the four canonical Gospels and in the apocryphal *Gospel of Thomas* as rejecting his biological parents and relatives (Mark 3:31–35; 13:17; Matt. 12:46–50; 24:19; Luke 8:19–21; 11:27; 23:28; John 2:4; 19:26–27; *Gospel of Thomas* 15; 79; 99; 105) in favor of a new "family" created by the mutual belonging of its members to one "father in heaven" (Matt. 23:9). Those who leave their biological families ("brothers or sisters or mother or father or children," Mark 10:29–30) and even "hate" their "parents, wife and children, brothers and sisters" (Luke 14:26; *Gospel of Thomas* 101; cf. the milder version in Matt. 10:37),[3] will be the members of the new community, which is already growing out of the present "adulterous and sinful generation" (Mark 8:38; Matt. 10:33; Luke 12:9). Within the households of this age, family members may even be set against each other in enmity as the age comes to an end (Luke 12:53; Matt. 10:34–36).

The group that surrounded Jesus and the first preachers of his appearance as the messiah seem to have been largely itinerant, depending on support from co-believers in the towns through which they passed (Matt. 4:23–25; 10:5–15; Mark 6:8–11; Luke 9:1–5; 10:1–12) or from the patronage of the well-to-do in the cities (1 Cor. 1:11, 16), or, in Paul's case, through supporting himself as an artisan (1 Cor. 9:6, 15; Acts 18:3; 28:30). That women were included among the itinerant followers of Jesus is clear from the mention of specific women by Luke as companions of Jesus and the Twelve in 8:2–3:

> And there were certain women who had been healed from evil spirits and debilities—Mary, called Magdalene, from whom he had cast out seven spirits, and Joanna the wife of Chuza (Herod's steward) and Susanna, and many others who served them out of their own resources.

What is of interest about this group, as Carla Ricci observes, is that these women appear to be "autonomous . . . , do not *belong* to male leaders of the group, [and] therefore have a direct relationship to Jesus outside the usual ones of clan, parental group or the structure of family relationships dominated by males."[4] Joanna, whose husband is mentioned along with his official function at the court, apparently acts independently of him, and it does not seem as though she has left him, as the married or engaged Christian heroines of the later Apocryphal Acts of the Apostles invariably do, because she is still called his wife. Moreover, she and Susanna and "many other" women are acting as patronesses of the group, supporting it out of their own "resources" (*hyparchonta*). In Luke's Gospel, these women from Galilee, among other women, follow Jesus to his crucifixion, and they alone note where he is buried (Luke 23:27–30, 49, 55–56). Luke also mentions Mary Magdalene and Joanna, with "Mary the mother of James," as members of this group; they are the first to discover the empty tomb (Luke 24:10).

Matthew's account of the Passion also mentions the women who had followed Jesus from Galilee and had "served" him, including Mary Magdalene, Mary the mother of James and Joseph, and the woman Matthew calls "the mother of the sons of Zebedee" (Matt. 27:55). Matthew incorporates the appearance of the angel at the empty tomb and a resurrection appearance by Jesus to the two Marys (Matt. 27:61; 28:1–10). Mark's account also includes the women who followed Jesus from Galilee and "provided" for him, naming Mary Magdalene, Mary "the mother of James the younger and of Joses," and Salome (cf. *Gospel of Thomas* 61), together with women from Jerusalem (Mark 15:40–41). The three named women are the ones who discover the empty tomb (Mark 16:1–8), while in the longer ending of Mark, Jesus appears and speaks to Mary Magdalene (Mark 16:9–11; cf. John 20:11–18). In the Gospel of John (19:25), the passion narrative includes among the women standing near the cross Jesus' mother, his aunt, "Mary the wife of Clopas," and Mary Magdalene, who is the only female character to appear consistently in all four canonical Gospels.[5] Found only in John, however, is the discovery of the empty tomb by Mary Magdalene (John 20:1–2) and an extensive narrative of the appearance of the resurrected Jesus to her (20:11–18). In chapter 11 is an account of Jesus' relationship with Mary and Martha of Bethany and their brother, Lazarus, whom Jesus raises from the dead. John says that Jesus "loved Martha and her sister and Lazarus" (11:5) and even identifies Bethany as the "village of Mary and her sister Martha" (11:1). After the resurrection of Lazarus by Jesus, Martha and Mary give a dinner, at which Martha serves and Mary anoints Jesus' feet with perfume costing the great sum of three hundred denarii, and wipes them with her hair, in an act both of service and of recognition of his death (John 12:1–3; cf. Mark 14:3–9; Matt. 26:6–13, in which the woman is unnamed; Luke 7:36–50, in which she is a "sinner").[6]

We may also count among prominent women in the Gospel of John the Samaritan woman, who meets Jesus at Jacob's well, is his dialogue partner in a revelatory discourse, and creates believers from the Samaritans with her testimony (John 4:7–30, 39–42). Thus in the canonical Gospels, as well as in the noncanonical gospels, in which Mary Magdalene and Salome also play prominent roles, several women are mentioned specifically as being followers of Jesus and as supporting him and the group, both on the road (Joanna, Susanna, Mary the mother of James, the mother of the sons of Zebedee, Mary the wife of Clopas, Mary of Nazareth) and in the towns (Mary and Martha of Bethany). Only in two cases are these women mentioned specifically as being someone's wife (Joanna, wife of Chuza; Mary, wife of Clopas) and in three cases as someone's mother (Mary, Jesus' mother; Mary, the mother of James and Joses or Joseph, who may possibly be the same person; and the mother of the sons of Zebedee). The householders Mary and Martha appear to be unmarried and heads of their own establishment (rather than their brother), and neither Mary Magdalene, Susanna, nor Salome is associated with a spouse. The Samaritan woman, who does not become one of the group following Jesus on the road, has had five "husbands" and is living with a sixth man who is not her husband (John 4:16–18). Of the male apostles, only Peter is mentioned as married, since he brings Jesus to his house to heal his mother-in-law of a fever, but that is early in the formation of the group around Jesus, and it is the mother-in-law who "serves" the group, the wife's presence being left out of the account (Mark 1:29–31; Matt. 4:23–25; Luke 4:42–44; cf., however, 1 Cor. 9:12).

In the Acts of the Apostles, Luke mentions that among the group in Jerusalem that devoted itself to prayer were "some women," including Jesus' mother Mary (Acts 1:14). Sapphira and her conniving husband Ananias are also members of this group until their deaths as a result of Peter's curse against them for withholding money (Acts 4:32; 5:1–11). Women as well as men belong to the group of believers in Jerusalem persecuted by Saul (later known as Paul) of Tarsus (Acts 8:3) and to the converts made by Philip from the followers of Simon in Samaria (Acts 8:12). "Widows" made up both a category for charitable support (6:1) and a group that did charitable work within the churches, among whom is specifically mentioned Tabitha (Dorcas) of Joppa (9: 36–43). Mary, the mother of John (Mark), is the owner of a house where Peter appears after his imprisonment under Herod Agrippa (12:12). Although women are not mentioned among the "prophets and teachers" of the congregation at Antioch, the preacher Philip has four unmarried (*parthenoi*, virgin) daughters who have the prophetic charisma (21:9), and Priscilla (or Prisca) of Corinth, in the business of tentmaking with her husband, Aquila, not only supports with him a congregation in their house (1 Cor. 16:9), but also houses their coworker Paul, makes a missionary journey with him and Aquila (Acts 18:1–5, 18), and works with her husband in explaining "more accurately" the "Way" to the charismatic preacher Apollos (18:26). Prominent female supporters and converts of

Paul include several of the "first women" of the synagogue in Thessalonica (17:4); Damaris, one of the few Athenians who is converted by Paul's Areopagus sermon (17:34); and a dealer in luxury goods, Lydia of Thyatira, a member of the "synagogue" of women in Philippi, who opens her house to Paul and Silas (16:13–15). Of these women, only Sapphira and Priscilla are specifically mentioned as having husbands, who are also presumably their business partners.

In defense of his apostolic status to the congregation in Corinth, Paul claims for himself the authority, among other privileges, to be accompanied on his travels by a "sister-wife" (*adelphe gynaika*), which can be translated as "a co-believer (sister) as a wife" (1 Cor. 9:4), perhaps along the model of the Corinthian husband-wife apostolic team of Prisca and Aquila (Rom. 16:3). Yet he renounces this privilege, although Jesus' brothers and Peter avail themselves of it (1 Cor. 9:12, 15; cf. 1 Cor. 7:7). Other possible male-female teams mentioned in the greetings appended to Paul's letter to the Roman congregation include Andronicus and Junia, "first among the apostles" (Rom. 16:7), and Nereus and his "sister," who may be his wife (Rom. 16:15). Apphia, mentioned among the three named addressees of the letter to Philemon as Paul's "sister" in the faith, may be the companion (wife? sister?) of either Philemon or Archippus of Colossae, but it is by no means certain that she has any marital relation with either. She may simply be one of the three leading members of the congregation in Philemon's house (Philemon 2).

Women named by Paul, like named men, are likely to be so because of their prominence within a congregation, their ministry, or their patronage of Paul. Among these is Chloe, whose "people" ("those belonging to Chloe") have reported the bad news of factionalism at Corinth to Paul (1 Cor. 1:11). Chloe's exact status is mysterious to us but apparently not to that congregation, who knows exactly who she is, most probably a householder. A list of such women in Romans 16 is headed by Phoebe, a *diakonos* from the congregation of Cenchreae (near Corinth), whom Paul commends to the beneficence of the Roman congregation, since she has herself been a "benefactor" or "patron" (*prostatis*) of many others, including himself (Rom. 16:1–2). Other named individual women (besides the already-mentioned Prisca and Junia) are Mary, who has "toiled much" in the Roman congregation; Tryphaena and Tryphosa, "toilers in the Lord"; the "beloved" Persis, who also has "toiled much in the Lord"; and Julia. Others are described according to familial relationships: Rufus's mother ("a mother to me also") and the previously mentioned sister (wife?) of Nereus.[7]

It is not unusual, therefore, though it later became so, for women of varying degrees of marital status to be involved in various ways in nascent Christian groups. The extensive research of Bernadette Brooten and Ross S. Kraemer, for example, has shown that Jewish women in the early centuries of the Common Era were prominent as patrons, benefactors, and leaders in the synagogues both in Palestine and the Diaspora, and not simply by virtue of being married to eminent men.[8] Among new or reformed philosophical movements like that of the Cynics, women were included as companions in study, in writing, and in adopting the itinerant lifestyle as a method of social reform. This does not mean, except perhaps in the latter instance, that full gender equality and sexual freedom can be presupposed.

Perhaps it is in the context of social reform that the question of female sexuality in formative Christianity needs to be addressed. The earliest written canonical Gospel, Mark, which is probably the first also to contain mention of Jesus' rejection of biological family ties (Mark 3:31–35), emphasizes, through its reliance on healing miracles and exorcisms, Jesus' challenge to the existing social situation, which is described as one of "sickness" (2:16–17). In Mark's view, the commandments of God are not the problem—the problem lies in their interpretation by the "human tradition" of "the elders," represented by the scribes and Pharisees (7:1–13). Therefore, when the latter ask Jesus whether he thinks it is permissible for a man to divorce his wife, he draws a careful distinction between what Moses commanded and what God intended. Moses allows divorce with the *get*, the certificate whereby a man can send away his wife for anything "objectionable" (Deut. 24:1–4; Mark 10:2–4), which Jesus calls evidence of "hardness of heart" (Mark 10:5). Instead, he says, God's commandment, as well as the intent of his creation of male and female, is the essential indissolubility of the sexual union of a man with a woman (Mark 10:6–9; Gen. 1:27; 2:24; cf. Matt. 19:3–8). He further tells his disciples that once a man divorces his wife and a woman divorces her husband, remarriage is adultery against the divorced partner (Mark 10:10–12), and he later quotes the Seventh Commandment as one whose observance will enable one to inherit "eternal life" (10:17–19; cf. Matt. 19:18).

In Matthew's Gospel, Jesus also insists on the primacy of the Law and the Prophets over against the practices and traditions of the Pharisees (Matt. 5:17). In the Sermon on the Mount (Matthew 5—7), he quotes the Decalogue prohibition against adultery (5:27) but insists that the lustful male gaze is as culpable as the act itself (5:28). While divorce is allowed by the Mosaic law (5:31; cf. Deuteronomy 1—4), Jesus would prevent a man from divorcing his wife, "except for the reason of *porneia*" (sexual unchastity, Matt. 5:32; cf. Matt. 19:9), and any man who marries a woman who has been divorced commits adultery (*moichatai*), presumably because she has been divorced because of sexual promiscuity, either prior to the marriage (during or before the betrothal period) or during the marriage.[9] Luke's briefer version (Luke 16:18), which G. J. Wenham believes is "the earliest and most demonstrably authentic form of Jesus' *logia* on divorce,"[10] conflates the Matthean saying, that men who marry divorced women commit adultery, with the Markan version, that a man who divorces his wife to marry another woman commits adultery. In neither Matthew's nor Luke's version is the woman the active partner in divorce or remarriage. Both Wenham and Will Deming note that these sayings on adultery and divorce are "new" and differ from the strictures in the Mosaic law in that they place a greater emphasis on male sexual responsibility, to the extent that a husband can commit adultery against his wife and may even *compel* his wife to commit adultery when he divorces her.[11] Deming in particular sees the Markan and Matthean versions sharing with developing Jewish tannaitic traditions (70–200 C.E.) a common concern with making legitimate male sexual desire within the bounds of marriage.[12] Consequently the man is even more responsible, since he must control his own sex drive as well as the sexual behavior of his wife.

The *Gospel of Thomas*, while not included in the New Testament canon, probably because of its advocacy of the extreme asceticism and secret revelation that have been attributed to Gnostic Christianity, nevertheless contains many sayings attributed to Jesus that may in fact date from a relatively early period of Christianity. According to Pheme Perkins, the *Gospel of Thomas* is "ambiguous" toward women's experience, including their sexuality.[13] Women must "become" male, but this is in order that all may be "living spirits" (*Gospel of Thomas* 114). Like the canonical Synoptic Gospels, *Thomas* devalues biological parenthood, earthly families, and indeed sexual intercourse of any kind. "Blessed are the solitary (or single, *monachoi*) and the elect," says Jesus (*Gospel of Thomas* 49; cf. *Gospel of Thomas* 75). The body itself and all concerns belonging to it, including intercourse and procreation, are scorned as material and "dead" (*Gospel of Thomas* 29; 56; 80; 87; 112).

Even with the exclusion of the *Gospel of Thomas*, marriage, together with sexual desire and reproduction, remains problematic within the canonical Gospels. In the three Synoptic Gospels, Jesus' knowledge and interpretation of the scriptures is tested by the Sadducees, a group of his opponents associated with the Second Temple priesthood who also happen to be opposed to the Pharisees on the subject of resurrection. Not finding resurrection in the Torah, the Sadducees reject it as an element of belief (Mark 12:18–27; Matt. 22:23–28; Luke 20:27–40). The challenge they propose, which is actually a mockery of the very idea of resurrection, revolves around the applicability of the law of levirate marriage (cf. Deut. 25:5–10; Genesis 38; Ruth 4). The case they choose is the hypothetical instance of a woman who is the wife of seven brothers, each of whom dies childless, followed (understandably!) by the still-childless woman herself. The question is, Whose wife will she be in the resurrection? Jesus' reply, alike in all three versions, separates the question of marital status in the resurrection from that of the idea of resurrection itself, accusing his opponents both of ignorance of the scriptures (Ex. 3:6) and of the power of God. In the present age, men marry and women are given in marriage, but in the next, they are "like angels in heaven." In Luke's version, "those who belong to this age" are differentiated from "those who are considered worthy of a place in that age," who are "children of the resurrection" and "children of God" (= angels; Luke 20:34–36, NRSV). The end of the present age will also be especially difficult for women who are pregnant and nursing children (Mark 13:17; Matt. 24:19; Luke 21:23); it will be "as in the days of Noah," with marrying and being given in marriage, eating and drinking, right up to the time of the Flood (Luke 17:27). Of the two in bed, one will be taken and the other left (Luke 17:34; cf. *Gospel of Thomas* 61).

This early Christian perception of marriage, sexual relations, and reproduction, as standing on an uneasy divide between the present (corrupt) age and the transformation of humanity back to its original splendor in the age to come, is further intensified in the Gospel of John, in which believers, like Jesus himself, undergo a spiritual birth that is differentiated from the fleshly one that is the result of "the desire of the flesh" and "the desire of a man" (John 3:6; 1:12–13). In this respect, John goes further than Matthew and Luke, who emphasize Jesus' miraculous birth from a virgin (*parthenos*) through a spiritual intercourse that is like that of YHWH and Israel, except that nearly all allusions to sexual contact are expunged from it, perhaps for apologetic purposes, against the suggestion that Jesus' birth was illegitimate (Matt. 1:18–25; Luke 1:26–38).[14] Luke's idea of the "power" of the "highest one" overshadowing and "coming upon" Mary, the submissive "slave-girl" (*doule*), the "most favored" one that the *kyrios* (master) has visited (Luke 1:35, 38, 28), has echoes of Greco-Roman stories of divine-human intercourse and of the sexual accessibility of a slave woman to a master (Ex. 21:7–11; Deut. 15:12, 17).[15] The emphasis here, however, as in Matthew, is on Mary's lack of sexual experience or aggressiveness, together with a corresponding denial to Joseph of any role in the biological parentage of Jesus. Matthew's Gospel, as might be expected of one so concerned with the Law and the Prophets, understands Mary's sexual situation both in terms of the women of Israel's past, who seemed to be sexual transgressors but were proven acceptable by God (Tamar, Rahab, Ruth, Bathsheba; Matt. 1:3, 5, 6), and in terms of the righteousness of Joseph under the law covering the case of a betrothed woman's suspected infidelity.[16] But here again the woman's sexual transgression only appears to be such, and although Joseph as husband has divine permission to "take Mary as his wife" (Matt. 1:20, 24), Matthew shows him as understanding this commandment not to include sexual rights, since he avoids marital relations with her until the birth of Jesus (1:25). Later versions of this story, such as the second-century *Protevangelium of James*, which reflects the increasingly ascetic tendencies within Christianity of all varieties, extended and reinforced both Mary's virginity and Joseph's lack of marital intercourse with her, further "protecting" Jesus from any taint of biological sex and hence of fallible flesh. Paul, on the other hand, with his characteristic lack of concern for Jesus' earthly life prior to the crucifixion, writes merely that Jesus was "born of the seed of David according to the flesh," but became "the son of God in power according to the spirit of holiness by resurrection from the dead" (Rom. 1:4).

Paul's training in the study of the Torah was initially Pharisaic (Phil. 3:4–6), and he appears to share the view of the Tannaim that marital relations restrain the lawlessness of desire (1 Thess. 4:3–8; 1 Cor. 7:2, 5–6, 9, 36–37). But Paul also partakes of the emerging Christian view that sexual relations were best avoided in light of the coming transformation of the world (1 Cor. 7:26–35). In 1 Corinthians 7, the longest passage on sexual relations serving as a reply to the Corinthian congregation's questions on the topic, Paul tries to achieve a balance between social and sexual relationships "in this world" or in the present age, whose *schema* (shape, form) is already changing (1 Cor. 7:31; cf. 1 Cor. 5:9–10), and those within the community "in Christ" that is preparing itself for the changed world. Paul wishes to reinforce the idea of a Christian congregation as an integral unit by continually employing the metaphor of a body that is composed of many members (1 Cor. 6:15; 12:12–27; cf. Rom. 12:4–8). This "body," however, like the individual human body, is not yet the "spiritual" one that it will become in the resurrection life (15:35–49), and it is still responsive to the desires of the flesh (*sarx;* cf. Rom. 7:5, 14).[17] Within this living "body" of Christ there are also, as in the present human body, sex organs ("the more shameful parts") and sexual feeling, which cannot be ignored and need to be treated respectfully (1 Cor. 12:23–24). Therefore, *porneia* ("unchastity") is to be shunned (6:18), and unchaste (*pornoi*) members of the community are to be avoided (5:9–11). Paul even gives examples of the kind of unchastity to be excluded from the Christian community: male patronage of prostitutes (6:13–20) and the even more serious crime of a member of the congregation having intercourse with his father's wife (5:1–8).[18] While the latter would have been forbidden by the law of Moses (Lev. 18:7–8), the former was not forbidden, although Paul considers it to be a kind of adultery or at least a prohibited "marriage" (1 Cor. 6:16). Conscious that he has little to pronounce on marriage from the tradition of Jesus' teaching (7:6, 25) except for the restrictions surrounding divorce and remarriage (7:10–11), Paul seems to regard it as necessary only to prevent *porneia* (7:2, 5; cf. 1 Thess. 4:3–6) and hence the only acceptable way to give way to the desires of the flesh.[19] Elsewhere, he emphatically declares that "the unchaste and adulterers," along with others he deems to be transgressors of acceptable sexual behavior, will not have a share in the kingdom of God (6:9–10; cf. Gal. 5:19; Rom. 1:26–27).

Although Paul's attitude toward women in his congregations has frequently been both vilified and defended,[20] it must be said that Paul is far more concerned with male sexual transgression than with female, perhaps because his advice restricts even what was considered to be permissible sexual behavior under the law of Moses, like male intercourse with prostitutes or with other women not "belonging to" another male (cf. 1 Cor. 6:15; 7:8–9, 36–38), while it remains permissive with respect to circumcision, the way in which Jewish males normally dedicated their sexual power to God.[21] Paul appears to advocate mutuality in marital sexual relations (1 Cor. 7:4–5, 12–16; 1 Thess. 4:6), and considers women free either to remain unmarried (as virgins or widows, 1 Cor. 7:8, 25–28) or to remarry once a husband is dead, although he states that he believes the widowed state is "more blessed" (1 Cor. 7:39–40; cf. Rom. 7:2–3). He also appears to have accepted widows and married and unmarried women as coworkers both in missionary work and in congregations (cf. Romans 16). For Paul, women, like men, may consider themselves free from the legitimate concerns of marriage only in order to devote themselves to "the Lord," rather than to indulge in sexual license (1 Cor. 7:32–35), although female adultery is not really an issue for him. What appears to be an issue, however, is his understanding of the "order" of women in creation and their "orderly" behavior in worship (1 Cor. 11:2–16).

"Order" is very important to Paul, both as a manifestation of the divine in the cosmic order and as harmony and stability within the "orders" existing in a congregation. In Romans 1:18–32, Paul describes the natural order of the universe created by one invisible deity as including the proper way to worship (avoid idolatry) and the ability to discern the proper sexual desires and relations in the world (heterosexual). In his mind, "knowledge" and sexuality are connected, as they are in the Tanakh, Paul's scripture. It is a lack of knowledge or improper knowledge of the divine that causes people's "senseless" and "debased" minds to lead them into a false sexual "knowledge" of each other, men exchanging "natural" intercourse with women for that with men, and women burning with passion for women (Rom. 1:26–27). But, while he clearly sees homosexual relations, if not homoerotic attraction, as "a violation of God's intention for creation,"[22] it is equally obvious that these are not the only sexual "errors" that can be committed by human beings (cf. Rom. 2:22). Sexual impropriety is one of many vices, and for Paul, as for the prophets, the greatest mistake and gravest sin is idolatry. Further, Paul does not seem to place any greater responsibility for transgression on either gender. Rather, he bases his idea of the appropriate expression of desire in human relationships here, as elsewhere, on his understanding of the creation narrative in Genesis, especially Genesis 1:27 ("Male and female he created them") and Genesis 2:24 ("Therefore a man will leave his father and mother and cling to his wife and the two shall become one flesh," 1 Cor. 6:15–16; 7:10–11; 11:7–9).

Paul also uses this concept of the order of creation in his comments on appropriate and inappropriate forms of worship in 1 Corinthians 11:2–16, where he once again perceives a violation of the created order when, during ecstatic "prophesying," married women cast off their head coverings, the signs of their "place" in creation (Gen. 2:21–23; 3:17). As Paul and his contemporaries described prophecy, or possession by the spirit, it was "conceived in terms redolent of sexual intercourse," the penetration of a body, the female being the more penetrable body and therefore symbolically "covered" against invasion by an illegitimate possessor.[23] Whatever else might be said about this passage, female sexuality in it threatens to destroy the proper order, as the married women prophets symbolically throw off their husband's control (the head covering as *exousia*, 1 Cor. 11:10) and expose themselves to the lustful gaze of and possible spiritual penetration by the "angels."[24] These "angels," the "sons of God" of Genesis 6:1–4, who fell in love with human women, appear in Jewish pseudepigraphical literature as rampantly lustful "Watchers" who taught the wiles of seduction to women, and whose intercourse with them resulted in "human evil and misfortune" (*Genesis Apocryphon; Testament of Reuben* 5:4–6).[25] Thus, the Corinthian women prophets could be "possessed" by spirits other than the appropriate one—Christ—who in the order of creation is "over" the woman in his place as head of her husband and below God. They would be opening themselves up to the possibility of committing a kind of "spiritual adultery," both against Christ and against their husbands.[26] The fact that Paul imposes this restriction on the spirit, despite endorsing spiritual gifts (14:1–5) and apparently sharing the early Christian belief that the spirit of the Lord will be "poured out" on all in the "latter days" (Acts 2:17–18; cf. Gal. 3:27–28), indicates that the "place" of women, particularly of sexually active (married) women within the borders of the Christian community against "the world," is, in Paul's view, still uncertain.

Paul has little to say elsewhere about women's sexuality, male control of it, or indeed of the control of married women by their husbands, unless we accept as genuine his letters to the Ephesians and the first and second letters to Timothy, a position that is rejected by most contemporary interpreters of Paul.[27] These pseudepigraphical epistles, probably written in the first part of the second century, expand Paul's teaching, intended for Christians on the margins of the present age, to apply to a more extended "present age" than Paul himself imagined, one that is complicated by the continuing need for the Christian communities and the "world" to come to some kind of rapprochement. Paul had already modified his own stance, from one of constant preparation for the imminent return of Christ, in which living and dead would be literally snatched up into the kingdom of heaven (1 Thess. 4:16–17) and in which total separation between believers in Christ and nonbelievers had to be maintained (2 Cor. 6:14–7:1), to one in which believers could not be taken "out of this world" but needed to concentrate on relations within the believing community itself (1 Cor. 5:9–13), and perhaps finally to one in which the existing political order was believed somehow to be a creation of God (Rom. 13:1–7).

PURE BRIDES, OLD WIVES, AND
LITTLE WOMEN IN POST-PAULINE CHRISTIANITY

The order and stability advocated by Paul within Christian congregations is already reflected in one of the "second generation" of Pauline letters, the epistle to the Ephesians, perhaps written about the end of the first century C.E., in which the author, purportedly Paul, warns his congregation to live "in humility and meekness," not like foolish children, "carried about by every wind of teaching" (Eph. 4:2, 14, NRSV; cf. Col. 3:12–13).[28] The church is now conceived of as a universal entity, rather than a particular congregation, the cosmic "body" of which Christ is the "head" (Eph. 1:22–23; 3:6; 4:4, 15–16; 5:29–31). The relationship between Christ and his "body," the church, is described in a long section (Eph. 5:22–33) as one between a husband and a wife, picking up the prophetic metaphor for the relationship between YHWH and Israel. Here, however, the weight of the metaphor falls upon the actual human relationships in marriage: a wife is to have a relationship to her husband as to "the Lord" (*kyrios*, which also means master). Since her husband is her head, as Christ is the head of the church, his "body," just as that body is "stationed under" Christ (*hypotasso* conveys a kind of military metaphor), so also the wife's station is under that of her husband "in everything" (Eph. 5:22–24; cf. Col. 3:18). Husbands are to love their wives as Christ loves the church, "washing her" with the water of the word to present her to himself "without stain or wrinkle, pure and blameless" (Eph. 5:25–26). This marital language recalls that of Paul's defense against the trickery of the super apostles in Corinth, which he calls the serpent that deludes the Eve-congregation and prevents Paul from giving it in marriage as a "pure virgin" to her one husband, Christ (2 Cor. 11:2–3), a metaphor that he himself describes as part of his "foolishness" or "lack of wit" (*aphrosyne*).

More disturbingly, however, the language of this passage in Ephesians recalls the rescue, bathing, and adorning of Jerusalem/Judah, the "bloody bride" of Ezekiel 16:9, without the explicitly sexual imagery, but with the same image of the bride as passive object—here, all body or "flesh" (*sarx*)— of her husband's self-love (Eph. 5:28–29). The "mystery" of marriage, the union of a man and a woman into one flesh, with reference to Genesis 2:24, describes the "great mystery" of Christ's union with the church (Eph. 5:31–32), but the husband is to love his wife, while the wife is to "fear" (revere) her husband (v. 33) and we are left with the metaphorical equation of church = body (flesh) = passive = wife, and Christ = head (ruling) = actively caring = husband.

We are also reminded that in Ephesians "flesh" is the locus of passions, desires, the realm of the senses that makes those who are disobedient to authority the "children of wrath" (2:1–3). The flesh is also antithetical to the enlightened minds who do not give themselves over to the "business of impurity" (4:17–19), the impurity from which the pure wife (body) of Christ has been washed. We are thus left with the disturbing impression that the wayward flesh that is the wife must be "care"-fully controlled by her head-husband to create a stable household in which the stability of the church is mirrored. Moreover, other members of the *oikos* (household), children and slaves, especially the latter, must also contribute to its stability by knowing their place within it and obeying its head as they would Christ, while the parent/master should behave as Christ behaves toward the church (6:1–9; Col. 3:20–4:1). However, despite its advocacy for the adoption of contemporaneous patriarchal "pagan and Jewish" philosophical models of "good household management" for the church in the Deutero-Pauline epistles,[29] the end of the letter to the church at Colossae sends greetings to "Nympha and the congregation in her house" (Col. 4:15), an indication of the fact that women still act as heads of households and churches in Christian communities.

The blurring of the boundaries between "the world" and the community "in Christ" is most obvious in the pastoral epistles, where instructions are given for the behavior of categories of Christians, presumably in the hope that they may contribute to a quiet, peaceful, and dignified life (1 Tim. 2:2; Titus 3:1–2), one that avoids conflict with the "outside" pagan authorities, and one that minimizes conflict within.[30] This behavior is reinforced by carefully constructed qualifications for various "offices," all of which contribute to a hierarchical order. The *episkopos*, or overseer of a congregation, must be a married male householder, whose management of his *oikia*, including wife, servants, and children, the latter especially, is a direct indication of his care for "God's church" (1 Tim. 3:1–7; cf. Titus 1:5–9). In the letter to Titus, the *episkopos* is called "God's household steward" (*oikonomos*; Titus 1:7). *Diakonoi*, the "ministers" or "servers" in the congregation, both male and female, are also distinguished by their serious conduct, by marrying only once, and by managing their children and households well (1 Tim. 3:8–13). Indeed, the church itself is imagined as "God's household" (3:15), those within it not as members of one body but as household utensils with different uses (2 Tim. 2:20–21). Timothy is to imagine himself treating an older man as a father, younger men as brothers, older women as mothers, and younger women as sisters, the latter "in total purity," lest anyone should interpret "sister" as a term in the erotic vocabulary of love poetry (1 Tim. 5:1–2). Elders (*presbyteres*) function as "rulers" and as preachers and teachers worthy of great honor, but it is not clear whether they are only men, as 5:1–2 seems to imply, or include both men and women (5:17). Slaves are to treat their masters as "worthy of all honor" (6:1–2), to be submissive and not to talk back or steal (Titus 2:9–10).

Women mentioned by name in the pastoral epistles are Prisca (with her husband Aquila) in the list of greetings at the end of 2 Timothy (4:19), perhaps to give a flavor of authenticity to this pseudonymous work, and Timothy's grandmother Lois and mother Eunice (2 Tim. 1:5), who preceded Timothy "in the faith." The name of Claudia is also included in the greetings list in 2 Timothy 4:21, together with that of Linus, with whom she may or may not be coupled. In general, however, the pastorals advocate the restriction of women's activities within the church and in public, especially for those who are married or of marriageable age. Extending Paul's advice to the prophetic women in Corinth to keep their head coverings on as an acknowledgment of their husbands' authority (1 Cor. 11:2–16), the author of Timothy, who has no special advice for men's appearance when praying, has very specific advice for women (or wives; Gk., *gynaikas*).[31] They are to dress themselves with "shame" (modesty) and "self-control," rather than in immodest or expensive clothing with braided (and perhaps uncovered) hair or gold or pearl ornaments (1 Tim. 2:8–9; cf. 1 Peter 3:3–5 for similar advice from a non-Pauline source).[32] But unlike Paul's own opinion on marriage, which is that it is a brake on *porneia*, primarily for men (1 Cor. 7:1–2), and that it is one of the anxieties of this world, creating disorder and detracting from devotion to the Lord (7:31–35), the pastorals extol marriage not only as an important element distinguishing orthodox from heterodox Christianity (1 Tim. 4:3), but as part of the created order and that which creates the proper order within society, which in the Deutero-Pauline and pastoral epistles definitely includes children. In the first letter to Timothy, potential wives are distinguished from the "true" widows, who are those over sixty with no family support, who have had only one husband and raised children, and live for God rather than "living lewdly" (1 Tim. 2:3–10). Widows of marriageable age are characterized as "behaving wantonly" toward Christ if they desire to remarry, but also as needing to be restrained by marriage from going from house to house and engaging in conversations with others that lead to their departure from the congregation and male authority: "I wish therefore, that younger widows would marry, have children, and manage households" (1 Tim. 5:11–14). The household itself may not be enough to prevent "little (silly or immature) women," mired as they are in their sins and led by their "many passions," from being taken captive by the teaching of those 1 Timothy opposes, but who never, despite constant instruction, are able to come to "knowledge of the truth" (2 Tim. 3:6–7; cf. 1 Tim. 5:15). Put in nonmisogynist terms, it may be that what these women are learning is the teaching of the Gnostics or the "spirituals," who emphasized both the androgyny of humanity and that of God, and who permitted women to have full partnership in study and worship. Or it may be that the traveling teachers include women, perhaps even older women, who have eschewed marriage (1 Tim. 4:3), and these are the ones who teach "profane old women's tales" (1 Tim. 4:7; cf. 6:20; 2 Tim. 2:16).[33] It is perhaps with the latter in mind that Titus is commanded to instruct older women to be sober and "teachers of good" to young women, who are to acquire through that instruction a loving attitude toward husbands and children, self-control, chastity, good household management, goodness, and submissiveness to their husbands, so as not to bring shame upon "the word of God" (Titus 2:3–5).

In general, the attitude toward sexuality reflected in the pastorals, as in the Deutero-Pauline epistles, is one that reflects the interests of a "householder" class, one that owns slaves and enough property to be concerned with household management and inheritance, and so is concerned with lines of descent and legitimacy of offspring. Sexual relations thus revolve around marriage and procreation. Itinerancy, including that of women, is discouraged as inimical to marriage and the creation of households (1 Tim. 4:3; 5:13; 2 Tim. 3:6–7; Titus 1:10–11). So important is reproduction that women, the deceived and transgressing descendants of their prototype, Eve, will be saved through childbearing (1 Tim. 2:15). Sexual self-control and chastity are therefore also important feminine virtues (1 Tim. 2:9, 15; Titus 2:5). Paramount, however, is the restriction of opportunities for learning or teaching nonapproved knowledge for married women and women of marriageable age. The first epistle to Timothy baldly states that an appropriately "God-fearing" woman (here, probably "wife") is to learn in silence and with total submission (1 Tim. 2:11); it sternly forbids a woman (wife) from instructing or "having full power over" (*authentein*) a man (husband), but she is instructed herself to remain "in silence" (2:12). The reason? Once again, the point of reference is the "order" of creation in Genesis 1—2, but not as in Paul's reference to the chronological creation of man first, woman second in 1 Corinthians 11:2–16. First Timothy nods to that "order," Adam first, then Eve, but places its emphasis on the entirely specious assertion that Adam was "not deceived" (by the "false" offer of knowledge by the serpent) but that "the woman" was deceived and thus "came into transgression" (1 Tim. 2:13–15). The issue, then, is not one of "the woman" seducing the man into trying to obtain the secret knowledge she possesses. If there is any hint of sexual knowledge here, the woman is the party who is seduced.[34] Even from the beginning, when a woman desires and seeks knowledge, it will inevitably be the wrong kind, that which is not "knowledge of the truth." To 1 Timothy, as to 2 Timothy and Titus, women as descendants of Eve are born heretics, and must not be allowed to develop their dangerous tendencies, so subversive of the household, both of the social realm and of the religious realm, and of male hegemony over both.[35] Women are also deprived by the pastorals of their connection with Wisdom, even with seductive Anti-Wisdom, since in this version of the story, Adam, the husband, has not been deceived and presumably remains faithful to God, another case when the metaphor does not entirely hold, dissolving itself into absurdity when we remember the rest of the story. Women who seek wisdom or knowledge, moreover, are called "silly," "idle," or "godless" and can never "come to the truth," however much they seek it. It is men in the world of the pastorals who alone possess or have control of knowledge.

CHRISTIAN WISDOM:
HEBREWS, JAMES, AND THE CATHOLIC EPISTLES

The texts of the canonical New Testament do not continue the representation of God's Wisdom as female that is found in the Tanakh and Apocrypha primarily because Christ takes her place as heavenly *Logos* (= Reason, Word; cf. John 1:1–14) and as the first creation and representative of God on earth (John 1:1–3; Col. 1:15–17; Heb. 1:1–3). Paul says quite succinctly that Christ is "the wisdom and power of God" through which the "wisdom of the world" becomes Anti-Wisdom, or Folly (1 Cor. 1:18–25), a sentiment echoed in the epistle of James, which is otherwise rather antagonistic to Paul's interpretation of the faith. James also posits two Wisdoms: one that is heavenly and is the righteousness obtained by doing good works, and one that is earthly and consists of selfishness and ambition (James 3:13–18). Thus, while the concept of a dual Wisdom, developed in Jewish wisdom literature, is retained in New Testament Christian teaching, it is not feminized. It is left to the noncanonical Gnostic literature, regarded as heretical by the orthodox writers and framers of the canon, to exploit both the duality and the femininity of Wisdom.[36]

The book of Hebrews, a second-generation Christian allegorical and typological interpretation of the Tanakh and the meaning of Christ for salvation, distances him from human birth by calling him the "reflection" of God's glory, the "imprint" of God's being (Heb. 1:3), and by comparing him to Melchizedek, the priest-king of Salem in Genesis 14:17–20, "without father, without mother, without genealogy" (Heb. 7:3, NRSV). For the writer of this text, steeped in Hellenistic Jewish philosophy, the history of salvation is a tale of faith "perfected" by the perfect Christ. In it, only two women are named: Sarah (11:11), but only as an adjunct to Abraham as an exemplar of faith, and Rahab the prostitute (11:31; cf. Judg. 2:1–21; 6:22–25). Rahab also appears with Abraham as examples of those who are justified by good works in the epistle of James (2:25), perhaps because of the Jewish legends that celebrated her as a convert, wife of Joshua and model of hospitality (cf. Matt. 1:5).[37] Without these legends, she would appear as an odd choice of role model in a text that advises all to hold marriage "honorable" and to keep the marriage bed "unstained," since *pornoi* and *moichoi* (unchaste and adulterous *men*) will be judged by God (Heb. 13:4). Once more, advice about sexual restraint is given to men, not to women, and marriage seems to be the means to restrict unruly male desire. Rahab is no more characterized by her gender or sexual activity than is Abraham, and she is spiritualized into a rather ironic model of faithful Christian conduct for both men and women.

In what has been called the wisdom-sermon of James,[38] of uncertain date but apparently written to counter an extreme interpretation of Paul's idea of "righteousness through faith alone" (James 2:14–26), the writer agrees nevertheless with the standard wisdom tradition that wisdom is from God (1:5) and with Paul (cf. 1 Cor. 1—4) that it is embodied in Christ as proper Christian teaching. James apparently believes that this teaching is a fulfillment of the "royal law," as contained in the Torah, particularly Leviticus 19:18 and the Decalogue (James 2:8–13). Transgressions of the law are the result of unfulfilled pleasures, cravings, and desires that injure others (4:1–3). In a direct address to adulterers (*moichalides*), the author chides them for their friendship (*philia*) with the world rather than with God, a God who they know from the scriptures "longs to the point of jealousy" after the spirit within them (4:4–5, NRSV), bringing to mind the image of God as the "jealous" husband of a faithless Israel (Ex. 20:5; cf. Num. 5:14; Zech. 8:2). James nevertheless does not dwell upon this particular sexual image, instead cautioning the members of the church against the pride that causes contentiousness (4:6–12), and the writer has no specific instructions about marriage itself. He does, however, draw a distinct contrast in 1:13–15 between the "God who tempts no one" and *epithymia*, or desire, which he personifies as "woman who seduces, conceives, and gives birth to destructive sinfulness, which in turn, leads to death."[39] Desire, which again is primarily envisioned as sexual and associated with a woman, is thus directly opposed to God.

The first epistle attributed to Peter, but probably belonging to the late first or early second century, is one that adopts a stance similar to that of the pastorals, that Christians are not to look like a countercultural fringe group but to both fear God and honor the emperor (1:17).[40] As in the Deutero-Pauline and pastoral letters, slaves are urged to respect and obey the masters they are "stationed under," even those who are pagan, or harsh and brutal, in order to imitate Christ (1 Peter 2:18–25). Wives are to accept their place under a husband's authority, following the example of Sarah, who eschewed worldly adornment for obedience to Abraham, whom she called "master" (*kyrios* = *ba'al*; 3:1–6). Even pagan husbands are to receive respect, because they may be won over by their wives' "purity and deference" (3:2). Christian husbands in their turn are to give honor to "the weaker womanly vessel" (3:7) so that their own prayers will be answered. In general, the letter advises social and sexual passivity and patient endurance on the part of those who are the "inferior" members of an already marginalized group. Making the most of an impossible situation, Christian slaves under pagan masters and Christian wives under pagan husbands are to hope that their refusal to subvert widely accepted social norms will persuade those in authority that to be Christian is not to be inimical to cultural stability.[41]

The concerns of 2 Peter and Jude, which also belong to the group of catholic (universal) epistles, exhibit the same universalizing tendency by inveighing against "false prophets" and "false teachers," those whom they regard as opponents of orthodox "truth" and the authority of apostolic teachers like Paul (2 Peter 3:15–16). The attack on their opponents in both includes accusations of sexual immorality, typical of inter- and inner-religious conflicts in antiquity, but of a rather vague and general nature. Second Peter accuses the "pseudo-prophets" and "pseudo-teachers," who may be Gnostics (2 Peter 1:16) of failure to follow authority in interpreting scripture, as in other things (1:19–21), and especially of "indulging their flesh in depraved lust" in their contempt for authority (2:10, NRSV), enticing others into error through appeal to "licentious desires of the flesh" (2:18, NRSV). They have "eyes filled with adultery, that cannot cease from sin" (2:14). Jude (vv. 4–16) likewise vilifies his opponents as "dreamers" who are guilty of three things: corrupting the flesh, having contempt for authority, and slandering reputations. The appearance of these dissenters, following their "lust for their own ungodly affairs," is regarded as a predicted sign of the end (v. 17). They are to be shunned or, if not too far gone, saved by the unwavering faithful (vv. 20–23), who are themselves to be "kept from falling" (*aptaistous*) into heresy by Christ. Marie-Eloise Rosenblatt comments that the adjective *aptaistos* has distinct sexual connotations, deriving from the father's preservation of his daughter's virginity for marriage, and here applied to the "blameless moral behavior of the community" (Eph. 5:27; Rev. 21:1), as opposed to the sexual immorality of the dissenters.[42]

In all of these writings, each of which gives advice in the form of a letter, sexual misbehavior is a metaphor for lack of respect for authority (*asebeia*), which, like adultery, threatens the stability of the church and a society that are based on a hierarchical structure that assumes increasingly authoritative "heads" over an undifferentiated "body" of those whose obedience needs to be reinforced. Slaves, wives, and the "body" of the church are thus in the same position, "stationed under" the appropriate "heads"—masters, husbands, Christ. Yet the concern in the catholic epistles seems not to be as much with female sexual unruliness as with males who disobey orthodox authority and thus commit a kind of adultery with the "property" of Christ, the bridal church. Women's sexuality does not appear to be an area of great concern, as married women and slaves are assumed to be under "control," and in these epistles the only female "state" that is addressed is that of heterosexual marriage. The "invasion" of the body of Christ by the lustful and lawless "false teachers," therefore, is like a rape or a seduction of the pure bride of Christ and not a betrayal of Christ by that body, which is even more sexless and passive than the "good" figure of Wisdom. "Church," already designated as a female figure and "pure virgin" by Paul (2 Cor. 11:1–3) and his followers (Eph. 5:25–33), continues to be addressed as female (1 Peter 5:13), even in the highly spiritual second letter of John (2:1: "To the elect lady and her children"), and finally appears as a full-blown character as the "Bride" opposed to the pagan "Whore" in the apocalyptic book of Revelation (Rev. 18:9, 21–24; 19:9; 21:2, 9).

6

Sinners, Adulteresses, Whores, and Brides

Imagining Women in the Gospels and Revelation

If he were a prophet, he would have known who and what sort of woman it is who is touching him—that she is a sinner. (Luke 7:39)

Sir, I perceive that you are a prophet. (John 4:19)

STRANGE ACTS AND OUTLAWS

One of the stranger stories shared by all four canonical Gospels is that of a woman who comes up to Jesus when he is a dinner guest and uses a costly ointment to anoint him. The details of the story vary in significant ways particular to the individual Gospels, but it has been regarded by Christians familiar with the tradition and not the different versions as a story illustrating the forgiving love of Jesus for the outcast. They believe that this woman is a prostitute, often identified with Mary of Magdala,[1] although in only one of the versions is she named, and that is as the decidedly righteous and prominent householder Mary of Bethany (John 12:3).

In the Gospel of Mark, whose account is first chronologically , the events presaging the coming of the "Son of Man" and the transformation of the present *kosmos* have just been cataloged (chapter 13). Two days before Passover, Jesus is dining in Bethany "in the house of Simon the leper," an admittedly unusual choice of venue because of the ritual and social impurity caused by the presence of lepers in some circles (cf. Lev. 13:9–17, 45–46). A woman breaks open a perfume jar containing a "very costly" (*poluteles*) ointment and pours it on his head (Mark 14:3; cf. Ps. 23:5). Those present complain about the foolish waste committed by the woman's extravagant gesture, because the unguent could have been sold at a price of more than three hundred denarii (about a year's salary) and the money given to the poor (14:4–5). Jesus tells her critics, "Leave her alone," and not to berate her, because she has done "a good/beautiful deed" (*kalon ergon*; 14:6). Those at dinner have the ability to do similar good deeds (*kala erga*; *mitzvoth*) for the poor, who are always with them, but she did what she could, the good deed of anointing his body for burial (14:6–8; cf. 16:1; Deut. 15:11).[2] This deed will be her "memorial" as a part of the gospel (14:9). As Elisabeth Schüssler Fiorenza and Mary Ann Tolbert point out, the anointing of the head is an old symbol of the recognition of "God's anointed one," the *christos* or *mashiach*, and in Mark's Gospel, having an un-known and silent woman perform this prophetic gesture, particularly after the prophecies about the coming of the ruler of Israel, is an appropriate but, in Schüssler Fiorenza's words, "politically dangerous" act.[3] The woman has no difficulty understanding that Jesus is going to die, as do the disciples and the "crowd," who have received three fairly explicit predictions of his death. Tolbert observes that this "lavishly loving act," regardless of its cost, con-trasts starkly with the subsequent action of Judas Iscariot, "one of the twelve," the inner circle, who immediately after the dinner promises to be-tray Jesus for money.[4]

Matthew's version of the story (Matt. 26:6–13) offers no significant dif-ferences from Mark's. The most significant differences from the story as told in Mark come in Luke and John. Luke puts the incident prior to Jesus' journey to Jerusalem, as an illustration of the inability of "this generation," even the interpreters of the law, to understand either John the Baptist or Jesus as messengers of heavenly Wisdom (7:29–35).[5] Luke places the din-ner in the house of Simon, who is here a Pharisee rather than a leper, and defines the still-unnamed woman as one "from the city" who is "a sinner" (*hamartolos*; 7:37, 39). Instead of anointing Jesus' head with the ointment, the woman, who weeps but does not speak and remains unnamed, bathes his feet with the ointment and her tears, and wipes them with her hair (7:38). This extravagant and self-abasing gesture does not bring forth the criticism of the woman for "wasting" the ointment, but instead provokes criticism of Jesus, since his host is making inaudible strictures against the supposed "prophet" for not knowing that a sinful woman is touching him (7:39). Jesus of course *is* a prophet and therefore knows what Simon is thinking. As is typical of Jesus in Luke, he tells a parable to illustrate a point. This one is about two debtors, both of whom have their debts canceled, but one of whom has a far greater debt and so will have a far greater love for his merciful creditor (7:40–43). When Simon admits this, Jesus points to the woman, who has outdone the host in the hospitable gestures of washing, kissing, and anointing. Because of her great love, which she has demon-strated with these dramatic and possibly erotic gestures,[6] says Jesus, she is forgiven her "many sins" (7:44–48; 50). Nothing is said about the exact na-ture of these "sins," although at least since Jerome they have been assumed

to be sexual transgressions.[7] As Jane Schaberg points out, Luke's "dangerous artistic ability" has caused his version, with its weeping, repentant sinner, the "outsider" who invades the banquet, to overshadow those in the
other three Gospels. By its placement directly before the listing of the
women who accompanied Jesus, some of whom, including Mary Magdalene, he had exorcized of "evil spirits" (Luke 8:2–3), Luke's version has cast
the shadow of sexual transgression over them all, particularly Mary.[8] There
may also be some connection between Jesus' forgiving attitude in this
episode and his forgiveness of the "woman caught in adultery," in John
7:53–8:11, an incident that also occurs in the context of a controversy with
the Pharisees, a story that some textual critics would like to assign to Luke,
perhaps because they assume the women's transgressions to be the same or
similar.[9]

The Johannine version, however, has nothing about sin. John preserves
elements of the Markan story, assigning the act of anointing to Mary of
Bethany, at a dinner given by her and her sister Martha in celebration of
Jesus' raising Lazarus their brother from the dead (John 12:1–2). It is
Mary's extravagant gesture of anointing Jesus' feet with the costly and fra-
grant perfume—the gesture of a wealthy householder and host—and wiping his feet with her hair, that calls forth Judas's criticism of the waste of
something that could be given to the poor (12:3–5; cf. 11:2). In a parenthetical comment, the author of the Gospel makes the point that Judas's
real concern was not the poor but his access to the money as keeper of the
common purse (12:6). Jesus' rebuke is similar to the one found in Mark's
and Matthew's versions, to let Mary alone because she has bought the ointment for his burial, and that the poor are always with them (vv. 7–8). Mary's
gesture, which is also mentioned in the previous chapter as a means of identifying her (John 11:2), may foreshadow the action of Jesus at the Passover
meal, in which his washing and wiping of the disciples' feet is a gesture both
of loving service and of preparatory "cleansing" for the days ahead (John
13:1–20).[10]

Unfortunately, however, the identification of Mary of Bethany as the
woman who anointed Jesus' feet and wiped them with her hair became
combined in later Western patristic exegetical and theological traditions
with the anonymous "sinner" of the Gospel of Luke (although Luke's portrait of Mary of Bethany as the ideal disciple in Luke 10:38–42 is quite distinct from this one), and even with the adulteress of John 7:53–8:11. The
crowning irony is the further application of this composite portrait to Mary
of Magdala, who is distinguished in all four canonical Gospels from Mary
of Bethany as the one woman who consistently appears in the crucifixion
and resurrection stories. Indeed, the first appearance of the risen Jesus in
the Gospel of John is to Mary Magdalene, and she is therefore his first evan-
gelist (John 20:11–18). The extrabiblical transformation of Mary Magda-

lene into the prototype of the "repentant prostitute" or first of the "harlot-saints" will be discussed in chapter 7, but it is sufficient here to say that this image represents an almost irresistible development in early Christianity, paralleled only to a small degree in emerging Judaism by the character of Beruriah. This development rhetorically converts stories of wise and sexually independent women into tales of women dependent upon holy or wise men, women who repent of or are punished for sexual "sins."

The Gospel of John provides us with several encounters with women who appear unmarried or in "irregular" marital situations. Mary and Martha of Bethany have a more prominent role in the story of Jesus and Lazarus than does their brother Lazarus, who does not even have a speaking part, although the Gospel mentions that Jesus "loved" all three (John 11:5). When Jesus comes to Bethany after "allowing" Lazarus's death, Martha's dialogue with him evokes the extent of her knowledge ("I know that God will give you whatever you ask of him"; "I know that he [my brother] will rise again in the resurrection on the last day"; John 11:22–23, NRSV) and her complete trust that Jesus is the Messiah (John 11:27). She summons Mary, who like her sister reproaches Jesus for letting Lazarus die, at the same time revealing utter confidence in Jesus' ability to prevent his death (11:21, 32). After the raising of Lazarus, the sisters both "serve" Jesus, Martha at the table and Mary by anointing him. In neither case is there any suggestion that they are or have been married, nor does that appear to matter in this Gospel in which those who have spiritual knowledge are not "of the flesh" or concerned with its desires (cf. 3:5–10).

This contrast between the "world" and its habit of judging by its own fleshly desires is clear in two other stories involving Jesus and women. One is a revelation-dialogue, in which a female interlocutor discovers Jesus' true identity and in which those who judge by appearance rather than spirit are deceived (John 4). The other is a controversy-story, in which the Pharisees, hoping to use an unknown woman as an object lesson to test Jesus, are shown to be blinded by their misunderstanding, both of the law and Jesus' true nature as "the light of the world" (John 7:53–8:11).[11] The first instance occurs early in Jesus' ministry, when he is recruiting disciples and testing both the depth of their knowledge and their belief (2:23–25). Jesus is going from Jerusalem in Judea to Galilee, his home territory, but has to pass through Samaria (4:1–4), where he rests at a well "near the plot of ground that Jacob had given to his son Joseph" (4:5). This connection with the foundation stories of Jewish history reminds the reader that now Samaria, the capital of ancient Israel, the Northern Kingdom, is regarded as not even Jewish, a point not missed by the author's parenthetical comment that "Jews do not associate with Samaritans" (4:9). Samaria, Ezekiel's "Oholah," was regarded by faithful Jews (Judeans) as an impious remnant of the apostate Northern Kingdom, Israel, which had been disloyal to the covenant

since the reign of Rehoboam (922 B.C.E.). Punished for this "whoring" by
falling to Assyria in 722 B.C.E., Samaria was still considered impure because
of its mixed marriages, and still was competing with the "true" place of worship, the Temple in Jerusalem, with an alternate shrine on Mount Gerizim.[12] Hence it is symbolically appropriate, especially in a gospel that
values symbols and "signs," that the first person Jesus meets in this suspect
and religiously irregular location is a woman whose own social position is
irregular. Because she is not named, she seems to be even more of a symbol, described merely as "a woman of Samaria" (4:7), an "outsider" woman,
both strange and foreign.[13]

The woman herself seems aware of the strangeness of the situation, asking Jesus why he, a Jew, is asking her, a Samaritan woman, for a drink (John
4:9). It is odd not only because of the Jewish-Samaritan enmity but also, as
it later appears, because Jesus is talking with a woman, a fact that "aston-
ishes" his disciples, presumably because they represent the principle also
advocated by some rabbis, that men should not have "excessive" speech
with women (4:27; cf. *Pirkē Aboth* 1.5; Sirach 42:9–14).[14] Jesus, as is typical
of him in this Gospel, does not respond directly to her question but to the
lack of knowledge revealed by it. If she "knew" the gift of God, and the true
identity of the one speaking to her, he says, she would ask the right question, to get him to give her "living water" (John 4:10). Again, she questions,
quite practically, where he will get this water to give her, and he again takes
the dialogue to the level of symbol, declaring that he himself is the fountain of living water, which comes from God (4:13–14; cf. Sirach 24:25–27).

When the Samaritan expresses again the practical wish to have this water, so that she will neither thirst nor have to come to the well to draw it,
Jesus abruptly commands her, "Go, call your husband (man) and bring him
here." This is a ruse to get her to admit that she has no husband to call,
whereupon Jesus replies that she has "spoken well" in saying that she has
no husband, for she has had five husbands, and "the one [man] you have
now is not your husband" (John 4:16–18). As Gail O'Day points out, both
the marital history and moral status of the Samaritan seem to intrigue commentators more than they do either Jesus or the narrator, who pass no judgment on them, but they are not totally without significance.[15] The
encounter at Jacob's well is probably not accidental in a Gospel that revels
in symbolism: it resembles a "biblical betrothal scene," like that of Isaac and
Rebekah (Genesis 24), Jacob and Rachel at the well of Haran (Gen.
29:1–20), or Moses and Zipporah and her sisters in Midian (Ex. 2:16–22).[16]
If we remember that Jesus is the representative of God, and that "Israel"
(now represented by its former capital, Samaria, and in the person of the
Samaritan woman) was often portrayed as God's errant wife, we might,
with Sandra M. Schneiders, envision this scene as the "wooing" of Samaria
back to membership in the "New Israel" by Jesus, the "new bridegroom."[17]

If we understand the marital metaphor a different way, however, in light of the self-understanding of the Johannine movement itself as being a marginal group rejected by formative Judaism, we could see Jesus, the rejected "outsider" bridegroom, himself rejecting Jerusalem as his bride and choosing instead an "outsider" or "outlaw" bride.[18] In any event, John's lack of emphasis on the woman's sexual history, given the biblical history of the metaphor, absolves her from being identified as the sexually promiscuous Strange Woman, even while it obscures the full embodied humanity of both the woman and Jesus.

When the Samaritan acknowledges that she "perceives" Jesus is a prophet because he has told her her marital history (John 4:19), the dialogue proceeds in a typically Johannine fashion to the difference between earthly appearance and spiritual understanding. The quarrel between the Jews and the Samaritans over the proper place to worship God, at the Temple or on Mount Gerizim, a question raised by the woman for the "prophet" to answer, elicits from Jesus the statement that God is spirit, and true worshipers worship "in the spirit" rather than either earthly locale (4:20–24). She replies that she "knows" the Messiah is coming, who will reveal all things, whereupon Jesus reveals that he is the Messiah (4:15–26). When the disciples intrude, "amazed" that Jesus is speaking to a woman, but afraid to question him, the Samaritan abandons her errand and summons her townspeople to come see the man who is probably the Messiah (vv. 29–31), convincing some by her testimony (v. 39) and leading others to "see for themselves" (vv. 40–42). The latter scorn her testimony as the basis for their belief, putting her into the category of those whose word and witness are rejected by those who cannot "receive the testimony" because they have to "see" Jesus to know he is "truly the savior of the world" (John 3:11). She is nevertheless ultimately responsible for their conversion, one of the laborers who sows while others reap (4:37–38).[19] Throughout, the emphasis of the passage is on the Samaritan's growing perception of Jesus' true identity and through him the nature of "the gift of God," and on her ability to share that with others. In contrast, the disciples appear to be still in the dark, as they do not understand Jesus' refusal to eat and his cryptic remarks about food and the harvest (4:31–38).

Jesus' dialogue with the Samaritan woman creates a temporary circle into which the disciples, who are usually members of the enclosed community with Jesus, intrude, or perhaps he is stepping to the edge of the boundary, the periphery that the woman as outsider always inhabits. In another episode, a woman is deliberately thrust into the circle formed by Jesus and his present and prospective disciples, in order to bring confusion, disruption, and the threat of death. This episode, the *Pericope de Adultera*, the Pericope, or passage, on the Adulteress, as it has been traditionally known, is assigned to John 7:53–8:11, and in the scheme of the text, takes place when

Jesus has come to Jerusalem to celebrate the Festival of Booths (Sukkoth), which commemorates the forging of Israel's identity in the wilderness of Sinai. Jesus is teaching in the Temple, and in chapter 8 is confronted by and confronts his usual Johannine opponents, the scribes and Pharisees, on the subject of his legitimacy as God's messenger and their own "illegitimate" understanding of the Law and the Prophets. Since the ostensible point at issue in the Pericope on the Adulteress is the interpretation of the law about adultery, it fits thematically within this section,[20] although its placement within the text of John has long been the subject of debate. It is not attested in the earliest manuscripts and is assigned by some to Luke, following Luke 21:38.[21] Recently, however, several scholars have suggested that the passage's "disappearance" from about 125 to about 300 C.E. has less to do with textual transmission than with the "danger" of the text—for patristic editors and exegetes—with Jesus' forgiveness of "the unlawful sexuality" of the female transgressor.[22] Even Augustine, who did not question the integrity of the text, was concerned lest it encourage wives to commit adultery, knowing that the Lord had once forgiven an adulteress (*On Adulterous Spouses* 2.6). As O'Day observes, "The history of interpretation of this text demonstrates the power of interpretive interests to read the text against its own shape," putting the woman's sexual transgression at its heart.[23]

As the episode opens, Jesus is teaching at the Temple, where "all the people" have come to hear him. The scribes and the Pharisees bring a woman "who had been caught in adultery, making her stand in their midst" (John 8:2–3), thus creating a circle of judges around her. Like the Samaritan, this woman is unnamed, but unlike the Samaritan, she is characterized solely by her supposed action and not even by her nationality.[24] Also unlike the Samaritan, she has no opportunity to converse with Jesus until the end of the episode, when she has little to say and does not take the initiative in speaking. Her accusers further dehumanize her when they make her the object of a challenge to Jesus' understanding of the law: "Teacher, this woman was taken in the very act of committing adultery. In the law Moses commanded us to stone such women, so what do you say?" (8:4–5; cf. Lev. 20:10; Deut. 17:2–7; 19:15; 22:22–24). For the time being, Jesus says nothing. He is as silent as the accused, being himself under judgment, for the scribes and Pharisees, according to the narratives, have brought this woman to him as a "test case," in order to find a charge with which to accuse him (8:6). Yet Jesus' silence, in contrast to that of the woman, who almost seems to disappear from the narrative, is active rather than passive; he bends down and writes something on the ground, an action that he repeats after his question to them (8:7– 8). Although many interpreters attempt to find the "key" to the episode in something that Jesus wrote on the ground, they have to largely ignore what Jesus *says* in favor of something he *might* have written, to which the text gives us no clue.[25] When Jesus breaks silence, he does not object to the punishment set down in the law, nor does he indict the law itself for being unjust or say that adultery is not the law's concern. Rather, he says, "Let the one among you who is sinless be the first to cast a stone," and bends over to write on the ground again (vv. 7–8). When he straightens up, the accusers have vanished, beginning with the elders, who would have had the right to execute punishment, leaving Jesus and the woman "in the midst," alone within the circle, as in John 4. Once more, John has shown Jesus as able to cross the boundaries of what is considered "inside" and "outside" behavior. Jesus speaks directly to the woman, "Woman, where are they? Has no one condemned you?" She replies simply, "No one, sir," her only utterance throughout (vv. 10–11). His reply, "Neither do I condemn you," the focus of so much controversy, is only the beginning, as he completes his final word to her, "On your way; sin no more." These closing remarks are scarcely an endorsement of adultery, as Augustine feared. Jesus appears to class adultery with other, not specifically sexual, sins (v. 7), but he nevertheless considers it a sin, something that Jesus in John's Gospel, as embodiment of God, can forgive. Moreover, although Jesus has clearly not sided with the accusers in their accusation, he has verbally placed himself with them, in that he, like they, does not condemn her.

There is, perhaps not surprisingly, little feminist commentary on this passage, and what there is, is recent. O'Day suggests that a centuries-old process of "mis-reading" the text is the result of an underlying fear of what Jesus' teaching and actions here might mean to male control of women's sexuality.[26] What Jesus' equating of adultery with other "sins"—those committed but not admitted by the men eager to close ranks against the woman whose act threatens their hegemonic solidarity—does, in fact, is to free adultery from the category of especially heinous "crimes." A sin like other sins, it can be forgiven, and no more or less than other sins, should be avoided, but since all are equally capable of sinning, women are not more prone to sexual sins than men. They do not lure men into sexual transgression, and female adultery in and of itself is not a great evil that must be purged from the community lest it collapse. As Luise Schottroff succinctly points out, Jesus' reply to the woman's accusers "puts adultery on the level of all other trespasses of God's will," as a sin, not a capital crime.[27] The Adultera does not repent publicly, and Jesus lets her "go her way," giving her, like her accusers, the responsibility for avoiding sin, a task in which her judges, no less than she, have failed (8:7). If we accept this pericope as it stands in John, its context is a typically Johannine polemic against the Pharisees, who "judge according to the flesh" (8:15), not rightly, according to the spirit, which has no concern with the desires of the flesh.[28] Naturally, Jesus will not fail the test of the Pharisees, who are "blinded" by their wrong judgment (cf. John 9).

Schottroff's interpretation is more typical than O'Day's of the way in which feminists have tended to read John 7:53–8:11, as an instance of the patriarchal "social praxis of getting rid of women by means of accusing them of adultery."[29] Unlike other feminist readers, however, Schottroff does not thereby simply dismiss this passage. She shows the chilling power of a code in which a sexually free woman's threat to her husband's honor theatens the male heterosexual hegemony of the community as a whole and therefore must be avenged through the termination of that threat by death. To this end, Schottroff cites the case of a modern stoning of an adulterous woman in Iran (1992), in which the woman is condemned to death by her father, and placed, like John's Adultera, "in the midst" of the male family and religious authorities, in a hole up to her shoulders. Exulting at her condemnation and calling her "Whore!" her father throws the first stone, followed by her husband, her two sons, and finally the *imam*, the male religious leader, holding the Qur'an as the symbol of God's will in one hand and a rock in the other. As in the case of the Adultera, her male partner is not apprehended.[30] Lest we find ourselves condemning Muslim men and Islam itself for allowing this outrage, just as Christian readers too often unthinkingly condemn the Pharisaic Jewish men in the Johannine story,[31] we would do well to remember that one of the points at issue in the biblical story is the same as that of the contemporary event. A community of men publicly reasserts their authority over one whose social independence threatens to dismantle it and hence to rob them of the honor that comes with being "in control." What gets "out of control" must be brought back under—or destroyed. In the Johannine story, Jesus no less than the Adultera is a threat to the Pharisees' authority and hence is also in danger of having a capital charge (blasphemy) found against him. Because Jesus' power in the Gospel of John is greater than that of the Pharisees, they are rendered powerless, unable to assert control and therefore themselves shamed and publicly dishonored, as they were hoping to do to the woman and Jesus. Jesus thereby gains honor, while the Adultera's honor can scarcely be said to be restored. One wonders what happened to her husband and *his* honor. In the cases of both the Pharisees in John and the Iranian men in Schottroff's example, however, female adultery as unrestrained female sexual power is so threatening to the fragile public honor of men that its perpetrator (the woman without male partner in both!) must be executed. In either case, men are the sole judges and executioners or pardoners.

Perhaps part of the Gospel of John's polemic against the Pharisees is to portray the very helplessness and isolation of the woman trapped in adultery in order to show the absurdity of regarding such a woman as a threat. It is indeed difficult to regard the Adultera in John 8 or even the Samaritan woman of John 4 as "evil," sexually threatening, or tempting. One was powerless and the other was a lone "outsider," little respected even in her own outsider community. Similarly, the unnamed woman of Jesus' anointing in

Matthew, Mark, and Luke is characterized as a "sinner" only in Luke, who uses her as John uses the unnamed Adultera, as the mere catalyst for a confrontation between Jesus and some unreasonable Pharisees.

Yet there is in Matthew and Mark the story of a wily and powerful woman who has the ability to seduce a ruler into doing evil despite his apparent intention: that woman is Herodias (Mark 6:17–29; Matt. 14:1–12).[32] In Mark's version of the story, Herod Antipas, ruler of Galilee, wonders whether the new Galilean prophet Jesus is John the Baptist, whom he beheaded, risen from the dead (Mark 6:16). Luke's version simply stops there, with Herod being assigned full responsibility for John's death (Luke 9:7–9). Mark and Matthew, who probably follows Mark's version, append a detailed story of how the prophet met his death. Mark says that Herod imprisoned John "on account of Herodias, his brother Philip's wife, because Herod had married her" (6:17). Matthew relates that Herod wanted to kill John because he had been openly critical of his marriage to Herodias for its being against the law, since she is his half-brother Philip's wife (Matt. 3—4; cf. Lev. 18:16; 20:1), but was afraid to do so because the people regarded the Baptist as a prophet (Matt. 14:5). Mark, however, presents Herod as putting John, whom he regarded with some fear, into protective custody for fear of Herodias, who "had a grudge against him and wanted to kill him" (Mark 6:19). In Mark's version, it is Herodias who resents John's criticism and wants him silenced, while Herod likes listening to the prophet. In both versions, however, Herodias's daughter, here unnamed (Josephus, *Antiquities of the Jews* xviii.5.4, gives it as "Salome"), dances at Herod's birthday banquet before the ruler and his guests, pleasing him so much that he rashly promises her "with an oath" whatever she desires (Mark 6:21–23; Matt. 14:6–7). At Herodias's prompting, she asks for the head of John the Baptist on a platter (Mark 6:23–25), in which the head is Herodias's idea, the platter is her daughter's addition (Matt. 14:8). In both versions, Herod is "grieved" and unwilling to grant the request, but "out of regard for his oaths and his guests," he gives the order and John is executed, his head presented to the girl, who gives it to her mother, while John's disciples bury his body (Mark 6:14–29; Matt. 14:9–12).

As sexually charged as plays like Oscar Wilde's *Salome* and Hollywood Bible movies like *King of Kings* have made this episode, it is important to remember that the focus in both versions of the story is on Herodias, not Salome, who is not named in either text. There is neither a suggestion nor an assumption that Herodias's daughter dances before an exclusively male audience, one such as Vashti in Esther refused to appear before, or that the dance was erotic in nature, only that it was pleasing to Herod. Mark even refers to the girl as *korasion*, "little girl," and in both versions she is clearly the instrument of her powerful mother. A.-J. Levine connects her "ill-fated dance" with the wisdom sayings in Matthew 11:17 about the children who refused to dance, a link that further de-eroticizes Salome's dancing.[33] While the dance does entice and entrap Herod, not to his own death, but to agreeing to the death of John (which in Matthew he clearly wanted), it is devised by Herodias. Herodias is the one in both versions of the story who has an "unlawful" sexual status, having been wife to two half-brothers, and the Markan Baptist's criticism of it earns him Herodias's determination to silence him. It is thus Herodias who is the sexual "suspect," the one whose "wiles" manipulate her daughter and her husband to contrive the doom of her husband's critic in the Matthean version, her own in the Markan. Maureen Mara poignantly "re-imagines" Herodias's own story, *not* "as told to" the biblical writers: "I have been condemned by Bible readers for a crime I never committed . . . my story has never been told."[34]

A queen's persecution of a critical prophet and her contriving the death of an obstacle to her own and her husband's power is a familiar tale, having been told already in 1 Kings 17—21 in the story of Jezebel, Ahab, Elijah, and Naboth. Since the resemblance of John the Baptist to Elijah is pointed to in both Gospels (Matt. 11:13–14; Mark 6:14–16), it is not hard to see a parallel between the biblical tales of the crafty Jezebel and the cunning Herodias. The strategies of both women, which from their perspective are undertaken to benefit their husbands and themselves, are portrayed in both texts as evil plots that lead to men's doom, and in Jezebel's case, eventually also to her own. Because of their ability to manipulate and control men, they are tainted by the biblical authors (and subsequent readers) with the reputation for sexual promiscuity, and hence, even though they are clever, are not representatives of Wisdom.[35] Rather, they embody Anti-Wisdom, female sagacity gone terribly "wrong," since it is out of male control, an Anti-Wisdom that appears, in the guise of the Strange Woman and Jezebel *rediviva* as manifestations of the Antichrist in the book of Revelation.

THE FALLEN, FALLEN, FALLEN WOMEN: JEZEBEL AND THE GREAT WHORE IN REVELATION

As Paula Fredriksen aptly observes, "Happy people do not write apocalypses."[36] The apocalypse belongs to a genre of prophetic literature whose core is a vision of the eventual triumph and reward of the currently suffering and wronged faithful (the righteous), and of the miserable end and punishment of their currently triumphant opponents (the wicked). This vision presents a mythic reversal of the present situation that, from the perspective of heavenly time, has already occurred. Apocalypses thus borrow symbols from the collective past (as Revelation borrows from Ezekiel, Zechariah, and Daniel, among others) to show that the struggle against the powers of darkness or the evil empire always emerges in victory. John Gager contends that this manipulation of symbols alters reality, giving writer and reader (or hearer) the ability "to transcend the time between a real present and a mythical future."[37] To put it another way, the "value" of apocalyptic is that it offers assurance that the future already belongs to those who share its worldview; they participate in the divine power to control events, to punish enemies and persecutors, secure in the knowledge that their worldview will eventually have complete and exclusive authority. The open-endedness of the symbol system, together with its use of a fairly standard repertoire of easily interpreted images for those who "know the code," continues to make apocalypses popular with those who, like the anonymous sign maker of I-40 mentioned in the introduction, are able to gain symbolic control over a cosmos that appears to be slipping ever farther into personal and communal chaos.[38] Thus, despite their often bizarre symbolism (bizarre only to "outsiders"), apocalypses also offer to their readers the comfort of the familiar, with heavenly warriors defeating bestial powers through superior cosmic means. Finally, the conquest of the threatening "outsiders" is, in apocalyptic writing, total and final. Hence the current fascination of certain Christian groups with "Armageddon," believed to be the "final battle" between the spirits of evil and those of God Almighty (Rev. 16:12–16).[39]

Historically, apocalyptic writing seems to emerge within Judaism and Christianity during periods of political powerlessness and challenges to their minority systems of belief from dominant ones. Apocalyptic, with its emphasis on prophetic visions relating to current events, seems to grow naturally out of classical Israelite prophecy, particularly in the troubling days of the exile and restoration in the sixth to fifth centuries B.C.E., producing passages in Ezekiel, Zechariah, and Third Isaiah. The bitter confrontation of Judaism with dominant pagan Hellenism and the later domination of Judea, first by the non-Davidic Hasmonean kings and then by the Romans, emerges in the apocalyptic book of Daniel, the pseudepigraphical *1 Enoch*, and the apocalypses of Qumran. Although only one full-length apocalypse, Revelation, is found in the New Testament canon, parts of the Synoptic Gospels, like Mark 13 and its parallels in Matthew 24 and Luke 21, some sayings of Jesus from the Sayings Source Q, and passages in the writings of Paul (1 Thess. 4:13–5:11; 1 Cor. 15:51–55) are heavily apocalyptic. Not surprisingly, given the antiestablishment nature of most of the apocalyptic writings, there are many more apocalypses found outside the canon than in it, like 2 Esdras (Apocrypha), the Syriac Baruch, and Gnostic apocalypses like the *Apocalypse of Peter*.

Common to all apocalyptic texts, however, is a very strong dualism. This may be a historical dualism, in which there is a marked division between "this present (evil) earthly age" and "the age to come," in which the world is transformed into an earthly paradise; or it may be a more universal "cosmic" dualism, in which there is a division between the evil forces of this world (the realm of "profane" time, in Eliade's sense) and the good forces of a transcendent heaven (the realm of "sacred" time). In Revelation, events contemporary with the apocalyptic prophet and his audience are mythically transformed into manifestations of cosmic significance, so that the persecutions and lapses in faith of the Christians in Asia Minor during the reign of Domitian (81–96 C.E.), when this text possibly was written, become "signs" of a cosmic war between the "kingdoms of this world" and those who hold satanic power in them, and the heavenly (and ultimately earthly) realm of God and the resurrected Christ. In both cases, however, the boundary between "outsider" and "insider" is sharply delineated and reinforced by a symbolism that often portrays outsiders as ravenous beasts of prey, "horns," statues, or humans who are part beast or who act in an inhuman and bestial manner.

In Revelation, the divide is also sexual, the righteous or "pure" insiders defined as those who have not had sexual contact, arrayed against the "impure" outsiders represented as sexually promiscuous women and those who "fornicate" with them (accept their authority). As Tina Pippin notes, "The boundary of the redeemed sets up a system of contrasts expressed as insider and outsider, Christian and non-Christian, fornicators and virgins. There is no room for dissent."[40] In Revelation 14:1–5 (cf. 7:5–8), the one hundred forty-four thousand "redeemed from the earth" with the name of the Lamb (Christ) and his Father on their foreheads (in contrast to the foreheads signed with the "mark of the beast" in 13:16 and the forehead of the Whore in 17:5) are the only ones who can learn the "new song" sung before the heavenly throne, because they "have not defiled themselves with women," and therefore have been saved to be the Lamb's companions. Intercourse with human women has thus become a symbol both of the stain of earthly existence and an evil that makes men morally impure.[41] One of two positive female characters in Revelation, the Bride of the Lamb, the heavenly Jerusalem (Rev. 19:7; 21:1–22:5, 17) is a virgin, symbolizing the church, which we have seen represented as a "pure bride" in the Deutero-Pauline, pastoral, and catholic epistles (e.g., Eph. 5:23–24). Her clothing is "fine linen," the pure white linen that clothes the faithful (Rev. 3:4–5), the righteous saints (19:8), and the "armies of heaven" (19:14), in contrast to the "fine linen" of purple and scarlet, the colors of luxury, wine, and blood worn by the Great Whore of Babylon (18:16). The other positive female image is that of the mysterious "woman clothed with the sun, with the moon under her feet, and on her head a crown of twelve stars" of chapter 12. Crying out with her childbirth agony, she is attacked by the evil red dragon that symbolizes Satan, and flees into the wilderness when her son, presumably the messiah, is snatched up by God. The dragon continues to pursue her and attempts to drown her, but God comes to her assistance, and the angry dragon then makes war upon her children. Although many interpretations of this figure have been offered, it seems most likely that the Woman Clothed with the Sun is a constellation of images, primarily of the mother of the messiah and the mother of the faithful, of the "new Israel," the church.[42]

Both positively portrayed women are also passive ones. The "bride, the wife of the Lamb" is displayed by an angel to the seer's gaze in 21:9–27, but there is little that is human about her. The description of the Bride, the new Jerusalem as a gated city, with "nothing unclean" permitted to enter her, recalls the metaphor of the "enclosed garden" used to describe the bride in Song of Songs (4:12–5:1) and the preferred locale of the chaste Susanna (Sus. 7–18). The Bride Jerusalem's designation as a "very rare jewel" reminds us of Wisdom and the *'ešet ḥayil* of Proverbs, both of whose worth is "far above jewels." The language quickly dissolves, however, into the nonhuman. Jerusalem is an "it," a perfect, measurable cube, composed of pure gold and precious gems. As an object of desire, moreover, the new Jerusalem, the Bride, is a pale foil to the Great Whore, identified with pagan Babylon (Rome), a woman who desires—and enjoys the desire of—many men who mourn for her destruction while the redeemed rejoice.[43] Perhaps the "measurable" and therefore controllable desexualized city is exactly the sort of ideal female the seer John has in mind, in distinct contrast to "the great city," Babylon (Rome), who is the all-too-feminine and all-too-powerful "Great Whore" (18:10, 16).

The Woman Clothed with the Sun, mother rather than bride or virgin, is perhaps a resexualized version of the Bride, now married and pregnant. She is obviously "good" because her son is God's chosen messiah and because she and her other children are the object of pursuit by the red dragon, but as a sexually mature female character, she is imperiled if not perilous. Because she must finally be rescued from the dragon's destructive bent by the eagle, sent (rather belatedly!) by God to help her, it seems rather an overstatement to say, *pace* Pippin, that she is an active heroine because she "takes the initiative" of fleeing into the wilderness at the dragon's pursuit.[44] The Woman's flight is reaction rather than initiative, undertaken solo because God is preoccupied, both with his holy war and with "snatching up" her son. (The narrator also periodically loses interest in her, being similarly preoccupied.) God has already prepared this place in the wilderness for her, and in Revelation 12:14, he rescues her on the wings of his agent, the "great eagle." When the serpent or dragon tries to drown her, it is the earth, not God, that comes to her rescue. This alternating attention and neglect of the Woman, who perhaps represents the church as new Israel, reminds us of Israel the bride of YHWH in Ezekiel 16, who was also alternately rescued and left in the wilderness. In any event, the ultimate interest of both the dragon (Satan) and God is not in the Woman, but in her children, first the messiah (12:5) and then the faithful "who keep the commandments of God and hold fast the witness of Jesus" (12:17). Both the Bride and her mature counter-

part, the Woman, have nonindependent and nonoppositional relationships to the Son (Lamb) and the Father, relationships that are
sanctioned in the text by portraying them as "good" female characters.

These positive albeit rather shadowy and passive female figures are over-
shadowed and nearly overpowered by negative images of female evil that
are active in an emphatically sexual way. Susan Garrett observes that, of the
four female characters in Revelation, "The wholly good are those whose
sexuality is effectively controlled; the wholly bad are those whose sexuality
escapes male management and manipulation."[45] The only real human female character in the whole of Revelation, mentioned in the fourth of seven
letters to the churches, that of Thyatira, is a prophet contemptuously called
"Jezebel" by the author (2:20). Indeed, the seer/author speaks with the
words of the Son of God when he condemns the church itself for its toler-
ating "Jezebel's" claim to prophecy, her teaching, and her "deceiving"
God's servants into practicing "fornication" (*porneusai*) and into eating
what is sacrificed to idols (cf. 2:14; 1 Cor. 8:1–13; Rom. 14:1–4). Although
she has been given time to repent, she "does not wish to repent of her fornication" (Rev. 2:21). For her punishment she will be "thrown on a bed,"
while those who have committed adultery with her (*moicheontas*) will be
thrown into great distress, unless they repent of her "works" (2:22). Her
children will be killed also (v. 23). The nexus of images employed here, particularly the evocation of Jezebel (1 Kings 16:31; 19:1–3; 2 Kings 9:22, 30),
recalls also her practice of a different, a foreign or "strange," religion, which
the priestly elite called idolatry and hence termed "fornication." The use of
Jezebel's name enables the author/seer John also to evoke the memory of
the prophet Elijah, her revered opponent, without having to name him, and
thus to identify himself with Elijah as a "true" prophet rather than the
"false" female prophet of Thyatira.[46] In the mythic time frame of apocalyptic, these linked images also help to remind the seer's audience that the
historical Jezebel was decisively defeated by the prophet of God. The fate
of the present "Jezebel," with that of her followers and children, has distinctly sexual overtones. I cannot accept the translation of *kline* (bed) as
"sickbed" (2:22), particularly since her followers are called "those who have
committed adultery with her."[47] Instead, given especially the symbolic connection to the prophets of ancient Israel, the term suggests a rape, the kind
of rape and punishment that are inflicted on the idolatrous Israel and Judea
in Ezekiel 16:35–43 and 23:22–34, 46–48. It has been suggested that the
followers of the Jezebel of Revelation 2:20–23, like the members of the
Nicolaitan sect that is also condemned, may have advocated sexual freedom
of a libertine type, in addition to advocating freedom with respect to eating
meat sacrificed to idols.[48] Given the persistent equation of the worship of
deities "other" than God with "fornication" or "harlotry" by the prophetic
literature of the Tanakh, however, it would not be necessary to preach ac-

tual sexual libertinism to be charged with it. It is therefore not surprising that this text also makes that connection, characterizing religious opposition as sexual infidelity, especially so when led by a woman, whose punishment, not unexpectedly, is envisioned in the form of sexual humiliation (rape) that involves her followers (lovers) and the death of her "children," perhaps her more innocently "deluded" rather than active disciples. The mention of the latter contrasts sharply with the fate of the Woman Clothed with the Sun and her children in chapter 12. The Woman's children are under attack by the evil dragon because of their fidelity to God and Christ; Jezebel's are under sentence of death by the Son of God because of her (and their) supposed infidelity. The contrast is made more terrible, however, if we recall the fact that the seer's "Jezebel," unlike the Woman Clothed with the Sun, is a real woman, destined for an inhuman punishment inflicted by a divine being.

Another, more dreadful punishment, as in other apocalypses an "ultimate" punishment, is meted out against the most prominent female figure in the text of Revelation, the Great Whore (*porne megale*), who is Babylon. As her epithet implies, she occupies a much greater proportion of the text than does any other female figure, whether good or evil (14:8, 17:1–19:4). The destruction of the Great Whore is the first of a series in which the most powerful forces of evil, including Satan, Death, and Hades, are overthrown, and is the prelude to the appearance of the Bride and the invitation to the marriage supper of the Lamb. The Great Whore also contrasts with the Woman Clothed with the Sun, in that while the latter is the mother of the messiah and of the faithful witnesses, the former is the "mother of whores and of the abominations of the earth" (17:5). She is the biblical epitome of female sexual evil, the "foreign" (outsider) power that preys upon, often to destruction, the righteous (insider) males who should be in power. The "wine" upon which the Whore is drunk is both the symbol of idolatry (= fornication) and the blood of those who will not submit to her, the "saints," the "undefiled" (14:8; 17:6).

The term "great" (*megale*), moreover, also means "large," and the image of the Whore is one of grotesque, even frightening size, with whom the adjectives "great," "many," and "full" are associated. Upon being shown the Whore by the seventh angel in the vision of the seven bowls, John the seer is "amazed with a great amazement" (17:6).[49] Indeed, the vision of the Whore is overwhelming, a kaleidoscope of images of insatiability in sex (the noun and verb forms of "whore" are used eleven times in this passage), wine, power, wealth, and violence. The Whore is "seated on many waters" (17:1), which the angel interprets as "peoples and multitudes and nations and tongues" (17:15), in a pile of images of power. She is also linked to the bestial, riding a scarlet beast with seven heads and ten horns, "full of blasphemous names" (17:3, 7, 9). The beast is also "amazing" and powerful,

needing to be destroyed in the war against the Lamb and his righteous allies (17:8–14), after turning on the Whore with hatred (17:16). The whore
is both literally and figuratively a "scarlet woman," in fact the original scarlet woman, clothed in scarlet and purple, the colors of luxurious wealth
(18:3, 14, 16) and adorned with gold, jewels, and pearls (17:4), the very
types of adornment Christian women were urged to avoid as provocative,
immodest, and flaunting of wealth (1 Tim. 2:9; 1 Peter 3:3–6).[50] The
Whore carries a golden cup that is also "full," filled with "abominations"
(idolatry) and the "uncleannesses of her fornication" (17:4). Here is impure
religion and deviant sex combined. Her sexual insatiability is also indicated
by the fact that both she and the "inhabitants of the earth" are drunk with
the "wine of fornication" (17:2; 18:3; cf. 14:8), which is also blood, "the
blood of the saints and the blood of the witnesses to Jesus" (17:6; 18:24).
Her terrifying power is symbolized by the "mystery" written on her forehead: "Babylon the great, mother of whores and of the abominations of the
earth" (17:5), and "the great city that rules over the kings of the earth"
(17:18). She exults in her power and wealth: "I am enthroned as queen, and
I am no widow; I will not see grief" (18:7, NRSV).

The only way in which she can be diminished is through an equally
"amazing" and terrifying violent death in which her naked flesh is devoured
by her quondam allies, the "horns" and the beast, and burnt (17:16). Her
lovers, "the kings of the earth," together with the merchants and seafarers
who both provided her wealth and enjoyed her patronage, will see the
"smoke of her burning" from afar, horrified and fearful of her "torment"
(18:9–10, 15, 18), while her judges and executioners, the "multitude" of
heaven and angels with "great authority" exult over her death, urging the
righteous also to rejoice and tauntingly comparing her former glory to her
complete downfall (18:31–19:3). This exultation over the fallen woman
Babylon is reminiscent of those in the prophets. Isaiah 47 envisions "virgin
Babylon" being stripped and sexually shamed. In Jeremiah 50— 51, the destruction of Babylon is envisioned through the image of a mother "shamed"
and "utterly disgraced," mocked by those who are "appalled" by her
wounds (50:11–16). The link to Jeremiah is especially intended by the author of Revelation, where the "voice from heaven" urges the faithful to
"Come out of her" (Babylon), in the language of Jeremiah 51:45 (Rev.
18:4).[51] Nahum portrays Nineveh (capital of the Assyrians) as a whore,
"mistress of sorcery" (cf. Rev. 18:23), whose "debaucheries" would be punished by sexual shaming and exposure to the mockery of the nations (3:4–7),
a punishment Jeremiah also prescribed for erring Jerusalem (5:1–3, 26–31).
The apocalyptic prophet Zechariah's vision (Zech. 5:5–11) of the woman
called "Wickedness" seated in a basket, taken by two women to be worshiped in Shinar (Babylon), may also have contributed to the depiction of
the Whore of Babylon, as the prophet's vision of the four chariots with dif-

ferently colored horses (Zech. 6:1–8) may have contributed to Revelation's four riders (Rev. 6:2–8).

As most interpreters have demonstrated, the Whore is not the historical Babylon but the "great city" contemporary with the seer and his audience, Rome. By referring to the city as Babylon, the author is thereby able to conjure up a wealth of prophetic references to that city as an idolatrous, "outsider" (pagan) domain that attempted to have power over the righteous faithful in the past but whose final destruction was prophesied, assured, and witnessed. Because of the symbol structure of apocalyptic, which not only refers to the past but is open-ended toward the future, "Babylon" can be any powerful city (Nineveh, Tyre, Rome—or any number of contemporary candidates, including Tehran and Baghdad) perceived to be exercising a political and religious authority that is deemed illegitimate by its opponents. In the words of Jacques Ellul, Rome/Babylon "is the historical actualization of the Power."[52] Since the image of a sexually promiscuous woman was employed so often in biblical literature to designate both a different (illegitimate) religious tradition, the worship of idols (multiple deities), and a threatened reversal of power, it was inevitable that John should employ this image to designate the powerful pagan empire under which he subsumes all forms of deviance from the "faithful and true," his version of a righteous cosmos. Rome/Babylon thus is the Great Whore religiously, economically, and politically, an enemy that must be defeated before the pure Bride, the "holy city" and the church, can emerge as the properly subordinate consort of her Lord. The absolute dualism of John's symbolic universe is played out, as in the prophetic and wisdom texts, in the arena of female sexual power. Notes Pippin, "The unconscious desires of the male reader [and of the author], not only for the destruction of the dominant political and economic power but for the destruction of the sexual power of the female, are found in the ideology of desire in the text. . . . Female desires for power are not allowed to continue."[53]

As in other biblical texts that believing women seek to reclaim for themselves, such symbols are profoundly disturbing. Margaret Miles observes that even "positive" images of women are those of "socially approved women, 'good' women from the perspective of the governing male collective," and "function not as 'rewards' for women, but as prescriptive messages."[54] Modern readers, sensitive to the empowerment that such authoritative texts provide, seek strategies of reading that nevertheless often deny or ignore the enduring power of such symbols, preferring, for example, to read Revelation as the struggle of those who are socially, economically, and politically oppressed against those who abuse power or have attained and sustain it through violence and exploitation. Such readings may point, quite rightly, to the fact that the "merchants of the earth" who are dispossessed by Babylon's fall supply her not only with luxury goods and supplies for the military (horses and chariots) but also with "slaves and human souls" (Rev. 18:11–13). What such readings fail to see is that the fall of such oppressive powers is itself engineered through violence, abuse, and persecution, however imaginary they may be.[55] More disturbing is the reflection that one of the most potent sources of evil is a figure whose power is undeniably linked to her female sexuality, and who is stripped naked, sexually humiliated, tortured, and burned—to the exultation of the righteous—under the unblinking gaze of the thunderstruck "seer." Still more disturbing is the fact that this event, the death of the Woman called the Whore, is not unique to Revelation but is so recurrent in the Bible—in Hosea, Jeremiah, Ezekiel, Second Isaiah, and Nahum—that it is employed in the symbolic back-reference system of this text. In the symbolic code of such texts, "uncontrolled" female sexuality means female power that threatens to overwhelm male hegemony. Notes Miles, "The female body . . . was a problem for men; the control of female sexuality, reproduction, and economic labor was a perennial preoccupation and anxiety in the male-defined and -administered communities of the Christian West."[56] In Revelation, "Jezebel" and the Whore represent such simply terrifying female power that they must be eliminated for righteous males to feel safe within their own boundaries. John's apocalyptic dynamic renders the powerful powerless, but in order to do so must first acknowledge, and let the reader feel, their power, if only to make its overturn more triumphant. Since power is often represented sexually, there is also something intoxicating about the sexual power of the Whore and Jezebel, symbolized in the former's case by the "wine of fornication." Both have "beguiled"—the standard biblical terminology for female sexual authority—many with that power, but in Revelation both are stopped by the assertion of male sexual authority, through exposure, abuse, rape, and the final destruction of the alluring and deadly female flesh, together with those who have succumbed to it, by those who are "pure"; that is, like the one hundred forty-four thousand male virgin warriors, they have not accepted an "illegitimate" inverse of sexual hierarchy by surrendering to female heterosexual attraction. The rhetoric and dynamic of power are indeed often expressed in sexual terms, but in the androcentric language that dominates biblical discourse, female sexual power is represented only by the nexus of seduction, wiles, and cunning, often leading to the death of males; while male sexual power is represented by rape, sexual abuse, and often the death of females. The latter is portrayed as perhaps unfortunate, but justified and even required by the evil of women. In his study of religion and female sexuality, Demosthenes Souramis notes that men represent women as wicked and dangerous: "If women were actually wicked and dangerous, men could emerge not only as 'good' but as 'generous' because they refrain from destroying the wicked sex."[57] They will only destroy those who embody female wickedness and have thus "deserved" their own destruction.

7

Confounding the Wisdom of the Wise

For it is written,
"I will destroy the wisdom of the wise,
  and the sagacity of the sages I will dissolve."
—1 Corinthians 1:19

THE HUMILIATION OF WISDOM: BERURIAH, MARY OF MAGDALA, AND OTHER WISE WOMEN

Both Judaism and Christianity are "scriptural" religions in that they rely on a body of authoritative and authorized texts, regarded to be divinely inspired, as their "mirrors of cultural identity."[1] The crises, controversies, and consensus within the social and religious fabric of the various communities out of which the biblical texts emerged, and within which they gained canonical status and became normative, both shaped and were shaped by this sacred literature. The traditions of Judaism and Christianity therefore embody, continue, and sometimes challenge the biblical texts, especially over important questions of religious values and social interactions that also include sexual relations. Indeed, constructions of sexuality and gender continue to be influenced if not governed by those found in scripture. We ought not, however, to fall into one of two traps common among Christian readers and exegetes, no matter how sophisticated. First is the "supercessionist" trap, the assumption that, because the Christian canon incorporates the Jewish Bible, the latter is therefore completely fulfilled, canceled out, or even surpassed by the scriptures of the New Testament. Second is what one of my former professors has provocatively called "the Great Protestant Fraud," the assumption that there are no writings important either to formative Judaism or formative Christianity outside the canon. The aim of this chapter, then, will be to avoid either pitfall while attempting to show how the connection between female power, wisdom, and sexuality is continued in some of the extracanonical materials of both scriptural traditions.

I suggest that, as in the canonical literature, there seems to be even here the remarkably consistent formulation that female power, linked as it is to a wisdom "mysterious" to men and therefore "strange," is desirable in the sexual sense but also ultimately dangerous, to men as well as women.

Daniel Boyarin points out the difference between formative Judaism and formative Christianity on the question of sexuality, in that the former, regarding people as bodies rather than spirits, seeks to recapture the original androgynous creation "in the image of God" in marriage, while the latter regards the asexual spirit as the perfect androgynous image (cf. Gen. 1:27; 5:1–2).[2] Both emerging traditions, however, seem to have agreed that heterosexual marriage was an acceptable means of keeping unruly sexual desire and its expression under control.[3] For both groups, however, female sexual autonomy seems to have been dangerous territory, and female freedom and authority, whether sexual or not, was often read as promiscuity. The only relatively autonomous women in the second-century book of rabbinic explications of religious law known as the Mishnah are those whose sexuality no man can claim, whose "biological function" no man owns.[4] Formative Christianity no less than its contemporary, formative Judaism, approved of a certain degree of autonomy for women to whom no man had a legitimate sexual claim. Unlike the Judaism of the Mishnah, however, Christianity did not assume that therefore the woman had some degree of sexual autonomy in the sense of her having a sexual choice. Women who had no husbands were to consider Christ their spiritual spouse and were to devote their energy to serving him (cf. 1 Tim. 5:11). For emergent Judaism, a prime concern in marriage remained the purity of the bride and her fidelity to her spouse, making adultery a grave matter. Early Christianity, especially that reflected in the canonical Gospels, seems not as concerned with marriage and hence less concerned with adultery per se, although marriage was deemed the only appropriate expression of sexuality if celibacy was not achievable. All else was "fornication" (*porneia*). Following Paul (1 Corinthians 6, for example) Christian authorities found male adultery as heinous as female, but increasingly portrayed women as a constant temptation to men, especially in the institution of celibate marriage.[5]

Sexual attitudes and concerns in both traditions also had an impact on how each regarded the relationship of women to knowledge. Women's wisdom, limited in biblical discourse to a kind of mysterious knowledge that often features underdog cunning, can either assist or hinder men. In this type of discourse, the woman is perpetually "strange," a foreigner who is always seeking to breach the limits set for her by the male community, either from the outside or, more threateningly, from within. "Unattached" women or wandering wives are considered "loose," needing to be connected, controlled, or in severe cases expelled from the community or killed. Androcentric discourse thus effectively "neutralizes" the power of wise women by overplaying their sexual perversity, so that all knowledge can be channeled through men. Men therefore have control both of sexual relations and of routes to wisdom. Two prototypical cases, one of a wise wife, Beruriah of rabbinic legend, and one of a wise disciple, Mary Magdalene of early Christianity, come to mind.

The story of Beruriah, according to Boyarin, establishes "an essential nexus between a woman studying Torah and the breakdown of the structure of monogamy. . . . There is an intrinsic and necessary connection between a scholarly woman and uncontrolled sexuality."[6] The male scholar, who from the time of the writing of Proverbs was urged to take Wisdom, or the Torah, which embodied Wisdom, for his bride, found an erotic dimension in study that for him was to be physically assuaged within the prescribed boundaries of marital intercourse. The eroticism of study may have resulted in the suspicion that women, assumed to be more sexual, were also more greatly aroused by learning, and may not have found an adequate sexual outlet in marriage. In discussing whether women should be admitted to studying the Torah at all, the Mishnah (m. *Soṭa* 3.4) relates that Ben Azzai, himself criticized for not marrying while he advocated marriage, comes down in favor of a father teaching his daughter the law, so that if she has to drink the bitter waters of the suspected adulteress, the merit acquired by her study will be a "good deed" mitigating her punishment. Rabbi Eliezer, however, claims that "Anyone who teaches his daughter Torah teaches her *tifluth*" ("trifles," foolishness or lasciviousness), to which Rabbi Joshua adds, "A woman prefers one measure (*qab*) of food or drink with lasciviousness to nine measures (*qabs*) with modesty."[7]

The Mishnah was compiled around 200 C.E. by rabbis in Roman Judea from existing, probably oral traditions. Later additions resulted in the Palestinian Talmud ("Teaching"), compiled around the third to fifth centuries C.E. and the Babylonian Talmud, compiled from the third to seventh centuries C.E. What these compilations reflect are the concerns of a particular group of male scholars to understand everything according to the orderly pattern of a kind of cosmic Torah, revealed at Sinai, but capable of being applied to new situations. The debate over women's learning in the Mishnah continues in the Babylonian Talmud, where Rabbi Abbahu explains Rabbi Eliezer's above comment thus: "As it is written, I am Wisdom, I dwell with guile (and knowledge will find intrigues) (Prov. 8:12). As soon as wisdom has entered a man [sic], with it has entered guile."[8] The learned woman Beruriah, who belongs to the generation known as the "Tannaim," around 200 C.E., is mentioned, not in the Mishnah, but in other related traditions, the Tosefta (*Tosefta Kelim Baba Qamma* 4:17; *Tosefta Kelim Baba Metzia* 1:6, both relating to *kelim*, or "vessels," and their purity) and the Babylonian Talmud itself as a profound adept in the laws of ritual purity. In the latter (b. *Pesahim* 62b), she is said to have learned three hundred ritual laws in one day from three hundred rabbis. She is also said to have known, and quoted to refute Rabbi Jose the Galilean, the rabbinic saying (*Pirkē 'Aboth* 1.5') that one should not speak too much with a woman (b. *Erubin* 53b). According to Léonie Archer, these and other stories about Beruriah's erudition, "unparalleled in other rabbinic literature," may have been intended only to enhance the status of her husband, Rabbi Meir, for marrying so wise a wife, skilled in the laws of domestic purity and aware of the temptation even women's speech poses for men.[9] In a much later commentary, an eleventh-century commentary on Rashi (on b. *'Aboda Zara* 18b), another, much more negative, story is found. Apparently miffed when his wife Beruriah scoffed at the saying, "Women are light-minded" (*Kiddushin* 80b), Meir decided to test her by ordering one of his students to seduce her. He succeeded, Beruriah hanged herself in disgrace, and Meir in shame fled Palestine for Babylonia.[10] Whether, as Boyarin claims, Beruriah is a "cultural fantasy," since the traditions relating to her as Meir's wife themselves are rather late, this story does illustrate "the extraordinary threat that the learned woman represented to Babylonian (and later European) rabbinic culture."[11] Like the tale of Hamlet, who is made insane with "too much learning," this tale relates how learned women cannot control their sexual appetites once they are aroused by a discipline much better left to men.

A similar fate is meted out by Christian patristic legend to Mary Magdalene. In the canonical Gospels, she appears as a loyal companion to Jesus, one of the group of women who were with him and the Twelve on the road (Luke 8:2–3), and as the first "witness" to the resurrected Christ (Mark 16:9, in the longer ending; John 20:11–18) or a consistent member of the group of two or three women at the empty tomb (Matt. 28:1–10; Luke 24:1–12, 22–24; cf. John 20:1–2). Yet even in the canon, there is an indication that Mary's witness, like that of the other women, is somehow inferior to that of the male disciples. In Luke's version of the story, it is called "nonsense" (*leros*), and even in the Gospel of John, where Mary is mentioned as the first to see and talk with the risen Jesus, her witness needs confirmation by the "beloved disciple" and Peter to be credited by the others. Perhaps this universal canonical disbelief in Mary's story reflects the fact that she was a far more important disciple in some Christian sects than in the orthodox group responsible for the New Testament canon. In many of the texts representing the esoteric wisdom sect of Christianity known as Gnosticism, Mary Magdalene is embodied Wisdom, the female partner of Jesus, the male Logos (*Gospel of Philip* 63.30–64.10; cf. 59.1–15), or the disciple who is supreme revealer not only of the Savior's true nature but also of the nature of the universe, "the All" (*Dialogue of the Savior* 139.10; *Pistis Sophia* 17.97). The Gnostic gospel attributed to her, the *Gospel of Mary*, employs the metaphor of adultery to illustrate "the adulterous union of spirit and matter," whether to the law, which in Gnostic texts is a product of a material deity, or to passion

(*Gospel of Mary* 7.15–16).[12] Although neither the metaphor nor its application to spiritual infidelity is new, nevertheless here, as in other Gnostic texts, the equation of "female" with sexual and "fallen" is not always total. Nor is Mary Magdalene herself characterized primarily as a female sexual being, although her opponents in the Gnostic texts attempt to make her so. Her superior wisdom and close companionship with the Savior (Jesus) angers male disciples like Peter, who challenges Mary's position in the *Gospel of Mary* (17.5–18.20), *Pistis Sophia* (36.71), and the *Gospel of Thomas* (51.18–25). In the *Gospel of Mary*, the brothers Peter and Andrew cannot believe that "the Lord" spoke privately with a woman and not "openly with us," but in the *Gospel of Thomas*, Jesus answers their objections by replying that he will "make Mary male," so that she too will be a worthy disciple.

While there appear to be obvious sexual overtones to the companionship between Mary and Jesus, the *Gospel of Philip* going so far as to say that he used to kiss her "often on the mouth" (*Gospel of Philip* 63.32–34), the nature of most of these Gnostic gospels is so anti-flesh and anti-sex that this relationship can only be one of intimate spiritual knowledge,[13] a knowledge of the divine that in biblical literature had long been expressed metaphorically in terms of sexual "knowledge," when such was clearly not the case. The "holy kiss," moreover, was even used by orthodox Christians as a sign of their companionship and equal, quasi-sibling relationship in Christ (1 Cor. 16:20; 2 Cor. 13:12; Rom. 16:16; 1 Thess. 5:26; 1 Peter 5:14). In Gnostic thought, it was the spiritual breath that helped in the process of the "perfection" (completion in knowledge) for those who would be saved (*Gospel of Philip* 59.1–5). But just as the holy kiss was misunderstood, perhaps deliberately, by pagan Romans as an indication of sexual promiscuity among Christians (Minucius Felix, *Octavius* 9.4; Eusebius, *Ecclesiastical History* 9.5.2), so also the orthodox opponents of these Gnostic texts and the female spiritual authority represented in them, misrepresented the metaphor of intercourse for the intimacy of knowledge as reflecting licentious sexual practices (Irenaeus, *Against Heresies* 1.23.4; Clement of Alexandria, *Stromateis* 3.2.10; 3.4.27–28).

Further, in a remarkably imaginative, or, if one prefers, perverse "reading" of the Gospels, Mary Magdalene became identified first in the Western church with Mary of Bethany as the woman who anointed Jesus' feet and dried them with her hair (John 12:3), then with the unnamed female "sinner" who performs the same deed in Luke 7:37–50, and finally with the legendary former prostitute, "Mary of Egypt" (sixth century). Eventually by the sixth century she became, both in popular legend and patristic belief, the prototypical "repentant harlot" of the New Testament, whom Jesus "redeemed" from the seven unnamed demons, in Luke 8:2, which are eventually characterized as those of lust or other deadly sins.[14] Mary is contrasted both with the Virgin Mary, who was free from sexual "sin," and also with Eve, the "first" sinner. Her life story, along with those of other repentant harlots, is balanced with those of "good" or ascetic Christian women.[15] Benedicta Ward explains the remarkable process of turning a disciple and faithful companion into a sexually promiscuous, "fallen" woman thus: "Mary Magdalene is a sinner, and takes to herself all the sins of mankind [sic] first seen in Eve as that fundamental turning away from God, which the Bible calls adultery."[16] Yet one is goaded by such a generous theological explanation of the transformation of Mary to ask why female sexuality is the prototypical "sin"? Why describe turning away from God as "adultery"? Is not this "prostituting" of Mary of Magdala in text, imagination, and belief, still widely held even by Protestants, the continuation of a long process, in which Beruriah and her legend also have a part, whereby resistance to or rejection of male authority in the religious realm is represented by wayward female sexuality?

The ascetic strain that characterized both orthodox and heterodox varieties of formative Christianity is not a dominant one in formative Judaism. In the latter, marriage is the usual means by which unruly sexuality, both male and female, can be held in check, although the men dominate in marriage and family as well as in the study and interpretation of the Torah. According to Turid Karlsen Seim, however, "In Judaism the case against celibacy is not as univocal as has been commonly assumed."[17] One celebrated exception is the first-century community of the Therapeutes and Therapeutrides, described by Philo of Alexandria (20 B.C.E.–50 C.E.) in his *On the Contemplative Life*. Philo relates how celibate men and women live a cenobitic life of self-denial combined with study. The women are elderly virgins who, according to Philo, retain their virginity so that they may zealously pursue Wisdom as her lovers, to bear offspring from the mind (*On the Contemplative Life* 68).

The wise and prophetic power of celibate female seers is also celebrated in the *Sibylline Oracles*. A series of prophecies composed in twelve books dating from the second century B.C.E. to the seventh century C.E., the Sibyllines take their name from the women prophets of the Gentile pagan world but are primarily Jewish texts with Christian interpolations and additions. Like their real pagan sisters, however, the probably fictional Sibyls of these texts embody what A.-J. Levine has called "the association of repudiated sexuality and a woman's prophetic ability."[18] There is a certain amount of confusion about the Sibyl's sexuality within the *Oracles*, however. While in *Sibylline Oracles* 2.1–5 and 11.322–324, the Sibyl claims to derive her "most perfectly wise song" from a prophetic ecstasy induced by God, she also "confesses" in 2.341–344 that she is "brazen," not caring for marriage, and knowingly has committed "lawless" and "shameless" deeds, thereby needing a savior.[19] In the Christian interpolations within Book 2, however, virgins and those who "love marriage and refrain from adultery" are given "an imperishable prize" in the contest to get into heaven (2.39–55), while the Virgin Mary is an intercessor for the penitent (2.311). Yet the earthly reign of women, actual or as feminized symbols of cities and kingdoms, is usually disastrous. Cleopatra VII, who governs the world "under the hands of a woman," presides over cosmic destruction (3.75–78). Macedonia, the kingdom of Alexander the Great, is a female who will "perish by an evil fate" (3.384–386). Rome is singled out as a "wicked city," a city rife with sexual crimes, in terms that recall the description of the Whore of Babylon in Revelation 18:7 (5.168–173). In Book 8, the Sibyl prays never to see the reign of "the abominable woman" (8.194–202), which presages eschatological woes in which "the power of the female will be great," but the "entire year will be turned upside down." As Levine points out, the Sibyl's status is an ambiguous one, particularly with regard to sexuality: while her now-celibate status allows her to be God's tool for prophecy, the prophecy is one of the destruction of powers that are characterized as predatory females who are indicted for sexual crimes, and punishment that is described "in terms of sexual humiliation."[20]

The connection between feminine wisdom and sexuality in the texts of formative Christianity reveals no less ambiguity. While nominally celebrating marriage, many early Christian authorities followed Paul in 1 Corinthians 7 in offering it "by way of concession" to those who could not keep their heterosexual impulses under control. Christian writing from the mid–second century C.E. onward, however, whether popular, learned, monastic, orthodox, or heterodox, whether Greek, Latin, or Syrian, praised the "solitary and elect," and represented the life free from sexual intercourse as a truly free life. It was also a life by which men and women to an even greater degree might achieve the reversal of the Fall into sin, increasingly understood primarily as sexual transgression and nearly exclusively identified with women's nature. Clerical authorities, however, were concerned lest the choice of a celibate life for women guarantee their equality with men. The heterodox apocryphal *Acts of Paul and Thecla*, dating from about the end of the second century C.E., is a case in point. According to this popular tale, a betrothed virgin of Iconium, Thecla, falls in love with the "word of the celibate life" as spoken by Paul, and determines to pursue it, to her great peril. Rejecting her fiancé, she is threatened with burning by the authorities of her family and her city, but miraculously escapes. Time and time again, as in nearly all of the apocryphal Acts and all of the hagiographies relating to women, Thecla's virginity is threatened but preserved. Even Paul keeps his distance from Thecla, arguing that she is beautiful and therefore a sexual temptation. Cutting her hair and donning men's clothing, she continues to seek Paul's blessing, although he refuses to baptize her and she finally baptizes herself. Ultimately, however, she does obtain his blessing, and continues teaching, preaching, and converting others, especially women. The response of the Christian bishop of Carthage, Tertullian (160–220), is to reject this text as authoritative, particularly for women, and he even calls it spurious. Paul, he fulminates in *On Baptism* 17.5, did not allow women to speak, let alone to baptize (cf. 1 Tim. 2:12). Tertullian nevertheless did not condemn Thecla's option for celibacy or portray her as sexually wanton; he objected to the use of the *Acts of Paul and Thecla* as legitimation for women's teaching and participation in ritual.[21] He did, however, attack the real Gnostic (Marcionite) teacher Philomena as an "angel of seduction" and an "insane whore" (*On the Prescription against Heresies* 6.5–6; 30.5–7).[22]

Other stories of wise and independent women fared similarly ill at the hands of the triumphant orthodox transmitters of tradition, with the unhappy result that, as Deirdre J. Good points out, "The chorus of outsiders' voices [i.e., the extracanonical, heterodox literature] is often the only place to hear women's stories."[23] The Latin theologian Jerome (342–420), who supported and was supported by intellectual Christian women like Marcella and Paula but who nevertheless regarded women as sources of temptation and praised the celibate life for women in preference to marriage, claimed that heretical Christian movements were successful because of the extensive involvement of women, including the "harlot" Helena among the followers of Simon Magus, the followers of the "unclean" Nicolas of Antioch, the anonymous apostle sent by the Gnostic teacher Marcion to "ensnare" men's minds; Prisca and Maximilla, the leaders of the New Prophecy of the late second to early third century, perverted by a male teacher; and the teachers Philomena, Agape, and Galla, all associated with "false doctrines," labeled "unclean" (and therefore sexually deviant).[24] The influential "Montanist" prophets, Prisca (Priscilla), Maxmilla, and Quintilla, are also attacked, together with Montanus, the only male leader associated with the New Prophecy, by the orthodox bishops Hippolytus of Rome (170–236) in his *Refutation of All Heresies*, Epiphanius of Salamis (mid-300s) in his *Medicine Box (Panarion) against Heresy*, and Eusebius of Caesarea (260–340), who was also an influential orthodox church historian, in his *Ecclesiastical History*. The sect was deemed heretical, not because of its visions (although Priscilla claimed to have had a vision of Christ dressed in women's garments predicting the coming of the new Jerusalem [Epiphanius, *Medicine Box* 49.1.3.]), nor even because of its ascetic practices, but apparently because of the leadership of women, including prophets, bishops, and presbyters (Epiphanius, *Medicine Box* 49.3). Maximilla asserted that Christ spoke through her, the eschatological prophet, and that she was sent by him as a conduit of knowledge. Priscilla also claimed to be the mouthpiece of God, "Word and Spirit and Power." Their influence is denounced by these male church authorities as "deranged," "mad," "seductive" of weak minds, and possessed by a "bastard" spirit, speaking "improperly" and "strangely" (Eusebius, *Ecclesiastical History* 5.16).[25]

STRANGE WOMEN REFORMED: ASENETH AND THE REPENTANT HARLOTS

In Judaism and Christianity alike, the connection between women, wisdom, and sexuality is negative when it challenges the prerogatives of the men who constitute communal religious authority, positive when it supports them or maintains a subordinate position. In the latter case, female Wisdom is either celibate (the Christian tendency) or a chaste wife, a "fit partner" to help the wise man. Even in heterodox circles like the various sects of Gnosticism, female Wisdom can be both "whore" and "holy one."[26] In all of these traditions, the possession of Wisdom, becoming "wise," is an important method of knowing the divine, but it is equally critical to have the "appropriate" knowledge, to embrace the "true" Wisdom. Metaphorically, following this "true" way is to embrace the "good" or "pure" Woman/Wisdom, as a man has intimate knowledge of a faithful wife; choosing the "false" or "strange" way of knowledge that characterizes one's opponents' views is to be seduced and ultimately betrayed by the slippery, deceptive wiles of the "wicked" Woman/Anti-Wisdom. The woman who wishes to be "wise" in these traditions will follow the example of the "good" and sexually "pure" woman (chaste wife, virgin, ascetic) and shun that of the "bad" and sexually "loose" woman, "impure" because she deviates from bounded sexual norms.

An example from Judaism is *Joseph and Aseneth*, a Jewish "novel" of the late first or early second century C.E., which is an expansion of the tale of Joseph and his marriage to Aseneth, the daughter of an Egyptian priest, Potiphera, here called Pentephres (Gen. 41:45). In it, the virgin Aseneth, whom Joseph, himself a virgin, initially shuns because he fears the seductive wiles of a foreign woman (*Joseph and Aseneth* 7.3; 7.6; 8.1; 8.4), provides an implicit contrast to the predatory and adulterous wife of Potiphar in the Genesis text (Genesis 39; cf. *Joseph and Aseneth* 4.14) and an explicit contrast to "all" the prominent women of Egypt, married and unmarried, who wish to sleep with Joseph. Aseneth, who is "not like the daughters of the Egyptians, but in all ways like the daughters of the Hebrews," Sarah, Rebekah, and Rachel especially (1.7–8), disdains all men and is enclosed within a tower so that no man has ever seen her (2.1), but when she first gazes at Joseph, whom she had formerly scorned as a bridegroom, believing the rumors about him true, she is "overwhelmed with fright," as if Joseph embodies God (6.1–2). When Joseph refuses to allow Aseneth to kiss him, even in sisterly fashion (although we are aware this term has a double meaning), because she is an "idolater," a strange woman and therefore impure, Aseneth weeps bitterly. Out of love for Joseph, she "repents of her gods," even though she had served them, as Joseph did his God, devotedly (9.1). Weeping, fasting, divesting herself of all her royal adornment and dressing in sackcloth and ashes, for seven days Aseneth performs the actions of penitence. Thus "purified," she prays to the God of Israel to save her, the sinner, "the desolate one" (12.1–11), imploring him to preserve the wisdom of Joseph and to allow her to serve him, "to be a slave to him for the rest of my life" (13.12). The image of Joseph appears to her and assures her that her prayer has been heard, that she is truly "a holy virgin," and that the

female Metanoia (Repentance), herself "the mother of virgins," has inter-
ceded for her (15.1–8). Arrayed now like a bride, Aseneth is given a miraculous honeycomb to taste, which reveals to her the secrets of God, and is
blessed along with her seven virgin companions. The figure then takes off
in the divine "chariot of fire" (17.6), having made Aseneth a fit bride for
Joseph. Like Wisdom, Aseneth invites Joseph to a banquet in her house,
and they are duly married. Aseneth conceives and bears Ephraim and Manasseh, the ancestors of the "Joseph tribes" of Canaan (Gen. 41:50–52).[27]

As Ross Kraemer points out, this "romance" is filled with images from
the Song of Songs and Proverbs, the marriage of Aseneth and Joseph being
"simultaneously the union of the Wise Man and Wisdom personified as female, and that of the lovers in Song of Songs."[28] But for Aseneth to represent Wisdom, she must first be transformed from the Strange Woman, the
Anti-Wisdom characterized by idolatry and its metaphorical concomitant,
sexual immorality.[29] Even her speech must be changed, purified from the
seductive speech of the Strange Woman by the honeycomb that represents
the Word of God. After she is suitably humbled, Aseneth directs her sexual services entirely to one "lord," humbly washing his feet, obeying Joseph
and his God and thus becoming Wisdom personified as "The Virtuous
Woman [Proverbs 31] . . . obedient, industrious, and fruitful," redeeming
the transgression of Eve, who sought knowledge without her husband's direction or consent.[30]

The ideal of the wise woman whose counsel helps her husband's own
wisdom to increase, contained but perverted in the Beruriah legend, is
not one that emerging Christianity, with its early and persistent am-
bivalence toward marriage and sexual fulfillment in it, readily adopted.
Instead, the ideal Christian woman, according to those tales that gained
the most currency and portraits of women drawn either from life or
imagination by male clerics and monastics, is not the fertile, chaste wife
but the virgin or widow who eschews all connection with sexuality as
part of "the world" that draws her away from devotion to Christ. Certainly Christian male authorities could not and did not criticize the
"good wife," and, as the case of Tertullian shows, could and did criticize
the celibate heroines of the apocryphal Acts, who abandoned fiancés and
spouses in order to pursue the wandering life of apostolic power and independence. Three categories of women, all ascetic and celibate, seem
to have drawn the most praise: the never-married virgin who sedulously
avoided any adornment or behavior that would attract the sexual interest of a man; the widow, whose obligations of marriage and childbearing were fulfilled (cf. 1 Tim. 5:3–16); and the repentant prostitute, the
wealthy *hetaira* whose conversion was indicated by her utter rejection of
sexual activity, sometimes even of her own gender, and adoption of severe bodily austerity, to the point that one of the most famous of the

penitents, Pelagia, supposedly changed her name to Pelagius and lived as an anchorite, no one discovering her sex until her burial.[31] One might argue, and argue with much textual warrant, that most if not all of those men who praise celibate and ascetic women have themselves foregone marriage, and, especially after the fourth century, when many of these penitents' "lives" appear, this is the case.[32] Moreover, stories of men who made the choice for the ascetic life, particularly after a life of license (the most famous case being that of Augustine, who made a drama out of his own conversion as an example for others), are not unknown in Christianity. But even these seize upon heterosexual desire as a besetting sin, which they frequently symbolize by a female or, as in the conversion stories of Anthony and Jerome, by multiple seductive female forms. As Geoffrey Galt Harpham points out, Augustine even "converts" his discourse from female desire to female chastity. Augustine relates in Book 8 of the *Confessions* how his choice for the new life was held back by "the bonds of woman's love," but how eventually the female allegorical figure Continence appears, "a fruitful mother of children, of joys born of you, O Lord, her spouse" (8.11).[33] Augustine symbolizes the "dynamics of conversion" by "purging" Continence of sexuality: "Within the allegory, sexuality has been liberated from its literalness, its roots in the world; the heaven signified by allegory is populated by eager bridegrooms, fertile mothers, and numerous children, begat without fornication."[34] Like other male heterosexual writers, Augustine envisions real females as dangerous sexual beings, linked to the world of flesh and desire that entrap the spirit, the world of "fornication" that is the enemy of continence and self-restraint. His own desires for women, which he depicts throughout the *Confessions* as being perversely "provoked" by women's own sexuality, must be symbolically defeated (or "purged"), transformed into the nonhuman and asexual female figure of Continence that contains (and therefore restrains) the threat of woman as virgin, mother, and wife, so that he can gain mastery over his own desire.

AMBIGUITY RETAINED:
WISDOM IN GNOSTIC THOUGHT

This problematic representation of female desire, both as desire for the female and female sexuality in general, reaches a kind of paradoxical resolution in some texts from the late antique phenomenon known as Gnosticism. The term "Gnosticism" itself embraces a variety of perspectives— philosophical, Jewish, and Christian—having in common only a pervasive sense of alienation from the material world and an emphasis on salvation through knowledge (*gnosis*) of how this world, the macrocosm, came to be and of the nature of the microcosm, the human person, within it. The myth that often appears in Gnostic texts and that underlies others, most of which date from the second to third centuries of the Common Era, is largely a *midrash* (narrative interpretation) on Genesis 1—3 and on wisdom texts, including Proverbs.[35] In it, Wisdom (Sophia), personified as a female figure, is a major character. One of the "emanations" or "aeons" emerging from the primal spirit, variously called the "All," the "Mother-Father," and "the invisible virgin Spirit," Sophia is unlike the others in that she, being female, is not perfect, lacking her male half (consort). Being a spiritual essence, albeit an incomplete one, she has within her the desire to create, but since she is "lacking," her desire becomes a creation that lacks complete knowledge and falls into the realm of the material. This creation, often identified in anti-Jewish Gnostic writing with the YHWH of the Torah, thus creates a material, imperfect world, based only on a reflection of the spiritual realm, which he seeks to capture in matter. He and his half-spiritual, half-material allies make an androgynous creature from matter, into whom they breathe a divine soul. Sophia, for her part, like a penitent harlot, aghast at this botched creation, "repents" of her deed and seeks to remedy her "lack" of a male consort by seeking to retrieve the fragments of divinity embedded in matter and to awaken the human creature to its true nature. Her efforts are furthered by various mediators, including in Christian Gnosticism "the Savior" (Christ), and thwarted in part by the creator of the material world, who seeks both to divide the originally androgynous human beings into male and female, to entice them into creating further material beings through sexual intercourse, and to drug or intoxicate them so that they will not awaken to their true origin, nature, and destiny, and thus attain salvation and the collapse of his illegitimate power.[36]

The role of Sophia, like the attitude toward sexuality and gender reflected in the Gnostic texts, is an ambiguous one.[37] In many of the texts employing the myth of Sophia, she is actually divided into two figures, a "higher" (divine) Sophia, the "female spiritual principle" (*Hypostasis of the Archons* 89.11–18) who is helper, savior, and instructor of primal humanity, like the Wisdom of Proverbs; and a "lower" (material) Sophia, called "the Whore," and "the Vulgar One" (*Prounikos*) (*Second Treatise of the Great Seth* 50.26–29). Like the Strange Woman/Anti-Wisdom of Proverbs, the lower Sophia seduces the unaware into her own delusion, that the fleshly world, especially sexual intercourse and procreation, matters, and hence she leads them to death (*Gospel of Philip* 60.10–15). In the *Gospel of Truth*, she is characterized as "Error" (*Plane*), whose "mistake" in getting involved with material creation can only be rectified by the male Wisdom, Christ the Logos, the "Word of Truth" that is "published" on the cross (*Gospel of Truth*

16.4–34; 20.10–21.3). In some Christian Gnostic texts, Sophia is also the spouse of the Logos. Hippolytus, in *Refutation of All Heresies* 6.31.5–6, claims that, according to some Gnostic beliefs, the lower Sophia took Jesus, the earthly (or lower) manifestation of the Savior, as her consort, in order to correct her defective female nature.

The soul or spirit itself, like Sophia, is often characterized as female in Gnostic texts. In the *Exegesis on the Soul*, dating from the early third century C.E., the virgin soul, living in her Father's "house" (the divine realm), "falls" into a body, becomes a prostitute, is abused by her lovers, "those adulterers, . . . pretending to be faithful, true husbands," and finally "a poor desolate widow," who cries to the "Father" to be restored (*Exegesis on the Soul* 127–129).[38] The author of the *Exegesis* finds a variety of proofs and prophecies of the soul's fate in the inspired writings of the wise, including Jeremiah 3:1–4, Hosea 2:2–7, and Ezekiel 16:23–26, all on the adultery of YHWH's "wife" Israel. The author interprets "sons of Egypt, men great of flesh" (i.e., big of phallus) in the passage from Ezekiel to mean "the domain of the flesh and the perceptible realm and the affairs of the earth, by which the soul has become defiled here." The redemption of the soul from its "defilement" takes place upon repentance, when she gives up "her former prostitution, . . . the pollutions of the adulterers," whereupon the Father sends "her man, who is her brother, the first-born," her bridegroom (*Exegesis* 132). Although the brother-sister language recalls the erotic terminology of the Song of Songs, their marriage is "not like carnal marriage," being without the "annoyance of physical desire," but a re-creation of the original androgynous human, before "the woman led astray the man" (*Exegesis* 133; cf. Gen. 2:24). The soul is thenceforth to be totally devoted to her spouse, "her true love, her real master" (*Exegesis* 133; cf. Gen. 3:16; 1 Cor. 11:1; Eph. 5:23). The soul's fate is also compared to the actions of the adulterous Helen in the *Odyssey* (IV, 260–261; 261–264): "For when the soul leaves her perfect husband because of the treachery of Aphrodite [goddess of desire], who exists here [in this world] in the act of begetting, then she will suffer harm" (*Exegesis* 137). But if she repents, she will be restored to her "house." Once again, although the author of the *Exegesis* uses language taken from such disparate sources as Hebrew prophecy and Homeric literature, the same image of female sexual promiscuity, the "fall" from virginity, adultery, and prostitution, is used to convey involvement with the material world. Like an erring virgin, the soul abandons "her" true home, the house of her "Father" God, which becomes the place of the "bridal chamber" of the chaste bride and her faithful, redeeming bridegroom, here, the Savior Christ.

In a remarkable Gnostic document that appears to be unrelated to Christian Gnosticism, *The Thunder, Perfect Mind,* a series of opposing images, mainly female, is used in a self-revelation of the divine intellect, which then calls to those who will listen, "Do not be ignorant of me":

> I am the first and the last.
> I am the honored one and the scorned one.
> I am the whore (*porne*) and the holy one (*semne*).
>
> I am knowledge and ignorance.
> I am shame and boldness . . .

Like both Wisdom and Anti-Wisdom of Proverbs, she claims,

> I am she who cries out,
>   and I am cast forth upon the face of the earth.
> I prepare the bread and my mind within.[39]

These paradoxes, interspersed with the call by "Perfect Mind" to self-knowledge as well as "knowledge of the All," like the apparently self-contradictory Zen koans, call into question the hearer's received perception of the world as the realm of polar opposites rather than their conjunction. As Anne McGuire observes in *The Thunder*, the use of terms that usually "serve to divide and reduce women" creates a single, powerful female entity that "exists in the violation and crossing of boundaries,"[40] just as Wisdom in Proverbs is not complete without her ultra-boundary opposite, the Strange Woman. *The Thunder, Perfect Mind* thus exemplifies a reading of wisdom literature that is the method we have attempted to undertake in the present text, in Claudia Camp's phrasing, "reading like a trickster," a reading that resists the oppositions and embraces the opposites without holding them in mutually contradictory tension.[41] Through such a subversive reading, we can become both Wise and Strange without being confined to or assigned to either. Thus we truly confound the "wisdom" of those who account themselves wise, bringing the creative chaos back into their cosmos.

Abbreviations

ATR	*Anglican Theological Review*
Bib	*Biblica*
BSac	*Bibliotheca Sacra*
CBQ	*Catholic Biblical Quarterly*
CH	*Church History*
HBT	*Horizons in Biblical Theology*
HTR	*Harvard Theological Review*
HUCA	*Hebrew Union College Annual*
JAAR	*Journal of the American Academy of Religion*
JBL	*Journal of Biblical Literature*
JETS	*Journal of the Evangelical Theological Society*
JSOT	*Journal for the Study of the Old Testament*
JSOT Sup	Journal for the Study of the Old Testament—Supplement Series
LXX	Septuagint
NOAB	*New Oxford Annotated Bible*
NovT	*Novum Testamentum*
NRSV	New Revised Standard Version
NT	New Testament
NTS	*New Testament Studies*
OT	Old Testament
SBL/AAR	Society of Biblical Literature/American Academy of Religion
SR	*Studies in Religion/Sciences religieuses*
TS	*Theological Studies*
VT	*Vetus Testamentum*
ZNW	*Zeitschrift für neutestamentliche Wissenschaft*

Notes

NOTES TO THE INTRODUCTION

1. Translation mine.
2. Susan Mitchell, ed., *The Official Guide to American Attitudes* (Ithaca, N.Y.: New Strategist Publications, 1996), 375, 385–87.
3. Jerry Allen, "Adultery: New Furor over an Old Sin," *Newsweek* (Sept. 30, 1996): 54–60.
4. John F. Burns, "Hard-line Taliban Stones Couple, Reviving Tradition," New York Times News Service, Nov. 3, 1996.
5. Judith Laws and Pepper Schwartz, *Sexual Scripts*, 139.
6. Mary McIntosh, "Who Needs Prostitutes?" 53–54.
7. See Laurie Shrage, *Moral Dilemmas of Feminism*, 52.
8. According to Daniel Boyarin, the *"yetser ha-rah"* is a "near synonym for sexual desire." Boyarin, "Body Politic among the Brides of Christ: Paul and the Origins of Christian Sexual Renunciation," in Wimbush and Valantasis, *Asceticism*, 460.
9. Paul Ricoeur, *The Symbolism of Evil*, 28.
10. See Tina Pippin, *Death and Desire*, esp. 65–68, for the connection between the Whore of Babylon and the rhetoric of desire in the Apocalypse.
11. Elena Ciletti, "Patriarchal Ideology in the Renaissance Iconography of Judith," in *Refiguring Woman: Perspectives in Gender and the Italian Renaissance*, edited, with an introduction, by Marilyn Migiel and Juliana Schiesari (Ithaca, N.Y.: Cornell University Press, 1991), 70.
12. Gale A. Yee, "'I Have Perfumed My Bed with Myrrh,'" 53.
13. Léonie J. Archer, *Her Price Is beyond Rubies*, 105.
14. Mark Taylor, "Of Monsters and Dances: Masculinity, White Supremacy, Ecclesial Practice," in Schüssler Fiorenza and Copeland, *Violence against Women*, 55–58.
15. Michael L. Satlow, "Shame and Sex in Late Antique Judaism," in Wimbush and Valantasis, *Asceticism*, 539.
16. Nancy Jay, "Sacrifice as Remedy for Having Been Born of Woman," 290.
17. Carol M. Meyers, "Procreation, Production, and Protection," 573–74.
18. See J. Cheryl Exum, *Fragmented Women*, 109, on the wife-sister stories of

Genesis 12, 20, and 26 as examples of the fear of the matriarch's having sexual relations with someone other than the patriarch because of "the threat to the purity of the line."

19. Henry McKeating, "Sanctions against Adultery in Ancient Israelite Society," 63–65.
20. Ibid., 69–71.
21. See Joseph Blenkinsopp, "Social Context of the 'Outsider Woman,'" 457–73.
22. YHWH is the English transliteration of the Hebrew tetragrammaton, a four-letter word for God that cannot be pronounced. When I am referring to the God of Israel in the exclusive sense, I will use the term "YHWH." YHWH is the God of Israel, a collective noun referring to the people of God. "Israel" is also the name of the Northern Kingdom, composed of ten tribes that split from the hegemony of the southern two (Benjamin and Judah, usually referred to as "Judah") in 922 B.C.E. after the reign of Solomon. I will distinguish when I am referring to the collective "people of God" (Israel) and when I mean the Northern Kingdom exclusively.
23. Archer, *Her Price Is beyond Rubies*, 106.
24. "Tanakh" is an acronym for the three parts of the Hebrew scriptures: Torah (Law); Nevi'im (Prophets), and Ketubhim (Writings). "Apocrypha" refers to those Greek texts that are related to characters and situations in the Tanakh but not considered part of it.
25. Judith Plaskow, *Standing Again at Sinai*, 183.
26. See notes to Matt. 12:38–42 in *NOAB*, NT 18.
27. See Amy-Jill Levine, "Matthew," in Newsom and Ringe, *Women's Bible Commentary*, 255.
28. Alicia Suskin Ostriker, *Feminist Revision*, 27.
29. Delores S. Williams, *Sisters in the Wilderness: The Challenge of Womanist God-Talk* (Maryknoll, N.Y.: Orbis Books, 1993), 187.
30. Daniel Boyarin, *Carnal Israel*, 2.
31. Williams, *Sisters*, 187. "Womanist" is the preferred self-description of African American feminists.
32. Ostriker, *Feminist Revision*, 30.
33. For the initial appearance of this neologism that indicates "rule of the (male) master," a more inclusive term than patriarchy, see Elisabeth Schüssler Fiorenza and Mary Shawn Copeland, eds., "Introduction," *Violence against Women*, vii–xxiv.
34. The sole exception is Gail R. O'Day's commentary on the Gospel of John in Newsom and Ringe, *Women's Bible Commentary*, 293–304, and her critique of previous scholarship on this particular passage, "John 7:53–8:11," 631–40. Adele Reinhartz, in her commentary, "The Gospel of John," in Schüssler Fiorenza, *Searching the Scriptures*, 2:578, follows the traditional scholarship and dismisses the "interruption" of the story of the woman caught in adultery as "non-Johannine."

35. Gail R. O'Day, "John 7:53–8:11," 631.
36. Ibid., 640.
37. Andrea Dworkin, *Our Blood*, 27–28.
38. Mary Daly, *Gyn/Ecology*, 339; see also Dworkin, *Our Blood*, 22–49.
39. Catharine A. MacKinnon, *Toward a Feminist Theory of the State*, 129.
40. Patricia Murphy Robinson, "The Historical Repression of Women's Sexuality," in Vance, *Pleasure and Danger*, 265.
41. Joanna Russ, "What Can a Heroine Do?" 9, 5.
42. So dominant, however, has been the androcentric interpretation and representation in various media of the adultery of David with Bathsheba, that many who supposedly are familiar with this text misread it and insist that Bathsheba "tempted" David's lust by bathing on her rooftop and thus was responsible for his "fall."
43. See Phyllis A. Bird, "The Harlot as Heroine," 119–39, for Rahab and Tamar among other examples.
44. David Halperin, *Seeking Ezekiel*, 208.
45. Mieke Bal, *Anti-Covenant*, 20; Ilana Pardes, *Countertraditions in the Bible*, 144; Claudia V. Camp, "Feminist Theological Hermeneutics: Canon and Christian Identity," in Schüssler Fiorenza, *Searching the Scriptures*, 1:167.
46. Camp, "Feminist Theological Hermeneutics," 1:167.
47. Plaskow, *Standing Again at Sinai*, 1, 174.
48. See Julia O'Brien, "Judah as Wife and Husband: Deconstructing Gender in Malachi," *JBL* 115, no. 2 (1996): 241–50, for a discussion of the different gender roles played by YHWH and Israel in prophetic texts.
49. Daly, *Gyn/Ecology*, 105, cited by Tina Pippin, "The Revelation to John," in Schüssler Fiorenza, *Searching the Scriptures*, 2:120.
50. Taylor, "Of Monsters and Dances," 58.
51. Pippin, *Death and Desire*, 86.
52. Howard Eilberg-Schwartz, *God's Phallus*, 3–5, 20.
53. MacKinnon, *Toward a Feminist Theory*, 239.
54. Susan Ashbrook Harvey, "The Odes of Solomon," in Schüssler Fiorenza, *Searching the Scriptures*, 2:87.
55. This is the criticism offered of my book, *Her Image of Salvation* by Schüssler Fiorenza in *Jesus*, 77–78. While I believe it is a misreading of my particular text, it is a valid general criticism.
56. Beruriah, the wife of the revered Rabbi Meir of the second century C.E., is cited for her knowledge of ritual laws and learning in *'Abot* 1.5, in passages from the Tosefta, and in several passages of the Babylonian Talmud, dating from about the fifth century C.E., including one in which she rebukes her husband (b. *Berakot* 10a). According to much later tradition (Rashi ad b. *'Aboda Zara* 18b), Rabbi Meir gets one of his students to seduce her because she made fun of the rabbinic saying that women were "light-minded" (lewd), and in disgrace she hanged herself. For

information on Beruriah and her legend, see Archer, *Her Price Is beyond Rubies*, 98–99, and Boyarin, *Carnal Israel*, 182–91. Mary of Magdala (Mary Magdalene), prominent in the New Testament Gospels as a follower of Jesus (see esp. Luke 8:1–3) and consistently in all four Gospels a witness to the resurrection, was also preeminent in heretical Gnostic Christian texts as a disciple. From the fifth century on, Mary Magdalene was portrayed as a woman posssessed by the "demons of sin" (Jerome, *Letters* 59.4) and as a prostitute whom Jesus had saved. For the subsequent Western church, Mary became the prototypical redeemed seductress, the "repentant Eve," in contrast to the pure Virgin Mary. For church lore relating to Mary, see Carla Ricci, *Mary Magdalene*, 30–39, 150, and Benedicta Ward, *Harlots of the Desert*, 7–21, 58.

NOTES TO CHAPTER 1.
ADULTERY AND OTHER SEX CRIMES

1. According to historian of religions Mircea Eliade, the sacralizing of ordinary or "profane" time is what makes the Judeo-Chrisian traditions unique among world religions. See Eliade, *The Sacred and the Profane*, 110–12.
2. Sandra M. Schneiders, *The Revelatory Text*, 181–83.
3. See, e.g., Edwin M. Schur, *Labeling Women Deviant*, esp. 52–53, 120; Gayle Rubin, "Thinking Sex: Notes for a Radical Theory of the Politics of Sexuality," in Vance, *Pleasure and Danger*, 288–309; Dworkin, *Our Blood*, 22–49.
4. Encyclopedia Judaica, s.v. "Oral Law," cited in Katheryn Pfisterer Darr, *Far More Precious than Jewels*, 27 n. 40.
5. Drorah O'Donnell Setel, "Exodus," in Newsom and Ringe, *Women's Bible Commentary*, 26.
6. See the introduction to Deuteronomy, *NOAB*, NRSV, OT 217; cf. Tikva Frymer-Kensky, "Deuteronomy," in Newsom and Ringe, *Women's Bible Commentary*, 52.
7. Gerda Lerner, *The Creation of Patriarchy*, 8–9, 78–83.
8. Judith Plaskow, *Standing Again at Sinai*, 178.
9. Judith Romney Wegner, *Chattel or Person?* 14, 114.
10. Léonie J. Archer, *Her Price Is beyond Rubies*, 25–26.
11. J. Cheryl Exum, *Fragmented Women*, 148–9.
12. This is despite the reprehension modern readers may have for the sexual exploitation of the matriarchs. See, e.g., Irmgard Fischer, "'Go and Suffer Oppression!' Said God's Messenger to Hagar: Repression of Women in Biblical Texts," in Schüssler Fiorenza and Copeland, *Violence against Women*, 75.
13. Susan Niditch, *Underdogs and Tricksters*, xi.
14. Ibid., 66
15. Exum, *Fragmented Women*, 16.

16. Footnote to Gen. 19:8 (*NOAB*, OT 23). A similar offer, made to protect a male guest from being sodomized by the men of the town, occurs in Judges 19:22–26. There the alien householder also offers his two virgin daughters to be sexually abused, and when this offer is spurned, throws out his male guest's concubine to be raped until she dies. The text presents this episode as a pretext for the other Israelite tribes to punish those responsible, the Benjaminites, by killing the men and raping their women. Through this rape, the "tribe of Benjamin" is preserved (Judges 21). See Phyllis Trible, *Texts of Terror*, 64–91.

17. Philo, *On the Contemplative Life*, 7.57–63.

18. See Mark Taylor, "Of Monsters and Dances," 54, where he suggests that the construction of a white male's sense of "masculinity" is both "over against" women and over people of color.

19. The *NOAB* commentary on Gen. 31:35, along with most commentators, including Susan Niditch in "Genesis," in Newsom and Ringe, *Women's Bible Commentary*, 21, assumes that "the way of women" refers to Rachel's menstrual "uncleanness," and therefore that the narrator thus "ridicules" Laban's "idols." The text, however, does not call them idols. Rachel's presumed "menstruous condition" may have prevented her from rising, but menstruation as a source of ritual uncleanness in the Levitical code (Lev. 15:19–24) may not apply here. This situation recalls a similar connection between female sexuality and property made by women in Haiti who refer to their genitals as their "land." See Karen McCarthy Brown, "Mama Lola and the Ezilis," in Falk and Gross, *Unspoken Worlds*, 241.

20. Niditch, "Genesis," 15.

21. Alice Ogden Bellis, *Helpmates, Harlots, and Heroes*, 89–90. A similar reaction to a sister's rape by a brother, with the inaction of a father, is seen in the story of the rape of David's daughter Tamar by Amnon and the vengeance of her brother Absalom (2 Samuel 13).

22. Niditch, "Genesis," 16.

23. Exum, *Fragmented Women*, 150.

24. Sharon H. Ringe, "When Women Interpret the Bible," in Newsom and Ringe, *Women's Bible Commentary*, 3.

25. Susan Niditch, "Wronged Woman Righted," 145–46.

26. Frymer-Kensky, "Deuteronomy," 53. See also Jon Levenson, *Sinai and Zion*, 75–80.

27. Levenson, *Sinai and Zion*, 78.

28. Wegner, *Chattel or Person?* 13.

29. Setel, "Exodus," 27.

30. Henry McKeating, "Sanctions against Adultery," 58. See also Michael Fishbane, "Accusations of Adultery," 44.

31. Setel, "Exodus," 29.

32. Plaskow, *Standing Again at Sinai*, 170-72.
33. Setel, "Exodus," 33.
34. Wegner, *Chattel or Person?* 13–14.
35. Setel, "Exodus," 34.
36. Cf. Deut. 15:12–18, where both male and female slaves are freed after seven years, and the female is not assumed to be her master's sexual property.
37. Wegner, "Leviticus," in Newsom and Ringe, *Women's Bible Commentary*, 36–38.
38. Ibid., 39. See also Mary Douglas, *Purity and Danger*, for the function of boundary systems and symbols within groups.
39. Howard Eilberg-Schwartz, *The Savage in Judaism*, 177–94.
40. Carol Meyers, "Procreation, Production, and Protection," 585–86. Meyers, however, finds that this valuation of females at about 40 percent of males reflects a "nearly balanced" situation that recognizes female contribution of labor to a subsistence economy, apart from their childbearing responsibilities. See also Wegner, "Leviticus," 43.
41. Fishbane, "Accusations of Adultery," 25 n. 1.
42. Rachel Biale, *Women and Jewish Law*, 155, 175.
43. Wegner, "Leviticus," 41.
44. In the case of a man who has intercourse with a slave woman who is "designated" for another man but is not freed or ransomed, neither he nor the woman are to be executed because she is not freed. Instead, "an inquiry shall be held," and he alone must bring a guilt-offering to expiate his sin. Female slaves intended to be concubines have a kind of liminal status (cf. Ex. 21:7–11) in which, while they are allowed some rights, they belong to a different category than full wives. This different category may account for the fact that this particular case does not incur the same penalty as adultery.
45. Commentary on Lev. 20:1–27, *NOAB*, OT 51.
46. Biale, *Women and Jewish Law*, 121.
47. Wegner, *Chattel or Person?* 13–14.
48. It has been assumed that the *qedeshoth* (consecrated women) and *qadeshim* (consecrated men) of Deut. 23:18 are "temple prostitutes," and Israelite fathers are prohibited from dedicating their female or male children to such service. For a discussion of the differences between *zonoth* ("prostitutes"; "harlots") and *qedeshoth* ("consecrated women," often translated "temple prostitutes"), see chapter 2.
49. Frymer-Kensky, "Deuteronomy," 57.
50. The situation of spousal jealousy that results in the ordeal of the accused wife (Num. 5:11–31) will be discussed more fully in chapter 2.
51. See Frymer-Kensky, "Deuteronomy," 59.
52. Cf. the special case of the daughters of Zelophehad, whose father died without sons to perpetuate his name and "portion" in Israel (Num. 27:1–11).
53. Frymer-Kensky, "Deuteronomy," 61; cf. Wegner, *Chattel or Person?* 114.

54. See Niditch, "Wronged Woman Righted," 148–49.
55. Numbers 31:13–20, which recounts the aftermath of a battle with the Midianites, presents an interesting version of this assumption, where the males of the defeated, even the infants, are killed, and among the women, only the virgins, the women who have not "known" men, are allowed to live. In this text, part of the Priestly strand of the Pentateuch, Moses gives as his reason for this action the fact that the women were responsible for persuading the Israelite men to apostasy at Peor (Numbers 25), thus attributing Israelite infidelity to YHWH to sexual seduction by foreign women, a recurrent theme in the Tanakh, especially in the prophetic literature.

NOTES TO CHAPTER 2.
WOMEN ON THE BOUNDARY: SEX AND SUBVERSION

1. See, e.g., Gerda Lerner, *The Creation of Patriarchy*, 89–91.
2. The Septuagint is the Greek translation of the Hebrew Bible and some of the related apocryphal writings. It was used by Greek-speaking Jews and constituted the scriptures for Greek-speaking Christians.
3. Athalya Brenner, *The Israelite Woman*, 78.
4. Mieke Bal, *Lethal Love*, 101.
5. Phyllis Bird, "The Harlot as Heroine," 126.
6. Phyllis Bird, "'To Play the Harlot': An Inquiry into an Old Testament Metaphor," in Day, *Gender and Difference*, 76; Tikva Frymer-Kensky, "Deuteronomy," in Newsom and Ringe, *Women's Bible Commentary*, 59.
7. Although Frymer-Kensky, in "Deuteronomy," suggests that these women were *qedeshoth*, the actual term is not used in the Hebrew text.
8. Michael D. Goulder, *The Song of Fourteen Songs*, 83, implies that Tamar is, like Ruth and the Shulammite of the Song of Songs, a foreign woman, but there is no evidence in Genesis 38 to support this claim.
9. The tale of Tobit (ca. third to second century B.C.E.) in the Apocrypha also features a bride, Sarah, whose seven prospective husbands are killed by a demon before the marriages can be consummated. Unlike Judah, however, the pious Tobit commands his son Tobias to marry Sarah despite the danger (Tobit 6:16), thus winning heavenly help and favor.
10. Susan Niditch, "The Wronged Woman Righted," 146.
11. Despite the fact that the Hebrew word being translated is *zonah*, the *NOAB* commentary on Genesis 38:15 explains that Tamar "was taken to be a cult prostitute, a devotee of the mother-goddess Ishtar. Prostitution was connected with the worship of the nature gods of fertility" (*NOAB*, OT 50).
12. The exchange occurs only in the Hebrew; the Greek translation of the Tanakh, the Septuagint, has *porne* (prostitute) in all instances.
13. The Levitical prohibition against a father-in-law having intercourse with

a daughter-in-law (Lev. 18:15) apparently is not applied here because of Tamar's liminal status: her husband, Judah's son Er, is no longer living.

14. Niditch, "Wronged Woman Righted," 144.
15. Ibid., 146.
16. Jane Schaberg, *The Illegitimacy of Jesus*, 25–26.
17. See Bird, "Harlot as Heroine"; Danna Nolan Fewell, "Joshua," in Newsom and Ringe, *Women's Bible Commentary*, 63–66. Rahab may in fact have been a woman of relatively high status in the Canaanite community. The employment of a "harlot" to avert danger to the community is known from the *Epic of Gilgamesh*, where a harlot is hired to civilize the wild man Enkidu and teach him the "woman's art."
18. Fewell, "Joshua," 65.
19. Ibid., 66; Bird, "Harlot as Heroine," 128.
20. Cf. *NOAB* commentary on Josh. 6:15–27, OT 276.
21. Bird, "To Play the Harlot," 76.
22. Ibid., 79.
23. Ibid., 77.
24. Her counterpart, the *qadesh*, is often distinguished by the translation, "male sacred prostitute."
25. Lerner, *Creation of Patriarchy*, 125–31.
26. Bird, "'To Play the Harlot,'" 75–76.
27. Frymer-Kensky, "Deuteronomy," 59–60.
28. Bird, "'To Play the Harlot,'" 75–76.
29. Howard Eilberg-Schwartz, *God's Phallus*, 84.
30. Niditch, "Genesis," in Newsom and Ringe, *Women's Bible Commentary*, 25.
31. See *NOAB* commentary on Gen. 37:36, 41:45. A Hellenistic Jewish romance, *Joseph and Aseneth*, makes much of Aseneth's purity, which matches Joseph's, and her eventual conversion to Judaism. For further discussion of the Joseph and Aseneth story, see chapter 7.
32. Danna Nolan Fewell, "Judges," in Newsom and Ringe, *Women's Bible Commentary*, 73.
33. Cf. J. Cheryl Exum, *Fragmented Women*, 70–71.
34. The distance and the height of ascent are given in the *NOAB* commentary on Judg. 16:3, OT 323.
35. Fewell, "Judges," 73.
36. Ibid., 74.
37. Ibid., 72; *NOAB* commentary on Judges 13:1–16:31, OT 323.
38. *NOAB* commentary on Judges. 5, OT 306.
39. Cf. Susan Niditch, "Eroticism and Death in the Tale of Jael," in Day, *Gender and Difference*, 52; Fewell and David M. Gunn, "Controlling Perspectives," 405–407.
40. Fewell and Gunn, "Controlling Perspectives," 406.
41. Fewell, "Judges," 69, points out that *raqaq*, "parted lips," is often "mis-

leadingly translated" as "temple." This translation blunts the sustained eroticism of the prose narrative.

42. Translation by Fewell and Gunn, "Controlling Perspectives," 407.

43. Ibid.

44. Fewell, "Judges," 69.

45. Niditch, "Eroticism and Death," 52. See also Jer. 31:22, where the "new thing" created by YHWH in restoring Judah is the unexpected "women surrounding the man (*geber*)." This phrase has also been translated as, "The woman surrounds [and thereby subdues?] the warrior."

46. Her husband's name, "Heber" (Joiner), and that of his clan, "Kenite" or "Smith," suggest further that their craft may support the Iron Age technology that gives the Canaanites their superiority over the Israelites. See Fewell, "Judges," 69; *NOAB* commentary on Judges 1:16, OT 301.

47. Fewell, "Judges," 69.

48. Niditch, "Eroticism and Death," 52.

49. Athalyah Brenner, *The Israelite Woman*, 120.

50. Joseph Blenkinsopp, "Social Context of the 'Outsider Woman,'" 457–61.

51. See Bird, "'To Play the Harlot,'" 75–94.

52. Claudia V. Camp, "1 and 2 Kings," in Newsom and Ringe, *Women's Bible Commentary*, 103.

53. Ibid., 104.

54. Tamara Cohn Eskenazi, "Ezra-Nehemiah," in Newsom and Ringe, *Women's Bible Commentary*, 117.

55. Léonie J. Archer, *Her Price Is beyond Rubies*, 106.

56. Eskenazi, "Ezra-Nehemiah," 120.

57. Ibid., 118.

58. See Amy-Jill Levine, "Ruth," in Newsom and Ringe, *Women's Bible Commentary*, 79; André Lacoque, *The Feminine Unconventional*, 2–5, 84–86, 93; Alice Ogden Bellis, *Helpmates, Harlots, and Heroes*, 217.

59. Levine, "Ruth," 79; Lacoque, *Feminine Unconventional*, 86.

60. Levine, "Ruth," 80.

61. Ibid.

62. "To speak to the heart" of is a familiar expression of wooing or seduction of a woman by a man, often in a context of sexual peril to the woman (cf. Gen. 34:3, Dinah's rape by Shechem; Judg. 19:3, the reconciliation of the Levite and his concubine; Hos. 2:14); see also Levine, "Ruth," 81.

63. Levine, "Ruth," 82.

64. Ibid., 81.

65. Ibid., 83–84; Lacoque, *Feminine Unconventional*, 93, 121.

66. I prefer to see Ruth, who disappears as an actor in her story once she has borne a son and heir, as being absorbed into the community rather than with Levine, "Ruth," 84, as being "erased."

67. Brenner, *Israelite Woman*, 121.

68. Marcia Falk, *Love Lyrics from the Bible*; Phyllis Trible, "Depatriarchalizing in Biblical Interpretation," *JAAR* 41 (1973): 45; Marvin Pope, *Song of Songs*, 210.

69. My thanks to my colleague Carey E. Walsh for sharing with me a preliminary version of her paper, "A Startling Voice: Women's Desire in the Song of Songs," read in the Theology of Hebrew Scriptures Section, SBL/AAR Annual Meeting, Nov. 23–26, 1996. What follows has been prompted by and depends in large part on Walsh's insights.

70. Renita J. Weems, "Song of Songs," in Newsom and Ringe, *Women's Bible Commentary*, 156.

71. Pope, *Song of Songs*, 89–90.

72. This is the NRSV translation; Falk, *Love Lyrics*, 115, translates the difficult *nidgalot* (sing., *diglo*, see 2:4, often translated, "His banner over me was love") as "glances," or "vision." The female beloved drives her lover wild with the sight of her.

73. Ibid., 111.

74. Ibid., 90; Weems, "Song of Songs," 159–60.

75. Goulder, *Song of Fourteen Songs*, 75, 86. Cf. Weems, "Song of Songs," 159–60.

76. Weems, "Song of Songs," 158.

77. Ibid., 160.

78. Exum, *Fragmented Women*, 76.

79. Bird, "'To Play the Harlot,'" 77, 80. "Ba'al" is the name of a Canaanite fertility god, of various male fertility deities of the land, and the name for both "master" and "husband."

NOTES TO CHAPTER 3.
JEALOUS HUSBAND AND WAYWARD WIFE:
SEXUAL CRIME AND PUNISHMENT

1. Miriam the prophet, Moses' sister, along with their brother Aaron, challenges Moses' leadership in Numbers 12. Only Miriam, however, is punished.

2. Judith Plaskow, *Standing Again at Sinai*, 4–5; Judith Romney Wegner, *Chattel or Person?* 3–5.

3. Claudia V. Camp, "1 and 2 Kings," 97–98.

4. Howard Eilberg-Schwartz, *God's Phallus*, 97.

5. Ibid., 128.

6. Phyllis Bird, "'To Play the Harlot,'" 75–76.

7. Ibid., 77.

8. Eilberg-Schwartz, *God's Phallus*, 3.

9. Ibid., 20.

10. Renita J. Weems, *Battered Love*, 70.

11. Tikva Frymer-Kensky, "Deuteronomy," 53.

12. Michael Fishbane, "Accusations of Adultery," 26.

13. Katharine Doob Sakenfeld, "Numbers," in Newsom and Ringe, *Women's Bible Commentary*, 49.
14. Mishnah Sotah 3.4; Daniel Boyarin, *Carnal Israel*, 171; Léonie J. Archer, *Her Price Is beyond Rubies*, 100 n. 1.
15. Frymer-Kensky, *In the Wake of the Goddesses*, 151.
16. Ibid., 149–51; Edwin LeBron Matthews, "The Use of the Adultery Motif in Hebrew Prophecy," Th.D. dissertation, New Orleans Baptist Theological Seminary, 1987, 8. See also Eilberg-Schwartz, *God's Phallus*, 112.
17. Gale A. Yee, "Hosea," in Newsom and Ringe, *Women's Bible Commentary*, 195.
18. Dwight H. Small, "The Prophet Hosea," 133–40.
19. Francis I. Anderson and David Noel Freedman, *Hosea: A New Translation with Introduction and Commentary*, Anchor Bible (Garden City, N.Y.: Doubleday, 1980), 221.
20. Yee, "Hosea," 195; T. Drorah Setel, "Prophets and Pornography," 86–95; Renita J. Weems, "Gomer," 87–104; Elisabeth Schüssler Fiorenza, "Interpreting Patriarchal Traditions," 39–61.
21. Bird, "'To Play the Harlot,'" 89.
22. Matthews, "Use of the Adultery Motif," 8.
23. See, e.g., the commentary on Hos. 1:2–9 in the *NOAB*, headed "The prophet marries the prostitute Gomer," and on Hos. 3:1–5, headed "The restoration of Gomer."
24. Yee, "Hosea," 199.
25. Weems, *Battered Love*, 51.
26. Weems, "Gomer," 97; cf. *NOAB* commentary on Hos. 1:2–3:5, which assumes that Hosea acts in chapter 2 toward Gomer as YHWH acts toward Israel, with "disciplinary action" and "temporary chastisement."
27. Fokkelien van Dijk-Hemmes, "The Metaphorization of Women in Prophetic Speech: An Analysis of Ezekiel 23," in Athalya Brenner and van Dijk-Hemmes, *On Gendering Texts*, 168.
28. Ibid.
29. Weems, "Gomer," 90. See also Yee, "Hosea," 199; Setel, "Prophets and Pornography," 92; Schüssler Fiorenza, "Interpreting Patriarchial Traditions," 47.
30. Setel, "Prophets and Pornography," 94.
31. Weems, *Battered Love*, 29.
32. Ibid., 93–94.
33. Bird, "'To Play the Harlot,'" 86.
34. Eilberg-Schwartz, *God's Phallus*, 3–5, 112.
35. Frymer-Kensky, *In the Wake of the Goddesses*, 149–151.
36. Setel, *Prophets and Pornography*, 86.
37. Kathleen M. O'Connor, "Jeremiah," in Newsom and Ringe, *Women's Bible Commentary*, 170.

38. Ibid.; Athalya Brenner, "On 'Jeremiah' and the Poetics of (Prophetic?) Pornography," in Brenner and van Dijk-Hemmes, *On Gendering Texts*, 185.
39. The "adornment" of the bride appears to attract the gaze of all toward her, as appropriate for the object possessed by the bridegroom. The bridegroom's munificence is the only fit ornament for the bride, who herself is his "adornment."
40. Brenner, "On 'Jeremiah,'" 182.
41. O'Connor, "Jeremiah," 171.
42. Rape is also envisioned as the appropriate retribution for "daughter Egypt" (Jer. 46:24) and for "daughter Babylon" (50:12; 51:47), Judah's quondam allies and later her betrayers.
43. Although there continues to be much debate on the composition of the book of Jeremiah, these chapters being attributed both to Jeremiah and his disciple Baruch (cf. O'Connor, "Jeremiah," 169; *NOAB* commentary on 30:1–31:40, OT 1007), for the sake of convenience, I will refer to the authorial "voice" as "Jeremiah."
44. O'Connor, "Jeremiah," 176.
45. Ibid.
46. Katheryn Pfisterer Darr, "Ezekiel," in Newsom and Ringe, *Women's Bible Commentary*, 183.
47. Matthews, "The Use of the Adultery Motif," 8.
48. David Halperin, *Seeking Ezekiel*, 148.
49. Weems, *Battered Love*, 41.
50. Darr, "Ezekiel," 187.
51. See Frymer-Kensky, "Deuteronomy," 53; Halperin, *Seeking Ezekiel*, 121.
52. Eilberg-Schwartz, *God's Phallus*, 112.
53. Halperin, *Seeking Ezekiel*, 121.
54. Darr, "Ezekiel," 187.
55. Halperin, *Seeking Ezekiel*, 142.
56. The Hebrew version of "full womanhood" is "ornament of ornaments," thus further directing the reader's eyes to the naked, sexually mature woman (*NOAB*, note on Ezek. 16:7, OT 1073).
57. Halperin, *Seeking Ezekiel*, 164.
58. The literal translation for "lustful" (Ezek. 16:26, NRSV); Eilberg-Schwartz, *God's Phallus*, 112.
59. Darr, "Ezekiel," 188.
60. Halperin, *Seeking Ezekiel*, 208.
61. Ibid., 150–51.
62. van Dijk-Hemmes, "Metaphorization of Women," 173.
63. Darr, "Ezekiel,"189.
64. Halperin, *Seeking Ezekiel*, 117–18.
65. Ibid.
66. Eilberg-Schwartz, *God's Phallus*, 112–15.

67. van Dijk-Hemmes, "Metaphorization of Women," 175.

68. See Darr, "Ezekiel," 190.

69. Weems, *Battered Love*, 109.

70. *NOAB* commentary on Micah 4:1–5:15, OT 1194.

71. Julia M. O'Brien, "Judah as Wife and Husband: Deconstructing Gender in Malachi," *JBL* 115, no. 2 (1996): 248–49.

72. Ibid., 249.

73. Beth Glazier-McDonald, "Zechariah," in Newsom and Ringe, *Women's Bible Commentary*, 230–31.

74. See van Dijk-Hemmes, "Metaphorization of Women," 175; Frymer-Kensky, *In the Wake of the Goddesses*, 151; Plaskow, *Standing Again at Sinai*, 175; Boyarin, *Carnal Israel*, 77.

NOTES TO CHAPTER 4.
THE WHORE AND THE HOLY ONE:
MIRROR IMAGES OF WISDOM

1. An alternate translation of "woman's art" is "woman's task." See Gerda Lerner, *The Creation of Patriarchy*, 132.

2. Howard Eilberg-Schwartz, *God's Phallus*, 91.

3. Nel Noddings, *Women and Evil*, 56.

4. An important exception is Genesis 19:4–5, where the term applies to men knowing men. See Eilberg-Schwartz, *God's Phallus*, 94.

5. The verse numbering is taken from the English text; in the Hebrew text, these verses are numbered 2:18–22.

6. Ilana Pardes, *Countertraditions in the Bible*, 123.

7. See Claudia V. Camp, "Wise and Strange," 14, 18–19; cf. Susan Niditch, *Underdogs and Tricksters*, xi.

8. Danna Nolan Fewell, "Judges," 69–70.

9. See Sidnie Ann White, "Esther," in Newsom and Ringe, *Women's Bible Commentary*, 127.

10. Niditch, *Underdogs and Tricksters*, 134.

11. Athalya Brenner, *The Israelite Woman*, 122.

12. Camp, "1 and 2 Kings," 102.

13. Tikva Frymer-Kensky, *In the Wake of the Goddesses*, 182–83.

14. Carole R. Fontaine, "Proverbs," in Newsom and Ringe, *Women's Bible Commentary*, 145.

15. Ibid.

16. Ibid.; Camp, "Wise and Strange," 21; Joseph Blenkinsopp, "The Social Context of the 'Outsider Woman,'" 457–61; Gale A. Yee, "'I Have Perfumed,'" 53 n. 1.

17. Blenkinsopp, "Social Context of the 'Outsider Woman,'" 457.

18. Ibid., 462.

19. Camp, "Wise and Strange," 20–21.

20. Ibid., 18–19.

21. Brenner, *Israelite Woman*, 44.

22. Henry McKeating, "Sanctions against Adultery," 59.

23. These are in the Masoretic Text of the Hebrew. A variant reading of *ra'* (evil) is *zarah* (strange). The Greek text (LXX) has, more mildly, "wife of another husband (man)," the reading preferred by the NRSV, which also rather inexplicably translates *nokriyyah* (Gk., *allotria*) as "adulteress," perhaps under the influence of 6:25–29.

24. Fokkelien van Dijk-Hemmes, "Traces of Women's Texts in the Hebrew Bible," in Brenner and van Dijk-Hemmes, *On Gendering Texts*, 57.

25. Yee, "Foreign Woman," 62.

26. That this is the exact behavior of Wisdom (Prov. 1:20–21; 8:1–4; 9:3–6) and also the appropriate behavior for an eager bride (Song 3:1–4), is noted by Yee (62) as part of the author's rhetorical strategy, and will be discussed later in connection with the construction of the figure of Wisdom as bride and wife.

27. Yee, "Foreign Woman," 62–63.

28. David Halperin, *Seeking Ezekiel*, 100.

29. Yee, "Foreign Woman," 62–63.

30. van Dijk-Hemmes, "Traces of Women's Texts," 63; *NOAB* commentary on Prov. 1:20–33, OT 803–4.

31. Yee, "Foreign Woman," 58.

32. The "high places" were the places in Jerusalem, Judah, and Israel where deities like Asherah were worshiped, so they are synonymous with "whoring" after foreign deities (cf. Jer. 2:20; Ezek. 16:24–25). The wise man will find Wisdom and the "knowledge of YHWH" there; the foolish one will find Folly and knowledge of other deities who will lead him away from YHWH into Sheol.

33. Even in the Song of Songs, the "public domain" is not the place for a woman to seek her lover. See Marcia Falk, *Love Lyrics from the Bible*, 90–94.

34. Eilberg-Schwartz, *God's Phallus*, 131.

35. Yee, "Foreign Woman," 66.

36. Eilberg-Schwartz, *God's Phallus*, 131, 138.

37. In many rabbinic texts, marriage assuages illicit sexual desire so that the sage can concentrate on the desirable wisdom contained in Torah. See Daniel Boyarin, *Carnal Israel*, 134–36.

38. Laurie Shrage, *Moral Dilemmas of Feminism*, 38, 52.

39. Job 9a–9e, LXX; cf. Carol A. Newsom, "Job," in Newsom and Ringe, *Women's Bible Commentary*, 132.

40. Rebecca Lesses, "The Daughters of Job," in Schüssler Fiorenza, *Searching the Scriptures*, 2:147.

41. Silvia Schroer, "The Book of Sophia," trans. Linda M. Mahoney, in Schüssler Fiorenza, *Searching the Scriptures*, 2:34.

42. Boyarin, *Carnal Israel*, 171–78.
43. Much of the discussion of Susanna has been stimulated by remarks by A.-J. Levine.
44. Boyarin, *Carnal Israel*, 134–36; Eilberg-Schwartz, *God's Phallus*, 20.
45. Noddings, *Women and Evil*, 60.
46. Camp, "Wise and Strange," 33.

NOTES TO CHAPTER 5.
SPIRITUALITY AND SEXUALITY IN THE BODY OF CHRIST

1. See esp. the landmark study by Elisabeth Schüssler Fiorenza, *In Memory of Her*.
2. The *Gospel of Thomas* is an apocryphal gospel with gnosticizing tendencies, consisting solely of Jesus' supposed sayings. In its present form, it probably dates from prior to the end of the second century, although some would date its putative original from the late first century. Many of the sayings in the *Gospel of Thomas* have parallels in the Synoptic Gospels.
3. The harsher saying in Luke is probably closer to the original source shared by Luke and Matthew, called Q (Ger., *Quelle*). Luke is usually supposed to have preserved versions of sayings that are closer to its Q version. See John S. Kloppenborg, *Q Parallels*.
4. Carla Ricci, *Mary Magdalene and Many Others*, 179.
5. Mary Magdalene also appears as a prominent disciple in many of the non-canonical gospels, including the *Gospel of Thomas*, *Gospel of Philip*, *Gospel of Peter*, and *Gospel of Mary*.
6. Martha and Mary are also mentioned by Luke, without their brother (Luke 10:38–42), in a story that contrasts the "typically female" role of serving (Martha) with that of discipleship (Mary).
7. It is not my intention here to recapitulate the fine work of many others on the active ministry of women in early Christianity, but simply to point out that it seems their marital status was not a special issue.
8. Bernadette Brooten, *Women Leaders in the Ancient Synagogue*, Brown Judaic Studies 36 (Chico, Calif.: Scholars Press, 1982); Ross S. Kraemer, *Her Share of the Blessings*, 106–27.
9. See Amy-Jill Levine, "Matthew," in Newsom and Ringe, *Women's Bible Commentary*, 255, for possible interpretations of *porneia*.
10. G. J. Wenham, "Gospel Definitions," 330.
11. Ibid., 331; Will Deming, "Mark 9:42–10:12," 141.
12. Deming, "Mark 9:42–10:12," 140; cf. Daniel Boyarin, *Carnal Israel*, 196; Rachel Biale, *Women and Jewish Law*, 121–22.
13. Pheme Perkins, "The Gospel of Thomas," in Schüssler Fiorenza, *Searching the Scriptures*, 2:539.

14. Jane Schaberg, "Luke," in Newsom and Ringe, *Women's Bible Commentary*, 284.
15. Gail Paterson Corrington, *Her Image of Salvation*, 161–65.
16. Levine, "Matthew," 255; Angelo Tosato, "Joseph," 547–51.
17. Dale B. Martin, *The Corinthian Body*, 174–75.
18. Jeremiah (5:7–8) also deems male adultery and patronage of prostitutes "crimes" worthy of prosecution by YHWH.
19. Martin, *Corinthian Body*, 209; cf. Jouette M. Bassler, "1 Corinthians," in Newsom and Ringe, *Women's Bible Commentary*, 323–26.
20. For a discussion of both attitudes, see Neil Elliott, *Liberating Paul*. I follow Elliott and most contemporary New Testament scholars in assuming that Paul's seven "genuine" letters (Romans, 1 and 2 Corinthians, Galatians, 1 Thessalonians, Philippians, and Philemon), with the possible exception of Philemon, were heavily edited by the followers of Paul who were also responsible for the Deutero-Pauline letters (Colossians, Ephesians, 2 Thessalonians) and the pastorals (1 and 2 Timothy, Titus). These latter especially represent a marked difference in thinking about sexuality and marriage from the "original" letters of Paul. See also Dennis R. MacDonald, *The Legend and the Apostle*.
21. J. Cheryl Exum, *Fragmented Women*, 124–25.
22. Beverly Roberts Gaventa, "Romans," in Newsom and Ringe, *Women's Bible Commentary*, 317. Gaventa makes it very clear that, while she does not herself subscribe to this idea, Paul does. I concur with both sentiments. See also Dale B. Martin, "Heterosexism," 332–55.
23. Martin, *Corinthian Body*, 239.
24. Corrington, "The 'Headless Woman'" 223–31; Martin, *Corinthian Body*, 242–49.
25. Howard Eilberg-Schwartz, *God's Phallus*, 139, 225.
26. Ibid., 139.
27. See above, n. 20.
28. See E. Elizabeth Johnson, "Ephesians," in Newsom and Ringe, *Women's Bible Commentary*, 338–39.
29. Ibid., 340.
30. Cf. Joanna Dewey, "1 Timothy," in Newsom and Ringe, *Women's Bible Commentary*, 355.
31. What often contributes to the confusion surrounding roles of women both in Judaism and Christianity is that the words for (adult) "woman" and "wife" are the same in Hebrew (*'iššah*) and Greek (*gyne*). Greek, however, has no special word for wife like the Hebrew *be'ulat ba'al*.
32. It may be, however, that this advice on women's clothing belongs more to the caution against conspicuous display of wealth (by wife or husband) by Christians than to sexual modesty.
33. Dewey, "1 Timothy," 356.

34. Dewey (ibid.) contends that the Greek of the text implies a belief that Eve was "seduced" by the serpent and that her transgression was in fact sexual. I am not as sure that the text supports that interpretation, but offer it as a distinct possibility.

35. I translate *gyne* as "wife" and *aner* as "husband" here, because I believe that restrictions on the active participation of women in the spiritual and intellectual life of the post-Pauline communities, like those in 1 Corinthians 11:2–16, pertain to married women only and reflect the long-standing relationship between women's religious behavior and their sexual control. The interpolated passage in 1 Corinthians 14:34–36, consistent rather with the view of 1 Timothy than 1 Corinthians, is a prime example. Married women are to remain silent "in all the churches of the saints" and are not permitted to speak. They are to be submissive, "as the law also says," and if they want to "learn" something, they are to ask their husbands about it in their own homes, for it is a "disgrace" (*aischron*) for a married woman to speak in an assembly. The presumed reference to the "law" is to Genesis 3:16, which has a sexual context, the wife's uncontrollable desire for her husband, despite her pain in childbirth, and his "rule" over her.

36. See Corrington, *Her Image of Salvation*, 123–39, for a description of this process.

37. Sharyn Dowd, "James," in Newsom and Ringe, *Women's Bible Commentary*, 369.

38. Introduction to the letter of James, *NOAB*, NT 331.

39. Alicia Batten, "An Asceticism of Resistance in James," 9. My thanks to Ms. Batten for permission to quote from her paper.

40. Sharyn Dowd, "1 Peter," in Newsom and Ringe, *Women's Bible Commentary*, 370.

41. Ibid., 371.

42. Marie-Eloise Rosenblatt, "Jude," in Schüssler Fiorenza, *Searching the Scriptures*, 2: 394.

NOTES TO CHAPTER 6.
SINNERS, ADULTERESSES, WHORES, AND BRIDES:
IMAGINING WOMEN IN THE GOSPELS AND REVELATION

1. Carla Ricci, *Mary Magdalene and Many Others*; Benedicta Ward, *Harlots of the Desert*.

2. The custom of using perfumed solid or liquid ointment at the banquets of the wealthy is well attested in antiquity; here it is transformed into a "sign" of the coming Passion.

3. Elisabeth Schüssler Fiorenza, *In Memory of Her*, xiii–xiv; 129–30; Mary Ann Tolbert, "Mark," in Newsom and Ringe, *Women's Bible Commentary*, 270–71.

4. Tolbert, "Mark," 271.

5. According to Schüssler Fiorenza (*In Memory of Her*, 129), Luke's version is closer to that of the Q source, which emphasizes Jesus as wisdom teacher and prophet.

6. Jane Schaberg, "Luke," 285–86.

7. Ricci, *Mary Magdalene*, 34–35.

8. Schaberg, "Luke," 285.

9. See, e.g., Michel Gourgues, "'Moi,'" 305–18; Hans Freiherr von Campenhausen, "Zur Perikope von der Ehebrecherin," 171, nn. 35–38.

10. Cf. Gail R. O'Day, "John," in Newsom and Ringe, *Women's Bible Commentary*, 299–300.

11. This attitude toward the Pharisees, as Jews deceived by their study of the scripture into rejecting Jesus as the messiah, is characteristic of John and must be carefully distinguished from what the Pharisees really taught. John's Gospel, like most of the New Testament, is polemical against any opponents, but particularly against other Jewish sects, who do not accept its version of the "truth."

12. O'Day, "John," 295.

13. In the Greek, she is "*gyne ek tes Samareias.*" Since "*gyne*" can also mean "wife," and since her marital status is of concern in this passage, the secondary meaning, "a wife of Samaria," is probably also intended. It was customary, as we have seen in the case of the prophets in chapter 3, to characterize cities as female.

14. Cf. Ricci, *Mary Magdalene and Many Others*, 64–65.

15. O'Day, "John," 296.

16. Adele Reinhartz, "The Gospel of John," in Schüssler Fiorenza, *Searching the Scriptures*, 2:572; Sandra M. Schneiders, *The Revelatory Text*, 187.

17. Schneiders, *Revelatory Text*, 190–91.

18. Jesus as "living water" and the encounter at a well further enhance the bridal imagery. The wise man is urged in Proverbs to "drink water from his own cistern," and to "let his fountain be blessed" (Prov. 5:15, 18), phrases that refer to a man's enjoyment of his own bride and staying away from the Strange Woman.

19. Cf. O'Day, "John," 296.

20. A. A. Trites, "The Woman Taken in Adultery," 138; cf. Dom Andrew Nugent, "What Did Jesus Write?" 193; François Rousseau, "La femme adultère," 463–80; James A. Sanders, "'Nor Do I . . . ,'" 337–47.

21. Bruce M. Metzger, *A Textual Commentary*, 219–22, discusses the textual history of the Pericope of the Adulteress and rejects it as Johannine, followed by Raymond E. Brown, "Roles of Women," 689 n. 4; and Adele Reinhartz, "The Gospel of John," 2:572, among others. Gourgues, "'Moi,'" 309, assigns it to Luke, while von Campenhausen, "Zur Perikope von der Ehebrecherin," represents those who believe the pericope is an authentic story from Jesus' ministry, whether it belongs here in John or not. Luise Schottroff, *Lydia's*

Impatient Sisters, 180, wants to consider Pericope of the Adulteress along with the Synoptic material. Gail R. O'Day, "John 7:53–8:11," 639, claims it as a "primitive piece of Jesus tradition," whether or not it is Johannine.

22. This view is supported by O'Day, "John 7:53–8:11," 635–38; Zane C. Hodges, "Woman Taken in Adultery," 331–32; Schottroff, *Lydia's Impatient Sisters*, 180; Harold Riesenfeld, "The Pericope *de adultera*," 95–110; John Paul Heil, "The Story of Jesus," 182–91; and, on the basis of new evidence, by Bart D. Ehrman, "Jesus and the Adulteress," 24–44.

23. O'Day, "John 7:53–8:11," 631; cf. Joseph Blinzler, "Die Strafe für Ehebruch," 32–47, who speculates exactly what form of adultery the woman had committed that required stoning as the form of punishment.

24. To simplify references to her and to distinguish her from other unnamed women in this section, I will run the risk of continuing to objectify her sexually and occasionally refer to her as the Adultera.

25. Nugent, "What Did Jesus Write?" 193–98, and Paul S. Minear, "Writing on the Ground," 23–37, both consider this action as a sign that Jesus writes "with the finger of God." O'Day, "John 7:53–8:11," 633, considers these and other examples as a form of "misreading" the text against its own shape.

26. O'Day, "John 7:53–8:11," 640.

27. Schottroff, *Lydia's Impatient Sisters*, 184.

28. Heil, "Story of Jesus," 190–91.

29. Schottroff, *Lydia's Impatient Sisters*, 181.

30. Ibid., 182–83, citing Freidoune Sahebjam, *Die gesteinigte Frau. Geschichte der Soraya Manoutcheri* (Reinbeck, 1992). Cf. the recent stoning of a couple "caught" in adultery in Afghanistan, mentioned in the introduction (John F. Burns, "Hard-line Taliban Stones Couple, Reviving Tradition," New York Times News Service, Nov. 3, 1996).

31. O'Day, "John 7:53–8:11," 634.

32. What follows is Herodias's story as her enemies have told it, not as the "historical re-imagination" might suggest. See Elisabeth Schüssler Fiorenza, *But She Said*, 48–50.

33. Levine, "Matthew," 258.

34. Maureen Mara, in Schüssler Fiorenza, *But She Said*, 48–50.

35. Levine, "Matthew," 258.

36. Paula Fredriksen, *From Jesus to Christ*, 82.

37. John G. Gager, *Kingdom and Community*, 51.

38. See Paul D. Hanson, "Introduction," in Hanson, *Visionaries and Their Apocalypses*, 1.

39. Despite the currency of the term "Armageddon" to conjure up a final, if not the final battle, the battle at the "hill of Megiddo" (Harmagedon) in Revelation is not the end but the sixth of seven plagues of the "wrath of God" poured out specifically on Babylon, who is judged and punished in chapters 17:1–19:8 as "the Great Whore."

40. Tina Pippin, *Death and Desire*, 56.

41. Adela Yarbro Collins, *Crisis and Catharsis*, 113.
42. See Susan Garrett, "Revelation," in Newsom and Ringe, *Women's Bible Commentary*, 381.
43. Pippin, *Death and Desire*, 69–74.
44. Ibid., 76.
45. Garrett, "Revelation," 383.
46. Cf. ibid., 378.
47. Cf. Pippin, *Death and Desire*, 72.
48. Garrett, "Revelation," 379.
49. Although Pippin (*Death and Desire*, 66), following Bakhtin, emphasizes the erotic nature of the seer's gaze, "amazement" (*thauma*) is a characteristic response to displays of power in the New Testament, such as miracles. It may be that the audience is meant to feel the erotic attraction that the "kings of the earth" had for the Whore, while at the same time rejecting it.
50. The Bride is also "adorned," but for her husband (Rev. 21:2), and is dressed in the white linen of holiness (19:8), the righteousness of the saints, rather than in scarlet, denoting their blood.
51. "Come out of her" perhaps also carries a sexually suggestive undertone, the refusal of further sexual relations, as the opposite of "Go in to her." See Pippin, *Death and Desire*, 82.
52. Jacques Ellul, *Apocalypse: The Book of Revelation* (New York: Seabury Press, 1977), 189; cited by Elisabeth Schüssler Fiorenza, *The Book of Revelation*, 185.
53. Pippin, *Death and Desire*, 84 and 86.
54. Margaret Miles, *Carnal Knowing*, 139.
55. The problems with such interpretations are indicated by Schüssler Fiorenza, *Book of Revelation*, 192–99.
56. Miles, *Carnal Knowing*, 17–18.
57. Demosthenes Souramis, *The Satanizing of Women*, 60–61.

NOTES TO CHAPTER 7.
CONFOUNDING THE WISDOM OF THE WISE

1. James Williams, "Scripture," in *Introduction to the Study of Religion*, T. William Hall, general editor (San Francisco: Harper & Row, 1978), 85.
2. Daniel Boyarin, *Carnal Israel*, 2–46.
3. Ibid., 134–36, 196; Michael L. Satlow, "Shame and Sex in Late Antique Judaism," in Wimbush and Valantasis, *Asceticism*, 535–43; Léonie Archer, *Her Price Is beyond Rubies*, 105.
4. Judith Romney Wegner, *Chattel or Person?* 114–115.
5. The obscure language of 1 Corinthians 7:36–38 may refer to this custom; see also Elizabeth A. Clark, "John Chrysostom and the Subintroductae," 171–85, for patristic approaches to the problems posed by celibate "marriage."

6. Boyarin, *Carnal Israel*, 191.
7. See ibid., 171; Wegner, *Chattel or Person?* 161.
8. Boyarin, *Carnal Israel*, 178.
9. Archer, *Her Price Is beyond Rubies*, 99.
10. Boyarin, *Carnal Israel*, 184–89.
11. Ibid., 189. Boyarin also theorizes that this story is an embroidery on the one in *'Aboda Zara* 18b, which is about Beruriah's sister, who is condemned by prostitution in Rome because her enticing walk attracted the Roman nobility. Meir rescues her from a brothel, but only after having discovered she has not done "forbidden things." This story is reminiscent of several tales of Christian virgin martyrs, who are condemned to brothels for their insistence on maintaining their faith, but who emerge virgins nonetheless.
12. Karen L. King, "The Gospel of Mary Magdalene," in Schüssler Fiorenza, *Searching the Scriptures*, 2:605–13; Anne Pasquier, *L'Évangile selon Marie*, Bibliothèque copte de Nag Hammadi, Section "Textes" 10 (Quebec: Université Laval, 1983), 14–17, cited by King, "Gospel of Mary Magdalene," 610.
13. King, "Gospel of Mary Magdalene," suggests that the text is "ambiguous" with regard to the existence of a sexual connection between the Savior and Mary. I believe that here, as elsewhere, spiritual intimacy is symbolized by sexual union. While spirituality does not automatically rule out sexuality, the Gnostic context suggests that the relationship is one of spiritual intercourse only.
14. Carla Ricci, *Mary Magdalene and Many Others*, 30–39; Benedicta Ward, *Harlots of the Desert*, 7, 10–21.
15. Ward, *Harlots of the Desert*, 58.
16. Ibid., 21.
17. Turid Karlsen Seim, "The Gospel of Luke," in Schüssler Fiorenza, *Searching the Scriptures*, 2:256.
18. A.-J. Levine, "The Sibylline Oracles," in Schüssler Fiorenza, *Searching the Scriptures*, 2:101.
19. English translation from J. J. Collins, "Sibylline Oracles: A New Translation and Introduction," in *The Old Testament Pseudepigrapha*, vol. 1: *Apocalyptic Literature and Testaments*, ed. James H. Charlesworth, 317–472.
20. Levine, "Sibylline Oracles," 108.
21. Feminist scholars of early Christianity have written a great deal on the subject of Thecla and her function as authoritative in heterodox Christianity. A recent treatment appears in Luise Schottroff, *Lydia's Impatient Sisters*, 105–9; cf. Sheila E. McGinn, "The Acts of Thecla," in Schüssler Fiorenza, *Searching the Scriptures*, 2:800–828.
22. See Anne Jensen, *God's Self-Confident Daughters*, 197–98.
23. Deirdre J. Good, "Early Extracanonical Writings," in Newsom and Ringe, *Women's Bible Commentary*, 383.

24. Jerome, *Letter* 133.4; Jensen, *God's Self-Confident Daughters*, 189–90.
25. Translations of the texts of these heresiologists may be found in Ross S. Kraemer, ed., *Maenads, Martyrs, Matrons, Monastics.*
26. *The Thunder, Perfect Mind* 13.16.
27. The D. Cook translation of this version, together with a summary of chapters 22–29 in the longer version, is found in Kraemer, *Maenads, Martyrs, Matrons, Monastics*, 263–79.
28. Ross S. Kraemer, "The Book of Aseneth," in Schüssler Fiorenza, *Searching the Scriptures*, 2:861.
29. Ibid., 863–64.
30. Ibid., 881.
31. This is not to say that orthodox Christians did not revere women martyrs, but even in the accounts of their martyrdom, these women "overcome the weakness" of their female flesh and, Christlike, often abandon their families. (See, e.g., the H. Musurillo translation of *The Martyrdom of Saints Perpetua and Felicitas* in Kraemer, *Maenads, Martyrs, Matrons, Monastics*, 96–107.)
32. For the idealization of virgin and celibate women in patristic writings, see Rosemary R. Ruether, "Misogynism and Virginal Feminism," 150–83.
33. Geoffrey Galt Harpham, *The Ascetic Imperative*, 101.
34. Ibid.
35. George W. MacRae, "Jewish Background," 86–101.
36. For an excellent synopsis of the classic Gnostic myth and the texts in which it is found, see Bentley Layton, *Gnostic Scriptures*, 5–22. See also the section "Sophia: The Saved Savior," in Corrington, *Her Image of Salvation*, 123–39.
37. Deidre Good, *"Pistis Sophia,"* in Schüssler Fiorenza, *Searching the Scriptures*, 2:683; cf. Michael A. Williams, "Variety in Gnostic Perspectives on Gender," in King, *Images of the Feminine*, 21–22.
38. Translation taken from the W. C. Robinson, Jr., version in Kraemer, *Maenads, Martyrs, Matrons, Monastics*, 386–92.
39. Translation taken from the G. W. McRae and W. M. Parrott version in ibid., 371–76.
40. Anne McGuire, "Thunder, Perfect Mind," in Schüssler Fiorenza, *Searching the Scriptures*, 2:48.
41. Claudia V. Camp, "Feminist Theological Hermeneutics: Canon and Christian Identity," in Schüssler Fiorenza, *Searching the Scriptures*, 1:167.

Bibliography

Archer, Léonie. *Her Price Is beyond Rubies: The Jewish Woman in Greco-Roman Palestine.* JSOT, 60. Sheffield: Sheffield Academic Press, 1990.

Bal, Mieke, ed. *Anti-Covenant: Counter-Reading Women's Lives in the Hebrew Bible.* Bible and Literature Series, 22. Sheffield: Almond Press, 1989.

———. *Lethal Love: Feminist Literary Readings of Biblical Love Stories.* Bloomington: Indiana University Press, 1987.

Batten, Alicia. "An Asceticism of Resistance in James." Paper presented at the conference Asceticism in the New Testament, Emmanuel College, Toronto School of Theology, Oct. 4–6, 1996.

Bellis, Alice Ogden. *Helpmates, Harlots, and Heroes: Women's Stories in the Hebrew Bible.* Foreword by Adela Yarbro Collins. Louisville, Ky: Westminster/John Knox Press, 1994.

Biale, Rachel. *Women and Jewish Law: An Exploration of Women's Issues in Halakhic Sources.* New York: Schocken Books, 1984.

Bird, Phyllis A. "The Harlot as Heroine: Narrative Art and Social Presupposition in Three Old Testament Texts." *Semeia* 46 (1989): 119–39.

Blenkinsopp, Joseph. "The Social Context of the 'Outsider Woman' in Proverbs 1—9." *Bib* 72, no. 4 (1991): 457–73.

Blinzler, Joseph. "Die Strafe für Ehebruch in Bibel u. Halacha: Zur Auslegung von Joh. VIII.5." *NTS* 4 (1957–58): 32–47.

Boyarin, Daniel. *Carnal Israel: Reading Sex in Talmudic Culture.* Berkeley: University of California Press, 1993.

Brenner, Athalya. *The Israelite Woman: Social Role and Literary Type in Biblical Narrative.* Sheffield: JSOT Press, 1985.

Brenner, Athalya, and Fokkelien van Dijk-Hemmes. *On Gendering Texts: Female and Male Voices in the Hebrew Bible.* Biblical Interpretation Series, 1. Leiden: E. J. Brill, 1993.

Brown, Raymond E. "Roles of Women in the Fourth Gospel." *TS* 36 (1975): 688–99.

Burrus, Virginia. *Chastity as Autonomy: Women in the Stories of the Apocryphal Acts.* Lewiston, N.Y.: Edwin Mellen Press, 1987.

Camp, Claudia V. *Wisdom and the Feminine in the Book of Proverbs.* Bible and Literature Series, 11. Sheffield: JSOT/Almond Press, 1985.

————."Wise and Strange: An Interpretation of the Female Imagery in Proverbs in Light of Trickster Mythology." *Semeia* 42 (1988): 14–36.

Charlesworth, James H., ed. *The Old Testament Pseudepigrapha*, vol. 1: *Apocalyptic Literature and Testaments*. Garden City, N.Y.: Doubleday, 1983.

Clark, Elizabeth A. "John Chrysostom and the Subintroductae." *CH* 46 (1977): 171–85.

Collins, Adela Yarbro. *Crisis and Catharsis: The Power of the Apocalypse*. Philadelphia: Westminster Press, 1984.

Corrington, Gail Paterson. "The 'Divine Woman': A Reconsideration." *ATR* 70 (July 1988): 207–20.

————. The 'Divine Woman'? Propaganda and the Power of Chastity in the New Testament Apocrypha." *Helios*, n.s., 13, no. 1 (1986): 151–62.

————. "The 'Headless Woman': Paul and the Language of the Body in 1 Cor. 11:2-16." *Perspectives in Religious Studies* 18 (1991): 223–31.

————. *Her Image of Salvation: Female Saviors and Formative Christianity*. Louisville, Ky.: Westminster/John Knox Press, 1992.

Daly, Mary. *Gyn/Ecology: The Metaethics of Radical Feminism*. Boston: Beacon Press, 1978.

Darr, Katheryn Pfisterer. *Far More Precious than Jewels: Perspectives on Biblical Women*. Gender and the Biblical Tradition. Louisville, Ky.: Westminster/John Knox Press, 1991.

Day, Peggy L., ed. *Gender and Difference in Ancient Israel*. Minneapolis: Fortress Press, 1989.

Deming, Will. "Mark 9.42–10.12, Matthew 5.27–32 and B. Nid. 13b: A First-Century Discussion of Male Sexuality." *NTS* 36 (1990): 130–41.

Douglas, Mary. *Purity and Danger: An Analysis of the Concepts of Religion and Taboo*. London: Routledge & Kegan Paul, 1966.

Dworkin, Andrea. *Our Blood: Prophecies and Discourses on Sexual Politics*. New York: Harper & Row, 1976.

Ehrman, Bart D. "Jesus and the Adulteress." *NTS* 34 (1988): 24–44.

Eilberg-Schwartz, Howard. *God's Phallus: And Other Problems for Men and Monotheism*. Boston: Beacon Press, 1994.

————. *The Savage in Judaism: An Anthropology of Israelite Religion and Ancient Judaism*. Bloomington: Indiana University Press, 1990.

Eliade, Mircea. *The Sacred and the Profane: The Nature of Religion*. Trans. Willard R. Trask from the French. New York: Harcourt Brace Jovanovich, 1959.

Elliott, Neil. *Liberating Paul*. Maryknoll, N.Y.: Orbis Books, 1995.

Exum, J. Cheryl. *Fragmented Women: Feminist (Sub)versions of Biblical Narratives*. *JSOT* 163. Sheffield: JSOT Press, 1993.

Falk, Marcia. *Love Lyrics from the Bible: A Translation and Literary Study of the Song of Songs*. Bible and Literature Series. Sheffield: Almond Press, 1982.

Falk, Nancy Auer, and Rita M. Gross, eds. *Unspoken Worlds: Women's Religious Lives*. Belmont, Calif.: Wadsworth, 1988.

Fewell, Danna Nolan, and David M. Gunn. "Controlling Perspectives: Women, Men, and the Authority of Violence in Judges 4 and 5." *JAAR* 58 (1990): 389–411.

Fishbane, Michael. "Accusations of Adultery: A Study of Law and Scribal Practice in Numbers 5:11–31." *HUCA* 45 (1974): 25–45.

Ford, J. Massingberd. "The Divorce Bill of the Lamb and the Scroll of the Suspected Adulteress: A Note on Apoc. 5,1 and 10, 8–11." *Journal for the Study of Judaism* 2, no. 2 (1971): 136–43.

Fredriksen, Paula. *From Jesus to Christ: The Origins of the New Testament Images of Jesus*. New Haven, Conn., and London: Yale University Press, 1988.

Frymer-Kensky, Tikva. *In the Wake of the Goddesses*. New York: Free Press, 1992.

———. "The Strange Case of the Suspected Sotah (Numbers 5. 11–31)." *VT* 34, no. 1 (1984): 11–26.

Gager, John. *Kingdom and Community: The Social World of Early Christianity*. Englewood Cliffs, N.J.: Prentice-Hall, 1975.

Gordis, Robert. "On Adultery in Biblical and Babylonian Law: A Note." *Judaism* 33, no. 2 (1989): 210–11.

Goulder, Michael D. *The Song of Fourteen Songs*. JSOT Sup, 36. Sheffield: JSOT Press, 1986.

Gourgues, Michel. "'Moi non plus je te condamne pas': Les mots et la théologie de Luc en Jean 8, 1–11 (la femme adultère)." *SR* 19, no. 3 (1990): 305–18.

Halperin, David. *Seeking Ezekiel: Text and Psychology*. University Park: Pennsylvania State University Press, 1993.

Hanson, Paul D. *Visionaries and Their Apocalypses*. Issues in Religion and Theology. Philadelphia: Fortress Press, 1983.

Harpham, Geoffrey Galt. *The Ascetic Imperative in Culture and Criticism*. Chicago and London: University of Chicago Press, 1987.

Heil, John Paul. "The Story of Jesus and the Adulteress (John 7,53–8,11) Reconsidered." *Bib* 72 (1991): 182–91.

Hodges, Zane C. "The Woman Taken in Adultery (John 7:53–8:11): The Text." *BSac* 136 (1979): 318–32.

James, Stephen A. "The Adulteress and the Death Penalty." *JETS* 22 (March 1979): 45–53.

Jay, Nancy. "Sacrifice as Remedy for Having Been Born of Woman." In *Immaculate and Powerful: The Female in Sacred Image and Social Reality*, ed. Clarissa W. Atkinson, Constance H. Buchanon, Margaret R. Miles. Boston: Beacon Press, 1985.

Jeansonne, Sharon Pace. *The Women of Genesis: From Sarah to Potiphar's Wife*. Minneapolis: Fortress Press, 1990.

Jensen, Anne. *God's Self-Confident Daughters: Early Christianity and the Liberation of Women*. Trans. O. C. Dean, Jr. Louisville, Ky.: Westminster John Knox Press, 1996.

King, Karen L., ed. *Images of the Feminine in Gnosticism*. Studies in Antiquity and Christianity. Philadelphia: Fortress Press, 1989.

Kloppenborg, John S. *Q Parallels: Synopsis, Critical Notes and Concordance*. Sonoma, Calif.: Polebridge Press, 1988.

Kraemer, Ross Shepard. *Her Share of the Blessings: Women's Religions among Pagans, Jews, and Christians in the Greco-Roman World*. New York and Oxford: Oxford University Press, 1992.

———, ed. *Maenads, Martyrs, Matrons, Monastics: A Sourcebook on Women's Religions in the Greco-Roman World*. Philadelphia: Fortress Press, 1988.

Lacoque, André. *The Feminine Unconventional: Four Subversive Figures in Israel's Tradition*. Overtures to Biblical Theology. Minneapolis: Augsburg/Fortress Press, 1990.

Laws, Judith, and Pepper Schwartz. *Sexual Scripts: The Social Construction of Female Sexuality*. Hinsdale, Ill.: Dryden Press, 1977.

Layton, Bentley, ed. and trans. *The Gnostic Scriptures*. Garden City, N.Y.: Doubleday, 1987.

Lerner, Gerda. *The Creation of Patriarchy*. New York and Oxford: Oxford University Press, 1986.

Levenson, Jon. *Sinai and Zion: An Entry into the Jewish Bible*. San Francisco: Harper & Row, 1987.

MacDonald, Dennis R. *The Legend and the Apostle: The Battle for Paul in Story and Canon*. Philadelphia: Westminster Press, 1983.

Macintosh, Mary. "Who Needs Prostitutes? The Ideology of Male Sexual Needs." In *Women, Sexuality, and Social Control*, ed. Carol Smart and Barry Smart. London: Routledge & Kegan Paul, 1994.

MacKinnon, Catharine A. *Toward a Feminist Theory of the State*. Cambridge, Mass.: Harvard University Press, 1989.

MacRae, George W. "The Jewish Background of the Sophia Myth." *NovT* 12 (1970): 86–101.

Martin, Dale B. *The Corinthian Body*. New Haven, Conn., and London: Yale University Press, 1995.

———. "Heterosexism and the Interpretation of Romans 1:18–32." *Biblical Interpretation* (1995): 332–55.

McKeating, Henry. "Sanctions against Adultery in Ancient Israelite Society, With Some Reflections on Methodology in the Study of Old Testament Ethics." *JSOT* 11 (1979): 57–72.

Metzger, Bruce M. *A Textual Commentary on the Greek New Testament*. New York: American Bible Society, 1966.

Meyer, Marvin W., trans. *The Secret Teachings of Jesus: Four Gnostic Gospels*. New York: Random House, 1984.

Meyers, Carol. "Procreation, Production, and Protection: Male-Female Balance in Early Israel." *JAAR* 51 (1983): 569–93.

Miles, Margaret R. *Carnal Knowing: Female Nakedness and Religious Meaning in the Christian West*. Boston: Beacon Press, 1989.

Minear, Paul S. "Writing on the Ground." *HBT* 13, no. 1 (1991): 23–37.

The New Oxford Annotated Bible (NOAB). Ed. Bruce M. Metzger and Roland E. Murphy. New York and Oxford: Oxford University Press, 1991.

Newsom, Carol A., and Sharon H. Ringe, eds. *The Women's Bible Commentary*. Louisville, Ky.: Westminster/John Knox Press, 1992.

Niditch, Susan. *Underdogs and Tricksters: A Prelude to Biblical Folklore*. San Francisco: Harper & Row, 1987.

———. "The Wronged Woman Righted: An Analysis of Genesis 38." *HTR* 72 (January–April 1979): 143–49.

Noddings, Nel. *Women and Evil*. Berkeley: University of California Press, 1989.

Nugent, Dom Andrew, O.S.B. "What Did Jesus Write? (John 7,53–8,11)." *Downside Review* 108 (1990): 193–98.

O'Day, Gail R. "John 7:53–8:11: A Study in Misreading." *JBL* 111 no. 4 (1992): 631–40.

Ostriker, Alicia Suskin. *Feminist Revision and the Bible*. Oxford: Basil Blackwell Publisher, 1993.

Pardes, Ilana. *Countertraditions in the Bible: A Feminist Approach*. Cambridge, Mass.: Harvard University Press, 1992.

Pippin, Tina. *Death and Desire: The Rhetoric of Gender in the Apocalypse of John*. Literary Currents in Biblical Interpretation. Louisville, Ky.: Westminster/John Knox Press, 1992.

———. "The Heroine and the Whore: Fantasy and the Female in the Apocalypse of John." *Semeia* 60 (1992): 67–82.

Plaskow, Judith. *Standing Again at Sinai: Judaism from a Feminist Perspective*. San Francisco: HarperCollins, 1991.

Pope, Marvin. *Song of Songs: A New Translation with Introduction and Commentary*. Anchor Bible. Garden City, N.Y.: Doubleday, 1977.

Ricci, Carla. *Mary Magdalene and Many Others: Women Who Followed Jesus*. Trans. Paul Burns from the Italian. Minneapolis: Fortress Press, 1994.

Ricoeur, Paul. *The Symbolism of Evil*. Trans. Emerson Buchanan. Religious Perspectives. New York: Harper & Row, 1967.

Riesenfeld, Harold. "The Pericope *de Adultera* in the Early Christian Tradition." In *The Gospel Tradition: Essays by Harold Riesenfeld*. Philadelphia: Fortress Press, 1970.

Rousseau, François. "La femme adultère Structure de Jn 7,53–8,11." *Bib* 59 (1978): 463–80.

Ruether, Rosemary R. "Misogynism and Virginal Feminism in the Fathers of the Church." In *Religion and Sexism: Images of Woman in Jewish and Christian Traditions*, ed. Rosemary R. Ruether. New York: Simon & Schuster, 1974.

Russ, Joanna. "What Can a Heroine Do? Or Why Women Can't Write." In

Images of Women in Fiction: Feminist Perspectives, ed. Susan Koppelman Cornillon. Bowling Green, Ohio: Bowling Green University Popular Press, 1972.

Sanders, James A. "'Nor Do I . . .' A Canonical Reading of the Challenge to Jesus in John 8." In *The Conversation Continues: Studies in Paul and John: In Honor of J. Louis Martyn*, ed. Robert T. Fortna and Beverly R. Gaventa. Nashville: Abingdon Press, 1990.

Schaberg, Jane. *The Illegitimacy of Jesus: A Feminist Interpretation of the Infancy Narratives*. San Francisco: Harper & Row, 1987.

Schnackenburg, Rudolf. *The Gospel according to St. John*. Vol. 2. New York: Crossroad/Seabury, 1980.

Schneemelcher, Wilhelm, ed. *New Testament Apocrypha*. Rev. ed. of the collection initiated by Edgar Hennecke. Vol. 2: *Writings Related to the Apostles*. Louisville, Ky.: Westminster/John Knox Press, 1992.

Schneiders, Sandra M. *The Revelatory Text: Interpreting the New Testament as Sacred Scriptures*. New York: HarperCollins, 1991.

Schottroff, Luise. *Lydia's Impatient Sisters: A Feminist Social History of Early Christianity*. Foreword by Dorothee Soelle. Trans. Barbara and Martin Reimscheidt. Louisville, Ky.: Westminster John Knox Press, 1995.

Schüssler Fiorenza, Elisabeth. *The Book of Revelation: Justice and Judgment*. Philadelphia: Fortress Press, 1985.

———. *But She Said: Feminist Practices of Biblical Interpretation*. Boston: Beacon Press, 1992.

———. *In Memory of Her: A Feminist Theological Reconstruction of Christian Origins*. New York: Crossroad, 1983.

———. "Interpreting Patriarchal Traditions." In *The Liberating Word: A Guide to Nonsexist Interpretation of the Bible*, ed. Letty M. Russell. Philadelphia: Westminster Press, 1976.

———. *Jesus: Miriam's Child, Sophia's Prophet*. New York: Continuum, 1994.

———, ed. *Searching the Scriptures*. Vol. 1: *A Feminist Introduction*. Vol. 2: *A Feminist Commentary*. New York: Crossroad, 1993–1994.

Schüssler Fiorenza, Elisabeth, and Mary Shawn Copeland, eds. *Violence against Women*. Concilium 1994/1. Maryknoll, N.Y.: Orbis Books, 1994.

Schur, Edwin M. *Labeling Women Deviant: Gender, Stigma, and Social Control*. Philadelphia: Temple University Press, 1983.

Setel, T. Drorah. "Prophets and Pornography: Female Sexual Imagery in Hosea." In *Feminist Interpretation of the Bible*, ed. Letty M. Russell. Philadelphia: Westminster Press, 1985.

Shrage, Laurie. *Moral Dilemmas of Feminism: Prostitution, Adultery, and Abortion*. New York and London: Routledge, 1994.

Small, Dwight Henry. "The Prophet Hosea: God's Alternative to Divorce for the Reason of Infidelity." *Journal of Psychology and Theology* 7, no. 2 (1979): 133–40.

Souramis, Demosthenes. *The Satanizing of Women: Religious versus Sexuality.* Trans. Martin Ebon from the German. Garden City, N.Y.: Doubleday, 1974.

Tosato, Angelo. "Joseph, Being a Just Man (Matt. 1:19)." *CBQ* 41 (October 1979): 547–51.

Trible, Phyllis. *God and the Rhetoric of Sexuality.* Overtures to Biblical Theology. Philadelphia: Fortress Press, 1978.

———. *Texts of Terror: Literary-Feminist Readings of Biblical Narratives.* Overtures to Biblical Theology. Philadelphia: Fortress Press, 1984.

Trites, A. A. "The Woman Taken in Adultery." *BSac* 131 (1974): 137–46.

Vance, Carole S., ed. *Pleasure and Danger: Exploring Female Sexuality.* Boston and London: Routledge & Kegan Paul, 1984.

von Campenhausen, Hans Freiherr. "Zur Perikope von der Ehebrecherin." *ZNW* 68 (1977): 164–75.

Walsh, Carey E. "A Startling Voice: Women's Desire in the Song of Songs." Paper presented at the Theology of Hebrew Scriptures Section, SBL/AAR Annual Meeting, New Orleans, Nov. 23–26, 1996.

Ward, Benedicta, S.L.G. *Harlots of the Desert: A Study of Repentance in Early Monastic Sources.* Cistercian Studies Series, 106. Kalamazoo, Mich.: Cistercian Publications, 1987.

Weems, Renita J. *Battered Love: Marriage, Sex, and Violence in the Hebrew Prophets.* Overtures to Biblical Theology. Minneapolis: Fortress Press, 1995.

———. "Gomer: Victim of Violence or Victim of Metaphor?" *Semeia* 47 (1989): 87–104.

Wegner, Judith Romney. *Chattel or Person? The Status of Women in the Mishnah.* New York and Oxford: Oxford University Press, 1988.

Wenham, G. J. "Gospel Definitions of Adultery and Women's Rights." *Expository Times* 95 (August 1984): 330–32.

Wimbush, Vincent L., and Richard R. Valantasis, eds. *Asceticism.* With the assistance of Gay L. Byron and William S. Love. New York and Oxford: Oxford University Press, 1995.

Yee, Gale A. "'I Have Perfumed My Bed with Myrrh': The Foreign Woman (*'iššā zārā*) in Proverbs 1–9." *JSOT* 43 (1989): 53–68.

Index of Passages

Index of Subjects

Abbahu, Rabbi, 161
Abraham, 24–25, 28–29, 68, 76, 101, 136–37
Adam, 4, 102, 135–36
Adultera, 145–49, 193 n.24
adulterer(s), 88, 129, 137–38, 190 n. 18. *See also: pornoi*
adulteress, 7–8, 18, 23, 32, 49, 53, 58, 63, 77, 80–81, 87, 95, 105–6, 110, 140, 146, 161, 188 n.23
Adulteress (figure), 16, 17, 19, 33, 119, 145–46, 192–93 n.21
Adventuress (figure), 16, 18, 19
Ahab, 62–64, 150
Ananias and Sapphira, 124–25
androgyny, 135, 160, 170
Anti-Wisdom, 105–7, 109–13, 136, 150, 170. *See also* Folly; Strange Woman
apostasy, 5, 8–9, 11, 19, 47, 58, 67, 83–84, 90, 98, 143, 181 n.55
apostles, 22, 121, 124, 132, 168
Aquila. *See* Prisca
asceticism, 5, 9, 11, 127–28, 164, 167, 169. *See also* celibacy
Aseneth, 53, 167–68, 182 n.31
Asherah, 50, 63, 81, 90, 98, 188 n.32
Athaliah, 64–65
Augustine, 3, 146–47, 169

ba'al, 16, 24, 36, 75, 82, 119, 137, 184 n.79
Ba'al (Canaanite god), 50, 63, 83, 184 n.79
Babylon, 4, 7–8, 66, 79, 95, 99, 152–53, 156–57, 186 n.42, 193 n.39

Barak. *See* Deborah
Bathsheba, 14–15, 30, 62, 116–17, 128, 177 n.42
Ben Azzai, 161
Beruriah, 19, 143, 161–64, 177–78 n. 56, 195 n.11. *See also* Meir, Rabbi
be'ulat ba'al, 23–24, 32, 38, 99, 110, 118, 190 n.31
Boaz, 17, 69–71, 92, 103. *See also* Naomi; Ruth
bride (Song of Songs), 17, 72, 109, 117, 188 n.26
Bride of the Lamb, 139, 152, 155, 157, 194 n. 50
bridegroom (Song of Songs), 17, 72–73
bridegroom (Jesus), 144–45, 171

celibacy, 122, 160, 164–66, 168–69, 194 n.5, 196 n.32
chastity, 11, 115, 135, 167–68
Chloe, of Corinth, 125
Church, 18–20, 72, 132–33, 138–39, 152, 157
church fathers, 72. *See also* names of individual church fathers
covenant, 32, 83, 94–96, 99, 100, 102, 107, 143
Covenant Code, 6, 23, 34–35
cunning, 19, 55–56, 103

Daniel, 9, 117–18
David, king, 14, 30, 46, 65, 67, 73, 128, 177 n.42
Deborah, 57–59, 60